VIRGINIA GHOSTS

By

MRS. MARGUERITE DU PONT LEE

REVISED EDITION

VIRGINIA BOOK COMPANY

BERRYVILLE, VIRGINIA

1966

BIBLIOGRAPHICAL NOTE

Mrs. Lee published *Virginia Ghosts* in 1930, and in 1932, she published *Virginia Ghosts and Others*. In the present, revised edition, all of the Virginia (and West Virginia) ghosts from the two earlier volumes are put into one "closet", and all non-Virginias ghosts are excluded. The photograph of Ash Lawn which appears in the present edition is by Philip I. Flournoy of the Virginia State Chamber of Commerce.

MARGUERITE DUPONT LEE

ARGUERITE DUPONT LEE was extraordinary. Exceptionally warm hearted and sympathetic, she had also a keenly inquiring mind and a strong will. She was a rebel against the complacent acceptance of conventional ideas, and she was, incidentally, a serious student of psychic phenomena.

She was born in 1862, the daughter of Eleuthère Irénée duPont and Charlotte Henderson. Her father was the resident manager of the DuPont powder mill on the Brandywine near Wilmington, Delaware. Her mother, a Virginian in all her family connections, was the daughter of Archibald Henderson, the long-time commandant of the Marine Corps.

Marguerite duPont was born into the Establishment, but the DuPont Company of her youth was not a vast, impersonal corporation. As manager of the powder mill, her father worked among his employees and knew them all by their first names. He lived near the plant, and his children's playmates were the children of the millhands who lived just across the road. Thus, Marguerite grew up in familiar contact, not only with the elite, but also with the industrial working class.

Eleuthère duPont and Charlotte Henderson both died in 1877, leaving five orphans in their big house, which was actually the property of the DuPont Company. After the second funeral, Alfred duPont, their uncle, came to tell the children that the family council had decided to parcel them out one by one among their relatives. He found them armed to defend their home and fireside: Anna (17) held an axe; Marguerite (15), a rolling pin; Alfred (13), a shotgun; Maurice (11), a pistol; Louis (9), a bow and arrow. Uncle Alfred was impressed, and the youngsters kept their castle.

But there were some constraints which even Marguerite's strong will could not overcome. She was unquestionably the best skater on Brandywine Creek, but the boys would not let her take part in their hockey games. Too rough for girls, they said. They probably knew that she would be as fierce a competitor as any of them but they never allowed her to prove it.

For all her tomboyishness, Marguerite was a girl, and a beautiful one at that. Soon there were beaux calling on her, and at the age of eighteen, she chose to marry a thirty year old Virginia cousin, Cazenove Gardner Lee. She became an ornament to the society of

MARGUERITE DU PONT LEE

Washington, where her husband was a lawyer. She spent her summers at "Menokin", a Lee family summer home on the outskirts of Alexandria, near the Virginia Theological Seminary. There, over the years, she entertained a long succession of Seminarians, and thus gained an extensive acquaintance among the Episcopal clergy.

In the later years of her marriage, Mrs. Lee became an aggressive campaigner for women's rights, as did many another Washington society matron. She marched in the great Washington parade for Woman's Suffrage.

Cazenove Lee died in 1912. At fifty, his widow found social life empty and unsatisfying. Her sons, Cazenove Gardner Lee, Jr., and Maurice duPont Lee, were already graduated from Cornell, and were well launched on careers in the DuPont Company. Mrs. Lee sold her fashionable residence on New Hampshire Avenue, and built a settlement house in the slums of old Georgetown. There she conducted a kindergarten, a boys' club, and various classes for the mothers of the neighborhood. At the same time, she devoted herself to less evident private benefactions, and to an endless correspondence with editors, clergymen and public authorities.

When Mrs. Lee freed herself from the demands of the social round in order to give her time to social service work in Georgetown, she also freed herself from the tyranny of fashion. A simple shirtwaist and skirt became her uniform. When she could no longer find what she wanted in the stores, she made her own clothes on her own sewing machine, and always in the same unchanging style. She depended on an old cobbler in Alexandria for a continuing supply of high button shoes, but when he died, she had to yield on that point.

After ten years in Georgetown, Mrs. Lee turned over her settlement house to the Salvation Army, and retired to a suite in the Powhatan Hotel. From there, she continued her private charities and her correspondence, but she also found time to indulge her interest in psychic phenomena, and to collect the stories that make up this book. She was Virginian enough to know that the stories were largely legendary, but at the same time, she was prepared to believe that underlying them, there was some genuine, inexplicable psychic manifestation.

Mrs. Lee died in 1936. Her spirit remains a strong presence among those who knew her.

LUDWELL LEE MONTAGUE

TABLE OF CONTENTS

_____

ALEXANDRIA AREA
City of Alexandria

Fairfax County

Prince William County

FREDERICKSBURG AREA

City of Fredericksburg

Stafford County

Spotsylvania County

TIDEWATER

RICHMOND AREA

City of Richmond

Charles City County

Chesterfield County

Fluvanna County

Goochland County

PIEDMONT

Albemarle County

Amherst County

Culpeper County

Fauquier County

SHENANDOAH VALLEY

SOUTHSIDE
Appomattox County

THE ANCHORAGE

PERHAPS soon after the little port was called Belle Haven, when both the earlier name Owl's Creek and the Indian had been forgotten; when casks of tobacco were rolled down a lane now Orinoco Street, and the white covered wagons began to end their long journeys at the river wharves, this ghost began to walk. In the far outskirts a rough path wended over the hill which later Braddock was destined to follow to defeat in the Western Wilderness. Close by on the hill amid trees and bushes stood on Red Lane a tiny cottage. This was the home of a sea captain and of his wife. They called it "The Anchorage."

Strangely enough all names have been forgotten save that of the house, and we know that where it stood is now the flower garden surrounding the home of Mrs. D. Mauchlin Niven.

Standing in the door of her cottage, shading her eyes with her hand, the sailor's wife watched her husband on his way to the ship anchored out in the river—and here she welcomed him home after many days. In course of time, from one cruise over the distant seas, as happens to all voyagers on the ocean of Life, he did not return. When the news reached the widow we are told she went out into the garden and shot herself.

The ghost of the sailor's wife has apparently been seen from time to time throughout the years by a number of the older residents of that now quite populous neighborhood.

Mrs. Niven writes me: "This is a true ghost story. Our house is located on what was known as Red Hill, adjoining the old Braddock Road, northwest of Alexandria, Virginia. One summer night as I was preparing to retire I glanced out into the garden through an open window and saw a woman not far away from and gazing towards the window out of which I was looking. Thinking she was a neighbor, I called out, 'Hello! Come in!' The figure vanished! The next day I related this incident to a woman who was born and had lived in the neighborhood all her life. She inquired, 'What did the woman look like?' I told her the woman was tall and rather slender, that she had dark hair and large lustrous eyes, and that she wore a cloak thrown carelessly over one shoulder. 'That,' my friend said, 'is the ghost of the sea captain's wife, and more than you have seen her wandering about your place and over Red Hill.' She then told me the tragic story."

COLROSS

A FINE old Virginia mansion is about to be moved from its ancient moorings. Kindly but alien hands hope that reconstructed in New Jersey, the scent of Virginia grown roses and the intangible sweetness of the little French bride, will cling round it still!

Colross, built in 1785, has its traditions deeply rooted in the soil of Virginia, and its history lends atmosphere, romance and charm to the old town of Alexandria, where it has stood for 140 years. It was built by Jonathan Swift, of New England, for his bride, with whom he eloped, Anne Foster, daughter of General Robedeau, a Revolutionary officer. Little is recorded of the life of the French girl in her beautiful home which she named Belle Air. The house is said to have been built upon ground rented from the old Alexander family, owners of an immense tract of land in the vicinity, and for whom the town was named.

One of the numerous remarkable incidents connected with this interesting mansion is that at the death of Jonathan Swift it reverted to the landowners, Lee Massey Alexander and his sister, Mrs. Chapman, to whom it belonged but a short time. They changed the name to Colross. The family to whom throughout its history Colross preëminently belonged, is one of Virginia's foremost—the Masons. Mrs. Virginia Mason Davidge stated to the writer of this sketch that her Father, Thomson Mason, won Colross at a game of cards from Lee Massey Alexander. Mason was the son of George Mason of Gunston Hall.

A high brick wall around this property was built by Thomson Mason and bears a tragic record unique in the annals of America's famous dwellings. "It was against this wall that the famous 'bounty jumper' Downey was shot after his capture in Alexandria, by his own troops;" and the late Julian Taylor, of Alexandria, long connected with the diplomatic bureau of the Department of State, Washington, related that when a boy during the Civil War, he saw two deserters shot standing with their backs against the Colross wall. Well may be possible the legend of the ghost of a soldier

Colross

Thomson Mason

seen haunting this old garden wall.

The lives of Thomson Mason and his wife in this fine old homestead, with its stately columns, wide halls and spacious rooms, were at least twice overshadowed by tragedy. The beautiful garden to the north, famous in its day for its great box bushes, lilacs and roses, had a path leading from the house and winding at last to a huge vault, with its great iron lock. To it, one by one, each member of the family passed through the doorway at Colross for the last time. The bodies of two little children rest in that vault, each having died under tragic circumstances. One was drowned while in the bathtub, one was killed while playing in the yard by a heavy coop falling upon her. Ever afterwards the old vault, with its heavy door and great iron lock, gave unique evidence of the ghostly haunting of Colross.

The property was purchased from the Masons by Mr. W. A. Smoot, of Alexandria, whose wife was an Alexander, a descendant of the former owners. Mr. Albert Smoot, his son, present Mayor of that city, states, "The door of the vault was locked with a large iron lock, and would never stay locked more than three days. Father would lock it himself, and open it would come! Never was the lock broken."

THE LAST VISIT

MANY years ago an old lady, more than eighty years of age, went to pass the summer on Seminary Hill, near Alexandria, Virginia.

As was courteous and customary, a visit of welcome was paid by Mrs. Harriet Cazenove, a resident of that locality, and a woman of about the same age as was the lady upon whom she called. Seating themselves upon the veranda, the visitor to Seminary Hill exclaimed, "My! how your name carries me back! Long, long ago, when I was a young girl, my favorite brother was an admirer of Miss Charlotte Cazenove, of Alexandria. He frequently called upon her and was always invited to remain and take supper with the family. One very dark evening when the hour drew near for the boat to leave Alexandria for Washington, such being the means of travel between the two towns in that day, Mr. Cazenove sent a colored man with a lantern to light the way to the ferry, through streets very dark in those early days. As soon as the lights on the boat could be seen, my brother dismissed the negro, telling him he could now see the way to his destination. It was a disastrous order, for not being familiar with the region surrounding the wharf, my brother fell into the river and was drowned.

"One summer evening at twilight, alone in the drawing-room, Miss Cazenove was seated at the piano playing reminiscently a familiar old air. She was startled to see the door open and the apparition of her friend pass silently through the room and out onto the veranda."

The stranger telling the story of bygone days was the sister of General Joseph E. Johnston of the Confederacy.

Gunston Hall

GUNSTON HALL

TO Helen Mason, great-granddaughter of George Mason of Gunston Hall, when a little, girl, seven years old, it was given to glance out of a window of that famous old mansion into the garden, one evening about supper time, and see the Spirit of her grandfather, Thomson Mason, who had at that hour died suddenly in his home, Hollin Hall, five miles away. Her mother, whom she called to the window, saw nothing! The experience seems to have been unique in this family and dwelling. Fortunately as the Spirit, released from the body, returned for a moment to the home of his childhood, where his body was to rest, the child not only saw the vision, spoke of it at the time, but when an old woman, her descendants listened as she described the scene indelibly printed upon her memory at Gunston Hall, one summer evening many, many years before.

Mrs. Mary Ellzey McCrary, granddaughter of Helen Mason, who saw the ghost of her grandfather Thomson Mason, writes of a member of the family talking with an old negro, Uncle Jasper, who actually witnessed the tragic death of the Master of Hollin Hall. Uncle Jasper said—

"Well, Miss Ca'line, you 'members hearin' how yo' great-gran'pa died in a kind er fit like, whiles he's shavin' hisse'f.

"I muster be'n a lil' brat, not mo'n five er six year old,—but hit was like dis, Mars Thomson was one er these here figity fo'kes, always a flyin' in er tantrum, an' he jes nachelly 'spise ter shave. He won't let nobody do it fer him, but 'sist on doin' it hisse'f, an' ever time he done it he raise de whole plantation, puttin nigh.

"An' dis day he done put it off 'till mos' tea-time—and den he call ole Ike ter fetch hot water, an' make Alec hol' de glass, an' den he fume 'roun', an' say hit too dark, an' make two mo' niggers come in to hol' de lights.

"An' me, hearin' all de runction, crope up to de do' to see what gwine on.

"Well, he fuss at ole Ike 'cause de razer wan't sharp 'nough. An' Alec he git so tired er holdin' dat mirrer out wid both han's dat hit wobble in spite'r ever'thing. An' massa, he cuss at him, an' holler at him to hol' it still—an' jes den Alec cotch my eye an' screw up he face an poke out his tong', behine de glass at Massa, an' hit so funny I buss right out laffin' *loud*. An' Mars, he turn 'roun' ragin' mad, wid de razer in he han'—an' he say, 'Jas, you lil' black imp er Satan, git er way fum der befor' I cut de —— '

"*An' right dar,* he fell down in er fit, an' ole Ike grab him quick, an' Alec drap de mirrer an' it bruk in ter a thousan' pieces—An' when dey lay yo' great-gran'pa on de sofa he is done stone daid.

"An', Miss Ca'line you sho 'members how at dis very place—fo' miles erway—*on de very same day,* lil' Miss Hel'n was a sittin' at her Ma's knee lookin' out on de gyardin jes' befo' tea-time. An', all on a sudden, '*O, ma!* she say—an' cotch hol' er her ma's dress wid bofe hans, an' 'pear like she powerful 'stonished—'*What* is gran'pa doin' out der in de gyardin in de wet? An' he's got he's neckcloth off, an' he's knee-buckles are undone,—*why, he must have been shaving!*' "

VAUCLUSE

THE property known originally as "Vaucluse" in Fairfax County, Virginia, ten miles from Washington and three miles from Alexandria, was named for Petrarch's home in Avignon, France, because of the closed-in-valleys which the name means. It was a grant of fifty thousand acres to Valentine Peyton, but disintegrated early in Colonial times. A part of the estate of George Mason of Gunston Hall on the Potomac was bought from the Vaucluse tract.

For more than one hundred years a spacious brick mansion stood on a hill commanding a view of the distant hills and surrounded by a large grove of fine trees. When during the Civil War the army of General McClellan occupied this part of Virginia and tore down the old dwelling, it had been owned and occupied for many years by the Fairfax family.

This was the age of large homes, unbounded hospitality, and many servants. During those days of the war guests have arrived at some big plantation in the South expecting to make a short visit and have remained several years.

Vaucluse was always filled with relatives and friends. Among the company at this time was a charming niece, Miss Constance Cary, of the Cary family of "Ampthill" on the James River—later Mrs. Burton Harrison.

Upon this well-wooded property was a group of beautiful springs, flowing eventually into a little stream falling through a deep ravine, famous as a trysting-place for lovers. In 1862 Federal pickets were stationed everywhere, and young Confederate soldiers trying to visit the lovely Constance, ran great danger of their fire. Thus it was that Vaucluse obtained its ghost, throughout the years seen from time to time by those walking in the ravine upon moonlight nights.

A handsome boy, taking his chance of seeing his sweetheart, was shot by a picket and fell beside the main spring whence a few stone steps up the hillside would have brought him to his love. He lies buried where he fell, near the spring. His name is forgotten, and all who could tell it have long since passed beyond mortal hearing; but the spirit of the brave young lover—perchance seeking once more his heart's desire, as on that fateful evening—or maybe just to revisit the scene of his last earthly experience, keeps ever in the minds of the youth of today the knowledge that he long years ago risked his life both to save his State and to see the girl he loved.

For years the land desolated by the fortunes of war was neglected. Pines, the aftermath of devastation, stand where once grew splendid forest trees. All that remains of that chapter in its history and of the once beautiful old garden are the hardy daffodils and narcissi, blooming here and there on the hillside in the spring sunshine; the thread of living water surging over the pebbles as of old, and the ghost of the unlucky lover, visible on moonlight nights, lying at full length among the ferns, violets and periwinkle beside the spring.

From the new Vaucluse, home of the well-known artist and writer, Mrs. Marietta Minnegerode Andrews, friends wander down the hill, and some have seen the boy in his gray uniform, his breast stained with a dark red, his youthful face turned upward to the leafy roof of the interlacing poplars. Children of a later generation bend over him and gaze in breathless wonder as through the soft grey of his Confederate uniform they see the little violets blooming on the sod! Gradually he fades from their sight. Mary Lord, Mrs. Andrews' daughter, had seen him several times e're she too essayed the "greatest adventure in life" on her twenty-second birthday; and, like the young soldier, returns again and again to testify to a life beyond this little day.

RIPPON LODGE

TODAY, in old Prince William County, Virginia, between the village of Occoquan and the still more ancient town of Dumfries, across Neabsco Creek, two miles west of the Potomac River, stands Rippon Lodge, built about 1720, and today renovated and remodeled to meet the needs of this generation.

Some years ago a private lane wandered between tall walnut trees and an old apple orchard to where has stood for two hundred years a big frame house, gray with age, and bearing some of those marks which years put upon houses as well as on men. A big Kentucky coffee-tree seldom seen in these forests stood nearby, having weathered the storms of winter and afforded shade through the hot summer suns of more than a century.

The multitudes have gone like the flowers and the weeds which wither away to let others succeed; but not so the plantain, familiar to all of us east of the Appalachians—the sturdy broad leaves and spikes of seed ripening in the sun at the doorstep of old Rippon Lodge, even the children's children of those first seeds brought from England in the garments of the Colonists, scattered, and taking root first in America along the shores of the Potomac River—called by the Indians, "the white man's footsteps"—for seeing it, an Indian knew a white man had passed.

A path extended south from the house through woods of oak and pine to the top of the ridge where all around in the woods are graves. A few stones are inscribed, but now scarcely legible—some are marked by rough native boulders, many have never been other than a grass-covered mound. One flat slab reads: "Here lieth the body of Collo. Richard Blackburn who departed this life July the 15th, 1757 in the 53rd year of his age. He was born in Rippon in England from whence he came to Va. where he acquired a reputable character. . . . He was a man of Consummate Prudence, Fru-

Rippon Lodge

gality and Indefatigable Industry Whereof he made a large fortune."

It was customary in those days to bury the slaves in the same large plot, where with their masters and mistresses finally one by one they found a resting-place upon the bosom of the Great Mother of us all. Doubtless it is to hover near one of these graves in which the ashes of a nameless slave child still lie beneath the oaks and the pines that gives to us the often repeated story of the ghost of old Rippon Lodge. For long years afterward untenanted, falling into decay—Ellen MacGregor, grandmother of the well-known Southern writer, Alice Maud Ewell, when a girl in Prince George County, Maryland, heard of the killing of the slave child.

A girl friend went to Rippon Lodge to spend the holidays. She saw, while at the dinner table Christmas day, a negro waitress crying. Having an opportunity afterward, she inquired what was the matter? The woman, still weeping, said her child got in Mrs. Blackburn's way and her mistress in a fit of temper angrily pushed it aside. The child fell against the stone jamb of a fireplace and afterwards died. The young visitor left the house as soon as she could get away.

This Mrs. Blackburn is said to have come of a well-known Prince William County family called "Rattlesnake Grahams," owing to high temper. After the child's death she seemed callous and indifferent, but later was said to have suffered from remorse. She doubtless lies buried at Rippon Lodge.

After Mrs. Blackburn's death the house remained vacant for many years. No one would live there. The *Manassas Journal*, May 19, 1911, gives a picture of Rippon Lodge and this information: "A very old house, near Dumfries, this county, once the home of the Blackburns, an old Prince William family, connected with the Washingtons, the 'Rattlesnake Grahams' and other people of note. The fine paneled woodwork of its interior is unusual in this part of Virginia.

"Many tragic stories are told of Rippon Lodge. More than one murder is said to have been committed there. A victim of a fatal duel bled to death on the parlor floor. This house is said to be haunted in such a ghostly and sinister fashion that no one will occupy it, and the public road has changed its course to avoid the neighborhood."

A Miss Atkinson at one time owned the place. She said the picture does not suggest the size of the house, as there was a back building. Miss Atkinson never saw anything unusual, but "sometimes hears strange and disturbing noises!"

To this building in 1808 was carried Bernard Hooe, in a dying condition, after a duel with William Kemp. For years the place was abandoned. During this period two young men from Alexandria were on a tramping tour. Night coming on they discovered an abandoned house where they elected to sleep. Very soon they began to hear loud and frequent noises. These were followed by shrieks and peals of unearthly laughter! Unable to rest, the young men struck a light and searched the house, but discovered no one and no thing. The place was deserted. They left at once. Inquiring in the morning at some little distance, they were told the house was called "Rippon Lodge," and was haunted! Reaching the house of a friend, Miss Alice Maud Ewell, near Haymarket, Virginia, the young men related their experience. Possibly the ghost has at times been seen as well as heard, but the chronicler of this little sketch has found no one who will admit it.

FEDERAL HILL

IN 1710 one of Virginia's greatest Colonial Governors, a Scotchman, Sir Alexander Spotswood, landed at Yorktown. A soldier with Marlborough and wounded at Blenheim, this picturesque leader of the Horseshoe Knights, and of many another adventure, rounded out his days in a land far from Caledonia's rockbound coast, and sleeps in an ancient burying-ground in Annapolis.

In old Fredericksburg stands today a charming mansion bearing the name "Federal Hill," believed to have been built by Governor Spotswood. In the heart of the town, and notwithstanding the changes and chances of its many years, the battle-scarred lawn is, in the springtime, golden with a wealth of daffodils, doubtless seeded beneath the eye of the color-loving old Scotchman. Birds sing in the trees shading the gunpits, recalling that a shell thrown from a gun stationed at Federal Hill killed General Thomas Rootes Cobb, at the foot of Marye's Heights.

A large two-story frame house is Federal Hill, wearing walls of solid brick beneath the white clapboard. The ghost of Governor Spotswood has been seen many times briskly mounting the steps leading to a porch, while his body lies a dim and shadowy column of dust beside the waters of the Severn. It is told there is a record in the Congressional Library stating that after the Revolutionary War, Robert Brooke bought a house in Fredericksburg, Virginia, and renamed it Federal Hill, after the Federalist Party of which he was one of the founders. He was also a Governor of Virginia.

It is delightful to know that the present owner of this historic dwelling, Mrs. Theodora Randolph Keim, answers frankly, "Yes," when asked if Federal Hill can boast a ghost. Twenty years ago, when her mother, Mrs. Henry Theodora Wight, bought the property she was told the place was haunted by the Spirit of Governor Spotswood.

It seems that in the dining-room there were built two spaces for sideboards, because in olden times huge hunt breakfasts were often

Sir Alexander Spotswood

Federal Hill

given by Governor Spotswood and his lady, and the smaller sideboard was used for the bowls of apple-toddy, eggnog, hot grog, etc., the customary drinks of the day.

Throughout the generations a story has been handed down by the various owners of the house that from time to time the Governor has been seen standing in front of this small sideboard, dressed in a pink coat and hunting breeches, pleasantly engaged in mixing drinks.

Mrs. Keim says she has never seen him, but in the Fall of the year Mrs. Margaret Halsey Weir has on two occasions been told of seeing a gentleman in hunting costume hurrying up the steps and onto the porch. Mrs. Weir, whose grandfather lived at Federal Hill for twenty-five years, has a most intriguing story to unfold. The story was told her by the late Mrs. Harriet Dickens Wight.

Mrs. Weir was invited to dine at Federal Hill with Mrs. Wight. "When I arrived Mrs. Wight received me with true Virginia cordiality, and explained the disappearance of the cook and waitress, owing to the tale of the cook's small daughter, who insisted she had seen standing by the sideboard 'an old gentleman, with boy's pants, with a white plait down he back, tied with a black string.' Furthermore, she declared 'he hand had a silver cup histed to de picture of a old gentleman on wall.'"

The child, Mrs. Wight said, was without any education and too young to have invented any story. The disappearance of the household staff was proof positive that the presence of a ghost and his story was unknown to them.

About a year later Mrs. Wight was sitting at her desk in the library in the twilight, transacting a business correspondence. She was about to ring for a light, when at her elbow at the corner of the desk appeared the same old gentleman of the child's story. "Boy's pants, pink coat, and plait! He was minus the silver cup. He lingered a long minute and then faded gently into the twilight, much as though a curtain of gauze shut him from sight!"

JOHN GLASSEL'S HOME

JOHN GLASSEL of "Long Middry," County of Haddington,
Scotland, was born in 1734. He emigrated to Virginia in 1756,
and married Helen Buchan, daughter of John Buchan of Lei-
tham, Scotland. John Glassel died in 1806. They had one daughter, Joanna, who was born in 1796 and died in 1828. Joanna Glassel
married, April 17, 1820, John Campbell, afterwards 7th Duke of
Argyle.

John Glassel lived in Fredericksburg before the Revolution, and
his house is still standing on Caroline Street. "He was a merchant
of large enterprises and fortune, with branches in Culpeper and
Fauquier." (Hayden.)

Evidently a staunch Royalist, at the beginning of the Revolution,
John Glassel deeded his very considerable property in America, in
fee simple to his brother Andrew—who apparently was in sympathy with the Colonists—and returned to Scotland, where he resided
on his estate "Long Middry" sixteen miles from Edinburgh.

His only child had a marriage portion of £50,000 sterling.
Joanna Glassel had one son, the 8th Duke of Argyle.

In 1883 while in America the Marquis of Lorne visited Fredericksburg and the house on Caroline Street, once the home of his
great-grandfather, John Glassel. After the Revolution Andrew
Glassel journeyed to Scotland to place his son John at school. "At
that time he returned to his brother John of "Long Middry" the full
value of the large estate the latter, before returning to Scotland, had
conveyed in fee simple to him." (Hayden.)

The old Glassel house in Fredericksburg has changed owners
many times since Andrew Glassel and his children each in due season found other places of rest. But that from time to time some
come again to Caroline Street we have reason to believe. It comes
to us that, in the twilight where her harp once stood, a singer of long
ago returns to listen to the strains of some familiar melody played
in the old parlor today.

One summer evening the front door closed and the other members of the family on the back porch, a young girl seated herself on

Johanna Glassel, Duchess of Argyle

Home of John Glassel, Fredericksburg, Virginia

the piano bench, and running her fingers over the keys, sang softly—

> "The light of other days is faded,
> And all their glories past."

Presently, hearing the front door open and close, she called, "Who is trying to frighten me?" There was no answer, but footsteps crossed the hall and their sound at length reaching the piano, some one sat down on the bench, placing a hand on the musician's shoulder! Unable to account for this mystery, the young girl arose and went to question the family. No one could tell who entered and sat by the piano, for no one had left the piazza since tea time.

One night, his two older brothers at a dance, a half grown boy was asleep in his big double bed by nine o'clock. During the night his mother feeling a cold breeze, decided to put a light blanket over the child. Entering the bedroom, she was astonished to find another boy also in the bed! His head was only half covered by the sheet. Covering both boys, the mother related the circumstance to her husband. He could not imagine who the boy could be, and saw no need of a blanket, declaring the night to be "very warm." At breakfast the boy said he had not left the house, and that no boy slept in his bed with him. His mother found no evidence that the bed had been occupied by two persons.

On several occasions door knobs have been turned by unseen hands and doors opened mysteriously. These phenomena accord with the testimony of Mr. Churchill Cooke, now 92 years of age, who told Mrs. Chewning of Fredericksburg that when he was young he was a frequent guest at the old Glassel house, and that Dr. Brodie Herndon, then the owner, always declared the house to be haunted.

One day a member of the household saw distinctly her uncle, apparently in perfect health, standing in the room. He died three days later.

The sound as of crashing china, heavy footsteps in the hall, doors slamming, and chairs rocking occurs very often in this charming and roomy old house .

HAZEL HILL

"HAZEL Hill," at the lower end of Princess Anne Street, Fredericksburg, was built by Gen. John Minor, third of the name, who was born in the home of his ancestors at Topping Castle, Caroline County, May 13, 1761.

When a youth, John Minor was at the battle of Yorktown, a commanding officer in the war of 1812, and later a distinguished lawyer. His first wife, Mary Berkeley, of Hanover County, lived but a few months. Later he married Lucy Landon Carter, of Cleve.

In June, 1816, General Minor was in Richmond attending a session of the court. His daughter, Mary, mother of Mr. Lancelot M. Blackford, principal for many years of the Episcopal High School near Alexandria, was at the time a girl of fifteen, and related the experience to her niece, Miss Mary Willis Minor.

One evening the family was at supper. Mr. McFarlane, a guest, entered the room after the others were seated at table and remarked, "The General has returned. He is wearing riding clothes and went upstairs, apparently preoccupied, not noticing me as he passed in the hall." Immediately Mrs. Minor left the table, but returned very shortly saying there was no one there. After the passing of as many hours as it took a man to ride from Richmond, they learned that at the hour Mr. McFarlane saw him—8 P. M, June 8, 1816—General Minor died at his lodging in Richmond.

Hazel Hill

KENMORE

FREDERICKSBURG, VIRGINIA, founded in 1727, was named for Frederick, son of George 2nd, King of England. Kenmore was built in 1752 by Fielding Lewis, who manufactured the first guns for the Revolutionary War, and married Betty, only sister of George Washington. It was their home for forty-five years. A beautiful specimen of Colonial architecture. The ceilings, we are told, were designed by Washington, and that he sent two Hessian prisoners captured at the battle of Trenton to carry out his artistic conception. The walls are very solid and the elaborate mantels undamaged after the passage of 177 years.

In 1775 the Virginia Assembly appointed Colonel Lewis Chief Commander of a "Manufactory of Small Arms" to be created at Fredericksburg. It was equipped and in running order early in 1776 and continued turning out arms throughout the war. The government failed to provide funds. Colonel Lewis used all his private fortune. At length Kenmore was sold to satisfy his creditors.

Fielding Lewis died in 1781. His last years must have been harassed by constant worry. It is therefore not surprising that at the present time, in the daytime and at night, those living in and caring for the interesting old landmark should hear in the halls and on the stairs the heavy tread of a man's foot. The crunching of gravel, the scraping of the foot on the stone step, can be heard, and the door knob seen to turn, but investigation shows no one in sight. Bedroom doorknobs turn, and footsteps are heard in the rooms as those of a mortal. One of the bedroom doors could not be opened for several days; it seemed to stick tightly, and at closing time one evening the caretaker said, "I must get a carpenter in the morning and get that door open." Next morning the door was found standing wide open!

No one knew what restless spirit revisited Kenmore until one day in broad daylight the lady in charge saw Col. Fielding Lewis standing in an upper room, where once he attended to business affairs. Col. Lewis held in his hand a paper and seemed to be reading it. He was wearing the costume of Revolutionary times.

Kenmore

Upon another occasion a young lady, passing along the corridor and glancing into the same bedchamber "over the greate room," beheld the former Master of the house seated as though poring over his accounts.

Betty Washington has not been seen, but we may believe Col. Fielding Lewis has not forgotten Kenmore.

Mrs. William Jeffries Chewning writes of an interesting experience at Kenmore. The day was hot and sultry, not a breath of air stirring, nevertheless she felt a cold draught blowing on the back of her head. That this experience is usual when a Spirit is close at hand is well known to students of psychic phenomena.

No one else in the room, Mrs. Chewning stood with two friends in Betty Washington Lewis' chamber, looking towards the wardrobe. She remarked: "I think this is the haunted room." At once they heard a click and the wardrobe door swung slowly open! Later investigation satisfied Mrs. Chewning the opening of the door was not due to a jar.

St. George's Church

ST. GEORGE'S CHURCH

IN 1732—seven years after the town of Fredericksburg was laid out—a small frame building was erected and named St. George's Church. The parish comprised the whole of Spotsylvania County. For the first two years of the varied vicissitudes inseparable from the beginnings of religious worship in Colonial days, Rev. Patrick Henry, uncle of the statesman, shepherded a tiny, but we may believe, resourceful flock.

The records of the County Court inform us that Thomas Moseley and John Shelton were committed by Larkin Chew upon the information of Thomas Chew, Church Warden, for taking upon themselves to baptise the child of one Ann Alsop. In default of bond for good behavior, these good churchmen were to receive thirty-one lashes on their bare back, sixteen in the evening and fifteen the next morning.

The first authentic beginning of Christianity in the Fredericksburg district is an old entry found in the records of Spotsylvania County, 1724: "Information brought by Thomas Chew, Church Warden, against John Diggs for absenting himself from the place of Divine worship; he is fined ten shillings, or 100 pounds of tobacco, or must receive corporal punishment in lieu thereof, as the law directs." Some of the parsons, it is revealed, were as zealous in supporting the law and doctrine as Mr. Thomas Chew, the Warden, appears to have been.

"In the main the character and manner of living of the early ministers of the Church of England here were not in accord with the dignity of their mission. Incidents so indicating were not at all unusual; on one occasion a clergyman of gigantic size and strength had a rough and tumble fight with members of his vestry, in which the laymen were knocked out. The burly Englishman took as his text the following Sunday, "And I contended with them, and cursed them, and smote certain of them, and plucked off their hair." Bishop Meade remarks, Surely God must have greatly loved this branch of his Holy Catholic Church, or he would not have borne so long with her unfaithfulness, and so readily forgiven her sins.

"In 1768 Lewis Craig, John Waller and James Chiles, Baptist preachers, were seized by the Sheriff of the County, tried by three magistrates in the yard of St. George's Church and confined in jail for 'preaching the Gospel contrary to law.' They were kept in confinement for several weeks and preached from the jail windows to the crowd gathered below. This jail was the handsomest jail in Virginia. Patrick Henry, apostle of religious liberty, pleaded their cause and they were finally released."

The little frame church, once enlarged, the scene of primitive and picturesque assemblages for worship, finally threatened to collapse one day while George Washington was attending Divine worship, "causing the people to leave by the doors and windows!" It was not, however, until 1849 that the present handsome stone edifice was erected upon the site of its modest predecessor. A beautiful window to her memory recalls that here Mary Washington worshipped in her day. The mortal remains of Col. Fielding Lewis rest beneath the front steps. The old communion silver was a thank offering on the part of John Gray, of "Traveller's Rest," his ships having been delivered out of the hands of pirates.

Rev. Alfred Randolph, later Bishop of Virginia, was the rector of St. George's in 1858. During this year a young lady, Miss Ella McCarty, who afterwards married Dr. Hugh Martin, was staying in Fredericksburg, and sang in the choir of St. George's Church. On this particular evening she went to church with Mr. Marshall Hall, and found only the organist had arrived. The body of the church was dark; one dim light burning in the choir loft, at that time over the vestibule of the church. Both men went in search of the sexton and more lamps. As Miss McCarty sat facing the chancel, there appeared to be a woman dressed in white with a veil over her face, kneeling at the rail; Miss McCarty watched the figure several moments before concluding she must be seeing a ghost. Presently the woman arose, and turning, gazed up with a sad expression at the mortal above her. Miss McCarty started to call to her when the figure vanished!

The two daughters of Mrs. Martin, Mrs. Gilmer Stoffegan and Mrs. Seddon, recall hearing their mother many times tell of the woman she saw kneeling one night at the rail in St. George's Church. The instantaneous vanishing is the assurance the figure in white was not mortal, but Spirit.

Towards the close of Bishop Randolph's life, two little children of Rev. and Mrs. George S. Vest having died at the same time, the clergyman told the Bishop that one night during his absence from home, Mrs. Vest awakened and saw the children standing at the foot of the bed. Mr. Vest asked his opinion of the matter. Virginia's great Bishop replied, "My son, years ago I would have called it an hallucination; but not today. The curtain was drawn aside, and for a moment their mother was permitted to see her children."

Aquia Church

AQUIA CHURCH

BETWEEN the Potomac and Rappahannock Rivers, on a commanding eminence in Stafford County, once part of Great Westmoreland, reaching from Georgetown to the Blue Ridge Mountains, stands, in Overwharton Parish, Aquia Church.

Built of brick and cruciform, it is unique in having a bell and clock tower; the hands of the old timepiece only within recent times disappearing beneath the corroding influence of the years. Over the south door in white letters strangers may read these words: "Built in 1751. Destroyed by fire in 1751. Rebuilt A.D. 1757 by Mourning Richards, Undertaker—William Copein, Mason."

For nearly two hundred years one of America's most beautiful churches has in this quiet spot survived many tides in the affairs of men. Its thick walls of checkered brickwork, sloping roof, square tower, "three decker" pulpit, overhanging sounding board and square pews remain, notwithstanding man's inhumanity and nature's storms.

The ashes of the parish's third rector Rev. John Moncure rest beneath the chancel, and under the Communion table is a marble slab with this inscription: "In memory of the Race of the House of Moncure."

The second rector of Overwharton Parish, Alexander Scott, A.M., was one of Scotland's most picturesque sons, finding in early life in the Colonies a flock to shepherd upon Virginian pastures, and for himself finally a resting place beneath her sod. A memorial of him is his gift of the massive beaten silver dish, chalice, cup and paten, each bearing the inscription, "The gift of the Rev. Mr. Alexander Scott, A.M., later minister of this parish." The date that of his death—April 1, 1739.

Three times in its history has this old silver been buried for safekeeping, as three great wars swept over the land.

Even as through the bitter cold of many winters and beneath summer's scorching heat, Alexander Scott gathered his flock into the Sanctuary to hear long, long sermons on Sunday morning, so has old Aquia throughout the years gathered her children one by one beneath her shadow, to wander forth no more! Upon one tomb can be read: "She was the daughter of Lady Baltimore by Henry Seawell, Esq., Secretary of Maryland—her age 35 years."

Mr. Thomas Waller, whose ancestors settled in Stafford County 260 years ago, tells of the tragedy of Aquia Church. All his life until very recently when a cement floor was laid in order to strengthen the walls, plainly could be seen in the center aisle on one of the flagstones, the blood stain where a woman was murdered in the church over a hundred years ago. The deed accomplished, her body, it is stated, was hidden in the belfry. So universal is the belief that the ghost of this woman walks at midnight, it is Mr. Waller's positive declaration that under no circumstances could any man in Stafford County be induced to enter the church late at night.

Mrs. Agnes Moncure of Stafford stated that she has lived close by Aquia Church all her life, always knew it was haunted and tells of the above tragedy enacted more than 150 years ago. Mrs. Moncure says: "Every one speaks of sounds in the church as though someone was running up and down stairs. A number of people have heard heavy noises, suggesting a struggle was taking place. Upon entering—all is quiet."

Mrs. Nellie Waller Wight also tells that throughout the years noisy disturbances have been reported heard in old Aquia. The woman was murdered during the unsettled period of the Revolution. She arrived, according to Stafford County tradition, in a stage coach. Probably no services were being held in the church during those days and the tragedy not discovered for some time.

Mr. G. V. and Margaret Moncure have from childhood heard this church mentioned as being haunted. Messrs. R. C. L. Moncure, Senior and Junior, have heard their fathers declare Aquia Church haunted. These gentlemen, also Messrs. W. F. Powers and J. A. MacGregor, state their grandfathers told them when they were young a ghost haunted Aquia Church.

Mr. John Waller of Fredericksburg relates that when he was a boy he used to sit and listen to Mr. Wm. Fitzhugh reminisce concerning the Civil War. One night Fitzhugh and another young soldier had had a hard day scouting and went into Aquia Church to sleep in the square pews, notwithstanding they knew the church was considered haunted. The moon was bright; presently they decided it safer to open the door. After resting some time both young men heard unmistakable footsteps at the rear of the church on the stone flagging. Soon the tune "The Campbells are Coming" was whistled. Then more footsteps and the whistling again. This was repeated until steps and tune reached the soldiers. They jumped up and struck a light. There was no one in sight, but chancing to go to the door, the Yankees were to be seen advancing along the road, planning doubtless to bivouac in the church. The Confederates jumped out a rear window, and in after life always attributed their escape to the whistling of the ghost.

A member of the Moncure family writes me that of recent years it has been the habit of a lady of independent fortune and social position to pass her summers in Stafford County. She became interested in the haunting of Aquia Church through the stories told her by the various maids she employed. This lady determined to make an investigation herself and sought the company of several Stafford County men in her proposed raid upon Aquia Church at midnight. Her overtures were respectfully but firmly declined. Nothing daunted, this doughty investigator motored to Washington to obtain the services of two "Scientists" whose duties were to record noises and sounds, she expected to hear. It was a very dark night they chose for their trip. The lady led the procession into the church, but just after entering the door, a hand slapped her in the face! It was a very severe blow inasmuch as the mark remained several days. The Scientists ran in, but nowhere could they discover any normal explanation, and created so much disturbance in their search no further sounds were recorded that night.

Mr. Mercer Waller of Stafford County states that he has always known Aquia Church to be haunted. As boys they were afraid to go in at night to see the ghost. The skeleton of the murdered woman, he says, was finally found, still bearing a beautiful suite of golden hair. Mr. Waller had many times heard his father Colonel

Thomas Waller tell that this woman was often seen looking out the window, and that no one would go there at night. One man of his father's generation declared he was not afraid to go in the church. He was given a hammer and nail and late one night told to go up in the belfry and hammer the nail into the wall, so they would know he had really been up there. He went but stayed so long people began to get anxious. Finally an hour elapsed, so with a lantern several men went in and climbed up into the belfry. There they found the man and the hammer beside him. In the dark he had nailed the nail through his coat into the wall. Evidently endeavoring to turn in order to descend, it held him fast. Thinking someone had grabbed him he actually died of fright!

In May 1931 a Washingtonian visited Aquia Church and surrounding grounds. Later in the day meeting a resident of the neighborhood he asked why they did not keep the church locked? The reply was: "For the very simple reason it will not stay locked!"

CHATHAM

IN Stafford County, upon a commanding eminence overlooking Fredericksburg, a great Georgian mansion has stood for two hundred years. Built in 1728 by William Fitzhugh, grandson of the Emigrant, he named his home for a classmate at Eton and Oxford—William Pitt, Earl of Chatham.

Washington wrote: "I have put my legs oftener under your mahogany at Chatham than anywhere else in the world, and have enjoyed your good dinners, good wine, and good company more than any other."

Those were the days of the crinoline and brocade, of knee-breeches and powdered wigs; when casks of Burgundy and Madeira graced the cellar, and mint juleps quenched the thirst at all seasons and at all hours. These, with the leisurely minuet and the famous race horses, have been swept from sight .

Generations of Virginia's aristocracy graced this splendid mansion with their presence and partook of its comfort and cheer. Amid all the changes and chances of the life of our day, their descendants, scattered by the winds of circumstance, or of destiny, have in the lives of their ancestors who gathered at Chatham in the heyday of its prosperity, a heritage which cannot be bought or sold and of which they cannot be deprived.

Chatham passed into the keeping of an officer of the Continental Army, Major Churchill Jones, and since that day has had many owners, touching whose lives from time to time has ever been the Spirit of one who, long before they were born, passed a few never-forgotten days at that Virginia mansion.

The late Mrs. Randolph Howard, for a short time Chatham's gracious hostess, related to friends that on several occasions she had seen the White Lady in the garden walking up and down a path, leading by way of some marble steps to the terrace below, known as the "Ghost Walk." The White Lady is reputed always seen once in seven years, on the 21st of June, between noon and midnight.

Mrs. Howard saw her in the afternoon. She had no idea of the

Chatham

ghost's name or history and seldom spoke freely on the subject, fearing the servants would be frightened. By great good fortune a Virginian, interested in Chatham and also a French scholar, chanced upon a very old book written in that language in a library in Newark, New Jersey. In discarding some delapidated old French books, the librarian showed the visitor one of early Nineteenth Century origin—a collection of ghost stories. Glancing here and there through the pages, her eye caught the names "Chatham" and "Geo. Washington" in one chapter. Sitting down she read an interesting story. One day Mrs. Howard invited this friend for afternoon tea at Chatham, to meet others, and to tell them of the story found in the dusty old volume in the Newark library.

The Frenchman who had been, during his travels, entertained at Chatham, heard the story of the White Lady and was preserving it to be told there once more upon a summer afternoon.

In life the White Lady was an English girl, the daughter of a distinguished man of letters, who fell madly in love with a drysalter, when, with tears and lamentations, she and her maid conveyed to him the mortal remains of her beloved parrot—to be preserved by his skill, in spite of death. The dry-salter reciprocated the lady's affection, and after a hurried courtship, plans were made for an elopement. Her Father discovered the plans in time to frustrate them by taking his daughter to America, where he hoped to marry her off.

On reaching America they were entertained by many friends who had left England to make their homes in the Western World. Meeting Mrs. Fitzhugh, they were invited to join a house party at Chatham. The White Lady languished in spite of the gay life at this charming place and mourned her dry-salter. However, he had followed almost at once, and finding she was in Virginia, succeeded in communicating with her without her Father's knowledge, and again an elopement was planned. Her Father heard that the suitor had reached American shores, so he locked the girl in her room each night.

Undaunted, the dry-salter procured a ropeladder which he threw up to her window and a boat was moored on the Rappahannock. All preparations were made when a servant of General Washington, who was visiting there at the time, told him, and he, counseling secrecy to her Father, had the dry-salter caught and locked up; and when the pale lady descended the ladder she was received not in her lover's arms, but in those of the General, who bore her with "a stout grip" into her Father's room! The Father hurried away and back to England, where he married her off to a man of his own choosing.

> "Oh, Time, whose verdicts mock our own,
> The only righteous judge art thou!

She lived long enough to have ten children, but died constant to the memory of the dry-salter.

On her death-bed she announced her intention of walking in Spirit on the anniversary of her death, in the Lady's Walk on the terrace at Chatham, a favorite spot with her. She died June 21, 1790.

CONCORD

I N Stafford County, Virginia, on a hill overlooking Aquia Creek, and from whence, in the far distance the Potomac River can be seen, a progenitor of the Waller family built a house of logs early in the eighteenth century and named it "Concord." In 1754 the present interesting old dwelling, with two big stone chimneys and high-pitched roof, was erected by the same family upon the site of the former house. The number of graves in the neglected and deserted old burying-ground, less than two hundred feet from the house, testify to the several generations living and dying in these pioneer homes.

A drive of about a mile from the highway through dense pine woods, or sometimes the country road fringed with cedars, sumach and elder, or with the tender green of Autumn's goldenrod mingling with the thick growth of blackberries ripening in the sunny open spaces, leads one to the kindly greeting of the present owner, Mr. I. Alaster MacGregor, whose Father, John Ridout MacGregor, bought the property from the Wallers in 1859. As the name suggests, Mr. MacGregor is of Scotch lineage, his forebears among Maryland's earliest settlers, and to this inheritance is probably due the interesting psychic experiences of several members of the family. Mr. MacGregor points out that the house, built of heart timber hewn from America's virgin forest of oak and poplar, is solid after the passing of 175 years. The roof in one long slope covers porch and house alike, and dormer windows afford light to the second story. Tall altheas and hollyhocks bloom in the sun by a fence close by; and through the little gate Mr. MacGregor has seen the ghosts of three women enter the yard at the same time, walk some little distance along the path and then disappear.

A visitor is interested and astonished to discover in the two steps leading to the porch, two handsome large marble tombstones resting upon carved sandstone pedestals. These latter were cut from the Aquia Creek quarries from whence came the stone of which the Capitol at Washington is built. It seems that a great many years ago these marble slabs, probably ordered from a distant

Concord

point, and destined for the Waller burying-ground, reached their destination a considerable time after there had been any deaths in the family. One man alone in the county knew to which graves these stones belonged. Unfortunately he delayed for one reason or another, coming to attend to the placing of these memorials, until he too was gathered to his Fathers. In course of time, Mr. MacGregor, needing some door steps, discovered the long forgotten stones, lying concealed by weeds and briars, so he put them to other use than that for which they were originally designed.

Even nearer the house than the Waller lot, is a trim and neat little plot planted with box, where rest all that is mortal of those MacGregors who have passed their lives in the old house nearby. Mr. MacGregor is most courteous in relating his very interesting and varied experiences upon many occasions with ghosts and apparitions.

So far as he knows, no tragedy has taken place in the history of this dwelling, and remarkable to relate, there is no evidence on record of any negro seeing an apparition in a house—as the owner expresses it—"chuck full of ghosts!"

No member of the family has even seen an apparition in the burying-grounds. In all the old rooms—one new one has been added—a woman has been seen many times by Mr. MacGregor, his mother, his father and his sister. When appearing to Mr. MacGregor the ghost was dressed in black. She would enter the house through the north wall, and walk about the corridor and rooms, as would a mortal. She did not appear either troubled or searching for any object. She endeavored always to peer into the faces of those she encountered, possibly hoping to find some particular person she knew while on earth. There is no record of her speaking, or having been spoken to. Each time, after a short visit, the apparition would vanish. Mr. MacGregor is quite sure his mother saw the ghost's face distinctly, having met her several times walking about the grounds. She passed through closed doors, and though often with the family upon different occasions, remained ever a mystery. No one ever discovered who she was.

Mr. MacGregor's wife never saw the unknown visitor, but would feel her touch. At night, at about half-past ten, upon three occasions Mr. MacGregor and his wife can recall being awakened by the ghost touching them on the shoulder. They never ascertained for what reason they were aroused.

This ghost appeared to Mr. MacGregor's sister early one morning after sunrise, standing by the window looking out into the yard. After her death Mr. MacGregor's father and brother both saw his sister in broad daylight. She was wearing a dress familiar to them, and passed quietly from the room in which they were sitting into the hall.

The ghost seen most frequently always entered the house through the north wall. This wall, at one side of the chimney, was found to be on fire one winter day. A man, ax in hand, ran to the second story, and chopping and pounding, knocked out the wall, while Mr. MacGregor performed the same feat below. Covering the burning timbers with snow, they in this manner saved the roof and the rest of the house; but the ghost was never seen again!

One night, when a child and preparing for bed, Mr. MacGregor relates he saw the door open and his mother looked in. She then crossed the hall, looking into the room where the girls slept. The next morning his mother declared she had not been upstairs that night.

It was the custom of the family to attend a weekly prayer-meeting at the Courthouse. Walking alone one evening, Mr. MacGregor relates he found in his pocket a small revolver with which he had been practicing that day and had forgotten to leave at home. His dog was with him, and suddenly the animal came running with his tail between his legs, unsuccessfully endeavoring to overtake a larger dog. Having heard of ghost dogs, Mr. MacGregor declares he fired, and plainly saw the bullet pass through the apparition and stir up the dust as it struck the road. There was no dog there!

Upon another night, coming from choir practice, and all dressed up, Mr. MacGregor declares, "I was walking carefully, as the road was very muddy. Suddenly someone grabbed me from behind! I though it must be a boy, but was nevertheless startled, and slipping into a ditch got all over mud. Jumping up, I decided to get that party and ran to the top of the hill. There was not a soul around."

Mr. MacGregor states that for the last eighteen years he has seen no ghost at Concord—they seem to visit it no more.

FOULKE

COLONEL GERARD FOULKE, born in Staffordshire, England, died in Virginia in 1669. He married Ann Chandler of Port Tobacco, Maryland. Colonel Foulke was "Gentlemen of the bed chamber to Charles I, and a Colonel in the Royal Army." He came to Virginia with his cousin George Mason of Staffordshire, England.

October 17, 1664 Foulke received six hundred acres of the Foster tract sold him by Governor Berkley, belonging to the King of Potomac. Colonel Foulke was Colonel of Troops for Westmoreland County in 1660. In 1661 charges were made against Captain Giles Brent, Colonel Gerard Foulke, Mr. John Lord and Captain George Mason, of having injured and affronted Wahonganocke, King of the Potomacs. The House of Burgesses investigated the charges and ordered that Foulke, Lord, and Mason pay the Indian King 100 arms length of Roanoke apiece, or match coats instead, at 20 arms length every coat. Roanoke was a cheap wampum made especially in Virginia from oyster shells; used only south of Delaware Bay.

The word match-coat is a Colonial American corruption of an Indian word, Ojibway in origin, which was spelled matshigode and referred to those fur mantles or cloaks the aborigines wore; also petticoats for the women.

Traders made match coats of a coarse woolen cloth, which they called match cloth. The cloth was measured by the length of the buyer's or the seller's arms.

September 7, 1664 Colonel Gerard Foulke deeded to his "beloved kinsman Richard Hope" 400 acres of his Foster tract. This land, September 18, 1672, Hope deeded to Ann Foulke for the consideration of £35. "Lands commonly called Mathapungo, formerly enjoyed by the King of the Potomacs," adjoining a piece of ground owned by said Gerard Foulke; said land being on record in Stafford County, Virginia. Upon his property Gerard Foulke built a house, still standing. It is typical of that early day in the wilderness. Of stout timber, with heavy chimneys, and as was often seen the high pitched roof sloped down over the porch.

Within a few hundred yards of the river's banks throughout 260 years this adventurer into the primeval forest from the Court of the Stuarts has slept near his homestead. An old mulberry tree today keeps guard at the spot. Ann survived her husband, and it was undoubtedly she who marked his grave with a large recumbent stone bearing a lengthy inscription. Mr. Edwin Kirk, present owner of the property, succeeding Mr. Logan Clare, has talked with those who have seen the stone, could describe it to him and point out just where under the mulberry tree it rested. The stone was brought from overseas in some little sailing vessel, Colonel Foulke's "beloved kinsman" Richard Hope probably seeing it start on the long voyage to far off Virginia.

Shortly after the year 1900 it seems that the brick in the old chimney fireplace gave way; probably in the winter when a fire was urgently needed, and the dweller beneath this old rooftree undertook to make use of Gerard Foulke's tombstone as a fireback. After putting the stone in place, undoubtedly a laborious and difficult undertaking, he probably warmed himself in front of the cheerful blaze on the hearth before mounting to bed in the cold room under the roof. During the night an apparition appeared in his bedroom, doubtless none other than Foulke himself, affording the desecrator of the grave a terrifying experience!—one he had no intention of having repeated. The next morning, fire or no fire, he disposed of the stone. It was probably dumped into the river, as no trace can be found of the slab that for 230 years guarded the dust of Gerard Foulke.

TRAVELLER'S REST

IN Stafford County, Virginia, on the King's Highway, can be found, five miles beyond Fredericksburg and encircled by splendid cedars, a large brick mansion, mellow with age, at ease after war; the custodian of many memories. Three stone steps lead to a sunken garden along the river's edge, and the old kitchen, smokehouse, and servants' quarters paint a picture of other days and other customs.

To this spot in 1809 journeyed a Scotchman who, like so many of his countrymen, came to Virginia to seek his fortune, perpetuate his name, and end his days in the land of his adoption.

John Gray found, amid the trees in a beautiful bend in the river, a square brick house, to which he added a wing of seven rooms and lovely dormer windows; three sons and three daughters, and called it "Traveller's Rest." His material hopes and interests centered in sailing-vessels, and for their safe return from sea he doubtless added his fervent petitions to those of the congregation; for the beautiful communion service today in use in St. George's Church, Fredericksburg, was his gift of thanksgiving that he was delivered out of the hands of pirates!

Today, beneath the shade of some great tree where sunlight is no longer necessary, for "the books have closed over; all the lessons are said;" stands the little brick schoolhouse, a feature of plantation life, and recalling the occupation of travelling tutor, long since passed away. A year or two under the roof of one manor house, and then he would drift elsewhere! In 1800 an Englishman, John Davis, staff in hand, tramped as far from New York as South Carolina, stopping here and there for a year or two, teaching. From the window of one tiny schoolhouse he could see the faroff Blue Ridge Mountains as he taught and fell in love with Virginia Ball.

Through the vista of much more than a hundred years, in fancy, we see Virginia standing in the schoolhouse door, her 'kerchief to her eyes, as her teacher, staff in hand once more, takes the path leading to Baltimore and to England. Virginia weeps no more, and has long since vanished beyond life's sorrows; but still lives the concluding entry in her lover's diary. "It was a killing circumstance to leave Virginia, but who can presume to contend against fate?"

Traveller's Rest is now the property of Mr. J. Bowie Gray, one of the Virginia Military Institute Cadets at the famous battle of New Market, and his daughter Miss Aylmer. From the latter I learn of a grandmother who will visit Traveller's Rest without invitation, and who disturbs the sleep of visitors by passing the night alternately walking up the stairs and rocking noisily in a campechee chair! Miss Gray declares it to be her grandmother and that she enters the room and remonstrates with her. The rocking ceases only so long as Miss Gray remains. "Grandmother rocks both day and night." The noise above became so annoying Mr. Gray advised the chair to be taken to the attic, from whence the rocking could not be heard.

Miss Gray writes me: "Uncle Tom, an old colored man, brings my Father's horse back and forth from the stable, and when he reaches a certain walnut-tree in the yard, the horse, at certain times, halts and refuses to move until after much coaxing. He then proceeds as usual. This Uncle Tom says is because 'the horse dun seen a spirit.' Only at a designated spot does he stop and none of the other horses do."

During the Civil War a guard was placed at Traveller's Rest to stop stealing and in order to guard the property. A Confederate soldier across the river, seeing the Federal uniform, fired, and nearly killed a member of the family! Both soldiers sleep on "fame's eternal camping ground." The member of the family rests beyond the rose-garden. The bullet is shown embedded in the porch pillar at Traveller's Rest.

Ruins of Mannsfield, Spotsylvania County, Virginia

MANNSFIELD

MANN PAGE, a member of the House of Burgesses and prominent in the affairs of the Colonies, built in 1749 a large two-story stone mansion near Fredericksburg in Spotsylvania and overlooking the waters of the Rappahannock. He called his home "Mannsfield," and hither he brought his bride, Mary Tayloe, from Mt. Airy. Celebrated for more than a century for its avenue and grove of magnificent chestnut trees, these were Mannsfield's pride and glory.

William Bernard of Belle Grove in King George County became the next owner of this fine estate. At the close of the Civil War, Union soldiers straggling north are supposed to have set it on fire by accident or otherwise, and old Mannsfield burned to the ground. For years the ruins, over which a tangle of wild grape gradually clambered, perfuming the air when in blossom, and the naked limbs of the dead chestnut trees etching the sky, alone recalled that here was once the beautiful home of the Pages and the Bernards.

And yet it was to Mannsfield a full generation after the destroying flames stained the sky crimson, and the smoke lingered a haze on the far horizon, that the most wonderful scenes were enacted beneath the chestnuts, and described by a "clear seeing" woman to a descendant of the William Bernard who long ago was master of Mannsfield.

In 1862 the house was used as headquarters by General Franklin, and also as a hospital. Here were brought the wounded from the battle then in progress at Hamilton's Crossing. Almost directly opposite and not quite one mile distant. This shady grove must have been a haven of rest and where first aid was given to those brought back from the front. It was in this grove that General Bayard and his friend Captain Gibson were just rising from the ground to go to lunch when a shot came. It cut off Captain Gibson's sword belt without doing further injury, and passing on, struck General Bayard.

Mr. William Bernard, Sr. of Fredericksburg writes me:

"The house was finally burned after the Surrender, by Union

troops on their way up north. The colored people born and raised here could never be induced to go to the grove or near the ruins after dark, declaring ghosts commenced to walk around at night. Of course nobody paid any attention to them. Finally some years later the farm was tenanted by a gentleman and his family who lived in a new home, the grove not far distant. They were people of culture whose ancestors sought and found homes in Virginia. Mrs. S. —now I think dead—was born and raised in Spotsylvania County and was endowed with what is called clairvoyance, a gift known among all people and in all races and times. Walking out into her yard and pointing to a certain chestnut tree, Mrs. S. would ask if you did not see men in uniform under the tree? She could see a doctor ministering to the wounded under another tree, officers with their side arms, all moving to and fro; orderlies holding two or more horses, etc. She could not understand why others could not see what she saw.

Mrs. S. has often told me that she saw men in Confederate uniforms walking back and forth under the trees and seemed annoyed that I could not do so."

Mr. William Bernard, Sr. recalls distinctly two others who saw soldiers reappearing in the vicinity of this interesting old mansion. A neighbor, a Mrs. Yerby, lived near them on the Hamilton Crossing battlefield, and told him she had a number of times seen the ghostly Confederate soldiers all about Mannsfield.

Many years after the Civil War Mr. Bernard was living *en garçon* in the tenant's house when his mother, Mrs. Isabella Roberts Bernard, came to visit him. She awoke one night to find a Confederate officer standing at the foot of her bed. Remembering Mrs. Yerby's experiences, Mrs. Bernard paid no attention to the soldier but again went to sleep.

KATINA

FRANCIS Thornton came from Yorkshire, England, to Virginia in 1673 and at the Falls of the Rappahannock occupied a vast plantation. Situated on a high eminence in Spotsylvania County, midway between Fredericksburg and Falmouth, stands today the interesting old house he built about 1680 and named "The Falls." His son Francis Thornton married Frances Gregory, daughter of Roger Gregory and Mildred Washington. Twenty years ago the old kitchen, office and slave quarters were still standing.

From this height one sees for miles the waters of the famous stream glistening in the sunlight, while cornfields and apple orchards color far and near the fertile valley. Flowing between the Potomac and the James, impressive to us as in the far-off days of the Powhatan Confederacy, is the rapid rise and quickly following ebb of its tide. The Indians along its banks were "Rapahanocks, or people of the alternating stream."

The Falls of the Rappahannock are today a wild, rugged and picturesque spot. The same countless age-old rocks, green with moss, over which the waters dash and sparkle as when Katina's forefathers stood in the wilderness beneath the shade of mighty oaks, watching old sycamores cast dancing shadows far over the swiftly flowing current.

Under an old cedar, doubtless hollowed out of a mighty boulder by Time, that tireless artisan, may be found, "Francis Thornton's punch bowl." Upon its rim he carved one day, over two hundred years ago, "F. T. 1720."

It is known that when Alexander Spotswood was Governor of Virginia an Indian girl became domesticated in his household. They called her Katina. Later, with her consent, she was transferred to the Thornton home, The Falls, becoming the nurse and devoted companion of Francis Thornton the younger and of his brothers and sisters.

On sunny days, passing out of the rear door and along the walk of square brick and marble blocks, past the big white swan from whose beak the water fell into the bowl of an iron fountain, still relics of those far-off days, they descended the long terraces then

Francis Thornton's Punch Bowl

leading to the river's edge and wandered far into the forest along the stream, learning much of Indian lore from their devoted attendant. Upon one occasion, heedless of the passing hours, these little pioneers in Virginia's solitary woods were discovered by their Father, far from home, playing with a covey of partridges Katina had cleverly enticed into a little basket woven by her dexterous fingers from the twigs of bushes and reeds plucked from the water's edge.

When Francis Thornton was about seventeen, probably 174 years ago, Katina died, and was buried in the garden at The Falls. Beside a little stream, with great boulders of granite gathered from her native hills marking the spot, this Indian sleeps her last sleep beneath a tree, up and over which climbs a wild grape vine, accredited "the most magnificent in Virginia." Sinking gradually throughout the years into the earth, only small portions of these stones are visible today.

Experience leads us to expect the Spirit of this Indian would be seen from time to time frequenting the house and woods where she spent a happy earth life. Mrs. Bessie Taylor Robinson lives in a mansion built later in life by Francis Thornton II and named Fall Hill, not far from the charming old brick house, hoary with age, steeped in tradition, and bearing that mystic atmosphere inseparable from the joys and sorrows of many life histories. She tells us that many persons—since Katina's death—have spoken of seeing her walking about the plantation as though looking for her companions of long ago.

One summer recently a young guest had been put to sleep in the old nursery, and awakened to see the Indian girl pulling back the covers of the bed, as if looking for her little charges who had slept there in far-off nights.

It is a fortunate circumstance that The Falls not only has weathered the vicissitudes of Time, but is still the property of descendants of that Francis Thornton and Frances Gregory who for maybe 150 years have slept in the little burying-ground surrounded

The Falls

Fall Hill

by the old brick wall. Mrs. Fred H. Robinson was Miss Bessie Forbes Taylor, and with her husband and children dwell upon the plantation of their forefathers and are playing their brief parts in the great pageant of earth's drama, e'er the curtain again falls, even as it fell when Katina and her little companions disappeared to wander, hand in hand, amid the woods of the "happy hunting-grounds."

Katina is not the only Spirit haunting her former home. June 12, 1930, Mrs. Robinson told Mrs. Chewning that last September she and her eldest son returned at midnight after passing an evening in Fredericksburg. As Mrs. Robinson walked in the hall, a small man came out of the downstairs bedroom in which her younger son slept. Passing her, he went down the hall, entering the back parlor. Mrs. Robinson, thinking it must be her youngest son, called to him. Receiving no answer, she went to his room, where he was sound asleep! She then went upstairs to her own room and found her husband asleep. Becoming alarmed, Mrs. Robinson sought her eldest son, and telling him the circumstances, together they searched the house. Every window was closed, every door locked. Undoubtedly some ghostly visitant had at midnight for one brief moment crossed the path of the mistress of Fall Hill.

LAMB'S CREEK CHURCH

IN King George County on the King's Highway about thirteen
miles from Fredericksburg, on the Rappahannock River side, an
interesting Colonial building may be found called Lamb's Creek
Church. Erected in 1769 it is now six miles from a lone gravestone
on Muddy Creek marking the site of the Mother Church in use as
early as 1710.

In Brunswick parish extending up to Stafford County, in days
almost forgotten, far beyond the tide of the years in which we live,
Sunday mornings the coaches of the aristocracy rolled from far distant points and over rough roads to the door of Lamb's Creek
Church.

In the company of family and friends and surrounded by retainers a large congregation listened to the delights of paradise glow-
ingly painted, and hell pictured as very real and very hot! The
lessons were read from the priceless old "Vinegar Bible," so called
owing to a typographical error in the edition, the heading of the
Parable of the Vineyard made to read "Parable of the Vinegar."
This Bible was given to Muddy Creek Church about 1716. Stolen
after the Civil War, by great good fortune it has been recovered
and is in use once each year when a service is held in the church.
The old prayer book, also inherited from the Mother Church, was
printed in 1739 when George II was King.

The devastating War of the Revolution scattered the faithful
and altered the lives and fortunes of the people. For fifty years the
church doors were closed.

Not until the Civil War did man's hand shatter and desecrate
this relic of a civilization of which the despoilers did not even
dream, and could not possibly appreciate. The woodwork was
pulled out, the windows and doors broken, and the church used
for a stable!

In a bend of the road this large country church may be seen from
quite a distance. A vital need in the lives of a generation long
passed away, it stands in an isolated spot abandoned and by the
world forgot—a mute witness to the transitoriness of all human
religious expression.

Lamb's Creek Church, Virginia

Just prior to the desecration of this house of worship by Federal soldiers two Confederate officers, one named Hunter, are said to have entered the church one night seeking refuge from a heavy thunder storm. The flashes of lightning were very vivid, and the thunder deafening. Running in they seated themselves at the door facing the chancel. Presently, for one brief moment the inky darkness was relieved by a great flash of lightning. The two men were dumfounded to see kneeling at the chancel rail as if in prayer a woman dressed in white! In pitchy darkness, silently and breathlessly they awaited the next flash. There still kneeled the woman! A third view of the figure was sufficient and both soldiers made a hasty exit into the teeth of the furious storm!

Mr. Thomas Lomax Hunter, a lawyer of King George County, very courteously makes reply to my letter of inqury as follows:

"My father and uncles were the only Hunters in the Civil War from this county, but I have never heard the story which you relate of them and Lamb's Creek Church.

"Lamb's Creek Church has however been long looked upon by the natives here as haunted, and while I cannot recite any detailed story about it I have no doubt that reputable witnesses of its neighborhood could be put upon the witness stand to prove its ghostly character."

Marmion

MARMION

MARMION, in King George County, Virginia, has been in the family of Mrs. Lucy Lewis Grymes for more than 150 years. Lord Marmion was the last of the title in England, and in his honor William Fitzhugh, emigrating to the Colonies in 1670, named this portion of his vast estate, erecting in 1674, between two splendid springs flowing in the primeval forest, the mansion still standing. One finds to the north the little house from the depths of which countless juleps were cooled; not far distant the old kitchen to which, from smokehouse and dairy, still standing, bacon, butter and cream flowed in a constant stream throughout the generations.

Behind the house the lovely old office stands in a garden, carpeted in spring with single blue hyacinths and yellow primroses, hardy descendants of flowers brought from England long ago. In the attic of this office quite recently Mrs. Grymes found a roll of Colonial money, signed by her husband's ancestor, Robert Carter Nicholas.

In 1719 John Fitzhugh took unto himself a wife, and Marmion was their home. A grove of pecans, walnuts and maples stand close to this sturdy and picturesque relic of a bygone age; its two secret rooms, one built in the huge chimney above the other, speaking to us of turbulence and of dangers unknown to our generation.

Marmion in 1785 became the property of Major George Lewis, son of Col. Fielding Lewis and Betty Washington. Their great-granddaughter, Mrs. Lucy Lewis Grymes, is the fortunate owner today. A mile and a half beyond flows the Potomac River, and in 1782 Philip Fitzhugh, the last of his name at Marmion, is said to have brought to his home, one day, one of those accomplished artisans, contributing by their skill to some of the most beautiful decorations remaining with us from their day. This Hessian soldier was in a dying condition when found by Philip Fitzhugh on the banks of the river. Recovering his health in course of time, the stranger was then desirous of contributing evidence of his skill in return for the kindness shown him. He decorated the walls of the parlor in lovely landscapes and cornucopias filled with flowers, making from Virginia clay and plants the paints he used—clear and beautiful after the passing of 150 years! Owing to Mrs. Grymes' willingness to share with countless others her treasures, the superb paneling, decorations and mirror in this beautiful parlor at Marmion were transferred into the keeping of the Metropolitan Museum in New York.

In the long ago when dangers threatened, before cannon balls from two wars were left embedded as relics in the brick walks leading from the mansion, a chest of valuables was buried. Whether discovered and carried off nobody knows. But Marmion possesses a charming ghost; thieves cannot break in and steal.

Some of the old darkies whose forefathers lived in the "Quarters" on the plantation claim today to have seen the "white lady" walking among the roses and the honesuckle in the little cemetery.

Mrs. Grymes writes: "Since my childhood, every now and then guests have spoken of a lovely young girl they have seen from time to time in the house. Twice, I myself, when in the guest-room, have felt there was someone in the room, but have never seen the ghost. During the summer of 1928 Miss Edmonia Goode, an elderly lady from Chase City, Virginia, was staying at Marmion with a group of young people whom she had been chaperoning at a house party in Fredericksburg. It was in the afternoon of a bright sunny day. Miss Goode was lying down on her bed resting, when the door opened and a very beautiful young girl came in and started to open the wardrobe. Miss Goode sat up and exclaimed: "Why, how do you do? I did not know there was another guest in this house beside our party." The girl turned and looked squarely at her. The face of the Spirit, Miss Goode would recognize anywhere. She arose advancing towards the visitor in order to shake hands. . . .

THE GHOST POOL

REV. JOHN BELL came from England in 1711, receiving the King's Bounty to pay the expenses of the trip. He was the minister of Christ Church until his death in 1743. With him came his daughter. Mr. Bell was a man of substance, his inventory showing land in Lancaster and Prince William Counties, forty-three slaves, etc. The Vestry book states prior to 1713, "The Glebe then as now, a good farm near the church."

April 1719 Rev. John Bell was absent when his name was called at the Convention held at William and Mary College. It is recorded —"October 23, 1723, Rev. John Bell was paid for 8 sermons at 450 pounds tobacco apiece."

In the year 1724 Mr. Bell informed the Bishop of London, "there were 300 families in it; that the Church was thronged; that almost all the white people attended; that there were a great many negroes who neither understood his language, nor he theirs, that the Church was open to them, and the Word preached, and the Sacraments administered with circumspection."

Christ Church is said never to have been repaired other than with some panes of glass; depredations following the Civil War; and of recent years a slate roof replacing shingles, the greater number of which are still serviceable.

Today, in an unfrequented region stands the old church, finished in 1732—upon the site of a still earlier house of worship built in 1670, not far from the Corotoman River. One finds woodland and undergrowth on two sides; here and there great walnut trees, nuts pressed into the earth by the feet of slaves felling their giant forbears; these trees living today in pulpit, table and panelling within this splendid relic of a bygone age. Beneath her shadows, here and there among the trees, interesting inscriptions may be deciphered on old stones, and a number of graves are within a crumbling wall. A heavy gate with immense iron lock was locked many years ago for the last time, and in order to prevent trespass the key thrown into the river.

"The will was obeyed, but a young tree sprang up on the inside of the enclosure near the wall and as the years have passed its roots have quietly found their way under the heavy masonry, and overturned the wall, and today the crumbling enclosure is a striking illustration of the futility of human commands."

The old cedar dial-post bearing the name John Carter, 1702, was removed into the Church from beside the door within recent years. The Church, in the form of a cross, is strong and impressive. Of checkered brick work; walls three feet thick; large windows with small square panes of glass. "King Carter" spared no expense when he built this house of God 200 years ago. Trimmed throughout with walnut, a massive Communion table, carved rail, panelled walls, high pulpit beneath its sounding board, clerk's desk below and a graceful winding stair. In the huge square pews, some capable of seating twenty people, worms are now silently contributing their work to Time's inevitable decree.

A splendid stone floor, bitterly cold in winter, is as smooth today as when "King Carter" drove through a cedar bordered road from Corotoman, dismounted from his coach, and amid a shivering congregation standing outside, walked to his pew beside the Chancel. One-fourth of the Church was reserved for his retainers!

A handful of a far off generation attends occasional services in the old Church today, while the sunshine streams through a great window onto "King Carter's" empty seat, and the dry leaves driven by the autumn winds eddy and whirl around his tomb.

The daughter of Mr. Bell was engaged to a young planter named Carter, who just before the day set for the wedding was killed in a fight with Indians. The girl pined and died. Sometime before death her father promised to bury her on the glebe beneath a certain old poplar, a happy trysting place. After her death he repented of the promise and had the body laid in the churchyard. Again and again the Spirit of the girl appeared in the night time, speaking to the minister, reminding him of his promise to put her body beneath the old tree. Finally wearied by the continued haunting, Mr. Bell had the coffin placed where his daughter requested. She appeared no more. Soon after this the grave began to sink and a pond of water sprang up covering the place of her burial. This pool can be seen today.

VERVILLE

L OST in the mists of Time is the early history of one of Virginia's old homesteads, standing as ever in an isolated spot in Lancaster County. Some authorities tell us it was built by a Doctor Madison; a Scotchman of means, we judge, from the fine woodwork and other evidences of refinement and of beauty. The site selected gives color to the tradition that Doctor Madison lived the life of a recluse. In the southern part of historic Northern Neck, about five miles from the village of Lancaster, "Verville" stands.

The house is said to have been built late in the seventeenth century, and rejoices in walls laid in Flemish bond, a hipped roof charming in all generations, lighted by dormer windows, and protected from rain and snow by those shingles so inflammable and so unfailingly picturesque! Beneath all we find deep cellars now used for storing fruit and vegetables. Above are large rooms with high ceilings, handsome wainscoting, beaded cornices, and carved mantels. These assure us that if Doctor Madison craved solitude he also loved beauty.

The detached buildings once standing here and there beneath the trees have vanished, but the old spring assuring the wandering Scot of a bountiful supply of water, after two hundred and fifty years flows beneath the shade of age-old trees, and carries to this generation the same assuring message. "Verville" at one time had in addition a deep well in a corner of the garden near the house. It is around this well and the Blue Room on the second story of the mansion that clings very interesting evidence of spirit return.

"This well suddenly went dry and the people attempted to fill it up," writes Mrs. Louisa Currie Hall of Amherst, who formerly lived at "Verville." "For years and years about every six months the soil where the well had once been would sink several inches. More soil would be placed in the depression and for a while all would be well, then it would sink again. The cause of the sinking was unknown, so the sinking and the filling would go on. According to the legend, from out the depths of this old well came the spirit of a lady and a little child. Quietly they came and quietly they made their

Verville, Lancaster County, Virginia

way to the Blue Room on the second floor. Always they came when the night was dark, and as soon as they entered the room they made a light. It is a fact that scores of times this light has been seen issuing from the high windows of the Blue Room by persons employed on the place, by neighbors, and by visitors approaching the house. Even guests sleeping in the room have been awakened suddenly and beheld this soft yellow light flooding the room. But nobody has ever seen the lady or the little child. Sometimes when the light was seen from the outside, some person more bold than the rest would dash madly up the winding stairs and throw open the door of the Blue Room to find—darkness, silence!

"Who this lady was, or why she came, we do not know, but the legend said that when the old well was made to stop sinking the lady and little child would come no more.

"One night in the spring of 1907 there came what has been spoken of as a 'young flood.' All night it rained in torrents; bridges were destroyed, the crops were washed away, level fields were covered with water, and the river was filled with landslides. The next morning when the storm had at last subsided every one was out viewing the destruction caused by the tempest. But the thing of most importance, that held the attention of all, was the fact that the old well had sunk about six feet! The sides were as smooth as if it had been freshly dug, and there six feet down lay the sod that had been a part of the field the day before. Again the old well was filled up, and not the slightest depression has been found since, and true to the legend the light has not been seen from that time either by persons in the house or outside."

After Doctor Madison's day "Verville" came into the possession of Colonel James Gordon. It was here that Rev. James Waddell, the famous blind Presbyterian preacher, mentioned in Wirt's "British Spy," was married to Miss Mary Gordon. Doctor Waddell from Ulster, Ireland, of Scotch parentage, settled in Pennsylvania in 1739. Colonel James Gordon was the wealthiest and most influential Presbyterian of his community. In 1778 Doctor Waddell moved to Augusta County.

Mt. Airy

MT. AIRY

CLOSE to the water's edge in Richmond County the little village of Tappahannock, not far distant, may still be found traces of the foundations of "Old Place Field," the early home of Col. John Tayloe.

Colonel Tayloe in 1758 built upon the same extensive plantation the splendid mansion called then, as now, Mt. Airy. Above the Rappahannock, and far beyond its reach, framed in a setting of sunny fields and shady forests of oak and cedar, it is the custodian of a superb collection of portraits and priceless heirlooms. Furniture, silver and china, have been treasured at Mt. Airy from generation to generation.

Built of native brown stone and of the white sandstone quarried on Aquia Creek, this imposing edifice is adorned by curved corridors extending to two-storied wings placed far from the dwelling. One of these additions was, before the Revolution, the Master's office, schoolroom, and guesthouse, and in it today is the haunted room where the ghost of a woman is still seen from time to time.

In days when foxes were plentiful and hunting a constant pastime, an ever-welcome visitor at Mt. Airy was Sir Jenings Beckwith —gay, debonaire, a devotee of pleasure, an ardent huntsman.

Sir Jenings first saw the light of day in Virginia, a son of Sir Marmaduke Beckwith, born at Aldborough, Yorkshire, England, in 1687, and the grandson of Sir Roger Beckwith and of his wife Elizabeth, daughter of Sir Edmund Jenings, sister of Edmund Jenings, Governor of Virginia in 1706, who gave his nephew, Sir Marmaduke, the clerkship of Richmond County.

Passing much of his time in the saddle at Mt. Airy, Sir Jenings was one day brought to bay in the great Race of Life, finally unhorsed, and his burial service read at the open door of the little vault beside the Rappahannock.

Sir Jenings had not, however, gone to that bourne from whence no traveller returns; as we shall presently learn, and more than one hundred years later, to rest in a little graveyard upon a bluff quite near the mansion he loved so well and to which his spirit returns throughout the years, his body was brought from the vault on the crumbling bank of the ceaselessly encroaching stream.

In 1850, during the lives of Mr. Henry A. Tayloe's Father and mother, whose granddaughters now live at Mt. Airy, a young lady—Miss Mary Leiper—arrived one Friday morning, having been engaged to teach the children of the household. The family were leaving in a few hours to be absent over the week-end, and Mrs. Tayloe remarked to the newcomer, as she was shown her room on the ground floor, that if she felt at all timid, there was an upstairs room.

That night Miss Leiper awoke during the night and was surprised to see an old woman, with white hair, in the room. She was dressed in an old-fashioned costume and coming towards the bed, with her hands extended as though to push the curtains apart, although they were already open.

Gazing at the figure for a moment, believing it must be a dream, she closed her eyes, then opened them again. There stood the woman! "This is very strange," Miss Leiper thought, "no one could get into this house."

Continuing to watch the apparition a few minutes, it gradually drifted into a corner of the room and disappeared, but the sound of sobbing and moaning could be heard for sometime.

Again on Saturday and Sunday nights Miss Mary had this identical experience. Monday morning the family returned, accompanied by some guests. At the dinner-table Miss Leiper related to one of them her strange experiences. Turning towards her, in a shocked voice, the lady exclaimed, "Mercy! You don't mean to tell me you slept in *that* room? Why, it's haunted!"

Later Mrs. Tayloe related to the governess an experience of her own. Coming to Mt. Airy a bride, one day she saw a man in the costume of the Revolutionary period walking in the hall. Speaking to her husband of this remarkable occurrence, he laughed and said, "Oh, that man has been seen in this house from time to time throughout the years, by many people, but never upstairs. If you feel nervous we will take a room on the second floor.

Miss Mary Willis Minor informed the writer of this sketch that she taught at Mt. Airy in 1877, and the room was then spoken of as being haunted.

SABINE HALL

I N Richmond County, Virginia, on the banks of the Rappahan-
nock River, has stood for the last two hundred years Sabine
Hall, one of Virginia's most beautiful homes; built for Landon
Carter, a son of Robert, "King" Carter, in 1730.

Greek porticos give entrance to a spacious hall panelled to the
ceiling in heart pine. A pillared portico extends across the rear of
the house overlooking the terraced garden. The stairway is unique
—of natural pine, it rises in a hallway of its own from the foot of
an archway between the main and transverse halls. Graced by
beautifully fluted balusters, the stair gradually ascends until broken
by the landing; the light from a large window floods the hall.
There the flight of steps reverses, mounting to the second floor.

Among the striking portraits in this magnificent inheritance
from a past century are those of Col. Landon Carter himself and of
the three stately ladies who in his time were successively the gracious mistresses of this beautiful home. Elizabeth Wormley, of
"Rosegill," Maria Byrd, of Westover, and Elizabeth Beale.

Sabine Hall descended to his son Robert Wormley Carter, whose
bride was Winifred Beale; and brides of Landon Carter 2nd were
Catherine Tayloe, of Mt. Airy, and Mary Armistead. Throughout
the generations it has been told that when the flowers bloom sweet
in the gardens, the winds whistle through the leafless branches of
the old walnut trees, or the snow falls in great white drifts; ever
as the newly-wedded couple cross the portico, enter the wide door,
turn through the arch and ascend the lovely stairway; on the landing, by the window, stands a little page in holiday attire to greet
the bride. Invisible at times to others, *she* always sees a welcoming
smile, and then he vanishes.

Sabine Hall

AYRFIELD

IN Westmoreland County a half mile from old YeocomicoChurch
on the road towards Kinsale may be found "Ayrfield." This
tract of land was purchased from Daniel Tebbs about the year
1770 by John Ballantine who came from Ayr, Scotland. His daughter married John Murphy about 1788, he also emigrating to Virginia from Caledonia. This John Murphy built the present homestead in 1806.

Mr. F. Marvin Murphy, the present owner, writes me the house
is of brick, nearly square, and two stories in height. It has a steep
shingled roof and very tall chimneys. The yard is shaded by some
good trees, while others give evidence of length of days. The yard
faces the county road, and the tract of 400 acres is bordered by a
stream. The Scotch forefathers and their children found rest after
life's meed of joy and of sorrow in the little burying ground not
far away.

John Ballantine Murphy, the son of the builder of "Ayrfield,"
was left a widower with five children, and lived in the homestead.
About 1840 he sent his eldest son Sidney W. Murphy as a medical
student to the University of Edinburgh, Scotland. One night shortly
after his son's graduation John Ballantine Murphy awakened and
noticed a light in his chamber. The light was sufficiently bright
to cause him to think the house must be on fire, not being able to
account otherwise for the light. He went out to investigate, but
found all dark outside of the room. Upon returning the light was
still to be seen. The source of the light was never discovered. In
those days communication was slow. Some time later word was received from the University of the death of his son, and the death
had occurred the night of the mysterious light. Mr. Murphy writes:

"I have no explanation for this occurrence. It was told me by my
father, coming from his father as a fact."

Old Mansion, Bowling Green, Virginia

OLD MANSION

IN 1670 land was granted Major John Hoomes by the British Crown, and his house is reputed to be the oldest in Caroline County. Erected not later than 1675 it stands just south of the corporate limits of Bowling Green. This relic of early Colonial days is built of brick, one and one-half stories high; a type of architecture then prevailing in as much as England levied a tax on houses of two or three stories. Massively built, a high pitched roof, very tall chimneys and the dormer windows still glazed with eighteen tiny panes of glass. Originally the plain doorway was guarded by a stoop; the large porch to be seen today being added seventy-five years ago.

We are told Major Hoomes was a sportsman and imported thoroughbred horses. We also believe he was a lover of trees and flowers. Acorns brought from his native land and planted 260 years ago are large oaks today. Other trees he started as saplings are now of great size and beauty. A race course encircles the lawn bordered with cherry trees, and from a bowling green in front, the estate derived its name. The giant cedars on either side of the avenue leading to the house were brought as switches in his saddle bag from Gloucester County; and to the south and north, rows of elms and aspens illustrate the saying "He who plants a tree loves others than himself."

Colonel John Waller Hoomes gave to the county the sites of the Court House and other public buildings, and also the name Bowling Green, afterwards designating his home "Old Mansion." The Colonel had one daughter, Sophia, who married a Major Allen, and for whom a frame addition was added to the house. Later Colonel Hoomes built his daughter a home at a little distance called "Oak Ridge." There is a well established tradition that Sophia never again visited her father's house by daylight, but her coachman averred she made long visits at night. There are those in the neighborhood who say that throughout the years her ghost has often been seen journeying to the "Old Mansion" in her coach.

John Waller Hoomes had a number of sons, stalwart men who followed in the footsteps of their sire. One night while seated in the long dining hall around the table which John Waller Hoomes according to a fancy of his own always had set for thirteen, those present heard distinctly the sound of horses' hoofs galloping rapidly around the track in front of the house. Knowing that all his horses should be in their stables at that hour and the grooms at their evening meal, Mr. Hoomes with several guests arose from the table and went to the door to see who the visitor might be. Peering into the twilight no traces of horse or rider could they see, but discernible at the far end of the track near the road gate was a group of children playing on the grass, clothed in light colored garments.

Little was thought of the occurrence, nor was inquiry made concerning children playing at that hour on the lawn, for on the morrow the eldest son was suddenly taken ill and died.

The next year at about the same time and under similar circumstances, the galloping hoofs were again heard and the children again seen, followed the next day by the death of the next son in line. This time all families in the neighborhood were questioned, but no children had been abroad at that hour. No one outside the house had seen or heard the horsemen.

The following year great apprehension was felt as the fatal time drew near. One night while all was light and cheerful within, although it was apparent most of the cheerfulness was forced, suddenly a deadly chill fell on those assembled at the table, for clearly came the rapid beats of hoofs up one side the gravel track, quickly to die away in the distance on the other side. Hastening to the door the family and guests saw the band of light clothed children or maidens on the far end of the lawn. The next day the third son was stricken and died. Several years elapsed, the rider again was heard, the children seen, and another son died. This strange occurrence was repeated until all the sons of John Waller Hoomes slept in the family burying ground beyond the box-hedge on the left side of the house. Never was that rider seen; nor were those appearing gaily dancing on the lawn, children of earth. After the death of the last Hoomes son never again were the hoof beats heard, nor the children seen.

Many hauntings are associated with this ancient dwelling. Records of these may be found in "The History of Caroline County," by Wingfield.

An old lady, Mrs. William Slaughter, née Battaille Hoomes, says: "I will tell you of the ghosts and haunting of Old Mansion. Child, isn't it a scandal that all Mr. Wingfield says is true? I have heard it all my life, and everyone in Caroline County has, but aren't they awful?"

Chief among the apparitions is that of Colonel John Waller Hoomes, who appeared to each member of his family before their death. He walked before them dressed in such clothes as those he wore while in the flesh. His appearance was an unfailing warning of the approaching death of some one of the family.

Some years after the house passed out of the hands of the Hoomes family, a man named Woodford lived at Old Mansion. His wife was very delicate, having serious heart trouble, therefore a housekeeper was employed—a buxom widow who with her children lived in the frame addition to the house, built by Mr. Hoomes for his daughter Sophia before he built for her a stately mansion across the road and about a mile south of the old home place. It was not very long before Mr. Woodford transferred his affections from his ailing wife to the handsome widow, but his wife lingered on, confined to her room and bed. One night, after a trying day during which his wife had suffered greatly, demanding his presence, and had only a few hours before fallen into a restless slumber, he heartlessly dressed himself in a sheet, and with a jack-o-lantern for an elevated head, slowly emerged from the Hoomes burying ground where several of his own and his wife's children were also buried. This was directly opposite Mrs. Woodford's chamber window, from which she in her high tester bed could plainly see him should she awaken. Aroused by the unusual light in that direction and startled by the frightful apparition she gave one terrified scream and expired. Mr. Woodford gave all necessary evidences of being greatly distressed at her death, even asking for a small sheet to wipe away his tears, his handkerchief not being sufficient, and trying to get on his horse backwards, not being in his grief able to tell its head from its tail.

Someway a neighbor heard of the little Hallowe'en trick he had played, and Mr. Woodford found it best to leave the country rather hastily. The widow very mysteriously soon followed.

Quite soon afterwards a family moved into the house, and the man and wife took as their bed-chamber the room in which Mrs. Woodford had died. One night they were awakened by groans which seemed to proceed from some place nearby. Going into the adjoining small room where the children slept, they assured themselves it was not any of them, and the groanings—somewhat stifled —continued. When this happened several nights in succession and one night was followed by the mysterious ringing of the bells which were on cords all over the house and used to call the slaves when desired, the family decided to seek other quarters.

The story goes, that several families moved in, all to leave very precipitately, each distinctly hearing the moans of Mrs. Woodford, and the ringing of the bells by unseen hands, all in the wee sma' hours of night. One family even left behind most of its furniture and family silver, so great was their haste in departing.

From 1804 for a period of about eight years the house was un-occupied as it was supposed to be haunted.

There is a tradition that General Washington and his weary soldiers camped here on the way to Yorktown. It is a fact that returning, they did camp, and held a banquet in Lafayette's honor.

In 1842 John Grymes Maury purchased "Old Mansion" and here brought up twelve children. In 1862 the property passed into the hands of his son-in-law Mr. J. T. White, and the family still retain possession.

BLANDFIELD

IN 1760, on the banks of that stream where in far-off times so many seeking an abiding place in a new country, finally settled, Robert, son of Capt. William Beverley, built a great mansion and named it in honor of his wife, Elizabeth Bland. It stands in Essex County upon the Tidewater Trail about ten miles from Tappahannock. With many huge trees on either side of the great wings, Blandfield is approached by means of a road winding through a thicket of fern, running cedar and densely-growing honeysuckle rioting beneath the tall cedars, spruce, and white pine; while far beyond, towards the gently-flowing river, stretches the great lawn, leading to a garden, the gate guarded by two cedars covered in the Springtime with yellow jassamine, for which throughout the years they have been an everpresent trellis. Roses planted by Colonel Beverley still blossom in the sunshine amid a wealth of pink crêpe myrtle and tall lilac bushes.

Blandfield is an imposing structure of brick, two stories in height, and today thickly draped with vines. Large white pillars grace the hospitable porch, and tall massive chimneys pierce the sloping roof. Long corridors on either side terminate in immense wing-rooms two stories high, such seemingly so necessary to the comfort and conveniences of many of the gentry of the Colonial period. The wing devoted to the kitchen has built-in dutch ovens and a fireplace ten feet in length, while the Master's office was opposite. The great central hall, seventy feet long, is imposing, and enormous twin-stairs ascend from the rear in separate passages, each with a huge fireplace and marble mantle.

Blandfield possesses a very interesting ghost, said to be the great-aunt of Capt. J. Bradshaw Beverley. She appeared to him about fifty years ago, and seemed solid and substantial, as one night he unwittingly followed her up the stairs.

Blandfield was in the hands of caretakers when late one autumn afternoon Captain Beverley arrived from "Avenel," and Mrs. Hutchinson asked if he objected to occupying a certain room which happened to be heated while the others were not.

"Why should I object?" Captain Beverley asked.

"Well," replied Mrs. Hutchinson with a smile, "the children say they see a woman go into that room."

Blandfield

"Oh, that's all right; I'm not afraid of Spirits and ghosts."

Captain Beverley told Mrs. Wm. Jeffries Chewning, of Fredericksburg, that he lingered a few days longer than necessary, hoping to see the ghost.

Very shortly the captain was again called to Blandfield, and about eleven at night, taking up a small lamp, he started to mount the stairs. Halfway up, a woman, candle in hand, passed him. The thought crossed his mind as he followed: I thought Mrs. Hutchinson had on a dark wool dress. At this point the woman and candle disappeared into his room and shut the door in his face!

"Mrs. Hutchinson," Captain Beverley called at the door. "Yes, Captain, what is it you want?" came from below stairs.

Instantly realizing the truth, Captain Beverley replied, "I have seen your ghost."

He examined every crack and crevice of the room, but his great-aunt and her candle had vanished!

Mrs. James J. Marshall, who was Miss Jane Hullihen of Staunton, had experiences of an interesting nature while she taught there in 1904, it being the home at that time of Mr. Robert Beverley. It is obvious from Mrs. Marshall's letter that Mr. Beverley had full knowledge of and was accustomed to, manifestations of a ghostly nature in this home of his ancestors.

"I had only been there a short time," writes Mrs. Marshall, "when Mr. Beverley announced that I was occupying the haunted room! This did not frighten me in the least, and months passed before the great uncle, Mr. Beverley declared, died in that room and was the ghost manifesting, appeared to me in any way.

"One morning I remarked to Mr. Beverley that I thought he had better have someone go up on the roof and examine the old chimney, as I had heard quite a number of bricks fall on the roof above my room during the night. Mr. Beverley laughed heartily and said: 'There is nothing the matter with the chimney. You've heard just what everyone hears sooner or later in that room!' Nothing could convince me, however, until I climbed up through the skylight, and found no loose bricks.

"Another night some weeks later, I wakened and saw a light just outside my window. There was no moon and the night was very dark when I retired. This puzzled me, so getting up to investigate, I discovered there was no light to be seen at the window! The light I saw from my bed was distinct, luminous, softly shining. This phenomenon was repeated upon three different occasions. No explanation was ever offered.

"Again one night in the late spring I was awakened by hearing very distinct footsteps on the brick walk connecting the wing with the main building, and leading to the large entrance door facing the river. The sound of footsteps passed around two sides of my room, and up the stone steps to the great double doors. There I heard knocking that resounded through the house. Curiosity taking me to the window overlooking the door, I was surprised to see no one, but in as much as Mr. Beverley occupied a chamber on the first floor, I imagined he had admitted the late arrival. When I inquired the next morning concerning the midnight guest, they told me no one had been there! Mr. Beverley said he 'presumed the old man was up to some of his tricks again.'"

THE MARINER RETURNS

PHANTOM ships are not unknown to the experience of students of psychic phenomena, but that within the borders of Virginia, and within the limited sphere of this little adventure two such apparitions can be chronicled, is of interest.

Two miles of a picturesque road such as the heavy coaches of the Colonists could scarcely travel, and today must be traversed on foot, winding up hill and down, through great banks of laurel, lovely in the springtime, bushes flaming in a garniture of Virginia creeper in late September, and tall cedars, and here and there lovely stretches of shady woods, leads finally to an abandoned old manorhouse standing in a lawn where clumps of untrimmed bushes, a rambling hedge of osage orange, over which old roses trail, and innumerable vines ramble and blossom.

Here, dilapidated and abandoned, though still unmistakably patrician, stands "Brooke's Bank." Not a large building, but in the Spring sunshine of today one catches a vision of the comfort enjoyed within its walls, the elegance of its hospitality two hundred years ago! Charming little brick wings, but ten feet square, graced by tiny dormer windows, are on either side of the main building, and mighty chimneys rising from the roof and more than twenty feet beyond, present a unique feature in the architecture of Colonial homes in Virginia. "They are decorated upon each end and side with contrasting headers laid to trace an effect of diamonds."

Through a hall, some thirty feet in length to the garden beyond, one can view the glories of the setting sun, or the wild ducks rise as they soar onward and upward from the marshes across the Rappahannock. The old kitchen with steep roof, quaint chimney and age-old shingles; the Master's office, following the same graceful lines, stand in the shade of great locusts, shedding their fragrance in May over the country side.

Untenanted for nearly half a century, the cornerstone tells us ground was broken in 1731 upon a grant of land from George the Second, King of England, to Sarah Taliaferro Brooke, after the death of her husband John Brooke, in a naval engagement between the French and English, and owing to the services he had rendered the English Crown.

Brooke's Bank

Situated upon an eminence, Brooke's Bank suffered during the Civil War. From the guns of the Pawnee a shell shattered the north window, then the east wall, leaving a great rent, an indelible scar. So terrific was the shock upon the wall that the parlor below was thrown completely out of place. Shattered in one moment of time were walls of splendid masonry that had already withstood the winds and storm of nearly half a century when the Declaration of Independence was signed!

Sarah Taliaferro Brooke erected the rooftree of one of Virginia's distinguished families. The memory of its long years of plenty and of hospitality are an enduring heritage.

It was recorded many years ago that upon one occasion only, at twilight, a month after the loss at sea, a phantom ship was seen to sail up the river. A man disembarked, and reaching the wharf walked towards a house and entered the door. The ship vanished

before the eyes of the astonished beholders. The apparition was declared to be that of John Brooke.

Elmwood, Essex County

ELMWOOD

ELMWOOD, Essex County, Virginia, was built prior to the Revolution by Muscoe Garnett as a home for his son, James Mercer Garnett. The estate comprised one thousand acres.

Today it is a grim and forbidding old house, in the midst of trees, the growth of many years, tangled with a riot of honeysuckle and sweet grape; the view of the river once beheld, now hidden from sight. To visitors no one is ever at home.

A road winding through the plantation is seldom travelled. The barn is empty. A narrow trail, then a sudden curve, and the old home of the Garnett family can be seen—quiet, depressing, alone. A sense of isolation without peace, remoteness without tranquility, pervades the air. A thicket of tall trees and underbrush stretches between the detached buildings and the mansion.

The silence is oppressive! Elmwood, forbidding and austere, holds out no welcoming hand. The air within, they say, is damp and mouldy. A weird influence permeates the abandoned structure, and one by one as the years glide by, the descendants of the pioneer builder rest for a few hours beneath the ancestral rooftree before finding a quiet home in the garden beyond, within the shadow of some tall pine, or where a pink crêpe myrtle sways in the breeze.

The air is heavy with the ghost of memories of happier days. In the great hall where once the minuet was danced, still lingers the furniture used by the Garnetts when the Georges ruled England. An old spinet stands in the corner with music scattered near.

Who can recall the girl who, playing some quaint melody, turned those pages for the last time?

In those halcyon days when here was the happy meeting-place of friend, neighbor and kin, when the coming guest was welcomed, and the partings delayed, one day a casual acquaintance arrived to make a short visit. Old age overtook him still occupying the greate room over the drawing-room, "a man of cheerful yesterdays, and confident tomorrows!" Today the room is completely furnished and one senses a purer atmosphere, a more cheerful air, happier memories than linger within the other rooms. May not the spirit of the man, graciously received and given a lasting welcome more than a century ago pervade this old and neglected room wherein he spent in peaceful contentment so many golden hours—a presence, no gloom, no mold, no inhospitality of today can shatter or dispel?

Throughout the years, far off and nearby, Elmwood is reputed to be haunted. In the dead of night the piercing cry of a youth, killed by the falling of a tree as he rode home at midnight in the midst of a storm, is still heard.

Nightly revels have been reported held within its walls and the old spinet is played by unseen hands. Many, many years ago, in the midst of a ball, as the hour grew late, a couple long since dead, dressed in the quaint costume of their day, descended the stair, hand in hand, and danced a stately minuet the entire length of the hall! Silent with amazement the gay revellers drew aside, giving ample space to the ghostly visitors, who leisurely and gracefully danced to the far end and out the door, disappearing in the darkness! So "The people sing, the people say!" Does the "Doctor," so cordially welcomed for forty years, love to return?

"Doors are opened and shut with great noise by an unseen hand supposed to be that of the 'Doctor' "—a visitor to whom no mortal has power to deny entrance. There are doors that will not open, and doors that no mortal can make stay shut!

In the garden amid magnolias and flowering shrubs, the old "Doctor" sleeps beneath a carpet of blue periwinkle beside the Virginia gentleman who, throughout so many years, was his gracious host.

KINLOCH

A DWELLER for a brief period in the tents of Kedar pitched beneath the shade trees for which Essex County is famous, writes of "Kinloch" and of its ghost.

Unoccupied for years, isolated and lonely, surrounded by mannificent trees, gracing a splendid park of many acres, "the atmosphere of solitude is oppressive." Norway spruce seventy-five feet tall, Irish and English yews, conceded to be the most beautiful in this country, chestnuts the blight has never found, pecans transplanted from their native soil, are among trees planted eighty years ago when Mr. Richard Baylor erected the mansion.

After a solitary drive of many miles, here and there at long intervals a negro cabin, maybe the tinkle of a cowbell breaking the oppressive silence, a pervading atmosphere of loneliness; miles of country road through dense woods. At a sudden turn, if it be sunrise, a startled deer bounds out of sight; or towards evening, framed in the colors of a gorgeous sunset, stands the stately mansion "Kinloch." Directly in front, in the center of a grass plot, stands a sundial throughout the years the silent unnoticed register of the flight of time.

Great box bushes guard either side of a marble porch none ever cross. Tall marble columns stand beside ever-closed doors. From the roof, far over the treetops, can be had a view of five counties and of Tidewater Trail as it wends its way through the vast estate. In the autumn the songbirds rise from the treetops for their long journey South, but the Rappahannock is an ever-present friend.

Among the trees stand little brick buildings so essential to the comfort of the household in those far-off days. Behind the mansion, the lovely rose garden, great box bushes, and splendid crêpe myrtle painting the surrounding green a gorgeous pink in the springtime.

A path of two hundred feet, bordered by all manner of flowering shrub, planted beneath the towering trees, leads to a quaint old summer-house standing beside the burying-ground. Old-fashioned roses bloom within the iron fence, and coral honeysuckle twining

Kinloch

in and out among the box adds to the scene the same note of beauty today the young tutor contemplated, these many years at rest beneath the shadow of old VaMter's Church, not far distant, and whose Spirit is chronicled on printed page, and told by guest, or wanderer through the park, to haunt the long walk, the old summer-house, and to be seen in the burying-ground. He was the tutor of the young son of the family and the lover of his sister.

A member of the family states it to have been known that failure to pass his examinations for the University of Virginia, rather than his hopeless love, lead one day to suicide at Kinloch.

Miss Mary Willis Minor states that her sister Kate, Mrs. Morris Fontaine, Beaver Dam, Hanover County, Virginia, when a young girl in 1866 went to Kinloch on a visit, occupying a room opposite that of Miss Nannie Baylor. Kate, being a great reader, retired early with her book. Presently she heard a deep sigh, followed at an interval by another. Arising, she looked under the bed, thinking a dog might be there. A third sigh interrupting her reading; she went across the hall, telling the experience to Miss Baylor who at once invited her guest to pass the night with her. Next day the room's history was revealed.

A young tutor from Vermont became much depressed, notwithstanding the best effort of the family to cheer him and make life pleasant. He would accept no invitations, go nowhere. One morning the maid informed Mr. Baylor she could not get into the tutor's room. A ladder from outside revealed the fact the young man had cut his throat.

Mrs. Carmichael informs me:

"I have slept in the room often but have seen nothing, and no member of the family has seen the ghost, but they do not deny the story." We may well believe that here, as has been frequently portrayed, where a tragedy has been enacted, the spirit of the discouraged student and disappointed lover returns from time to time.

It is recorded—

"He appears periodically, a slender, tall young man, strolling in the rose-garden at evening, towards the iron fence of the cemetery."

McCall House, Tappahannock, Virginia

THE CALL OF THE WILD

ARCHIBALD McCALL was one of the many Scottish youths trusting themselves in the course of the eighteenth century to those little cockle shells leaving the safety that rockbound coast afforded, and so frequently never reaching the shores of that wilderness for which they set sail. This particular ship was named The Betty. William Dunlop was the master, and she belonged to Samuel McCall, a merchant of Glasgow.

In Scottish parlance, Archibald McCall was "born on the Nith," and upon a Kello-side farm, the property of his family for generations. Born April 28, 1734, he had an older brother George who was for a few years a merchant in Fredericksburg. True to Scottish psychology one of the brothers—George—returned to Scotland to tend the fire upon that commercial hearthstone. Archibald prospered in the wilderness and married Katharine, only daughter of Dr. Nicholas and Eliza Flood. Their home was "Cedar Grove," three miles from Farnham. Katharine must still have been young when, in 1767, the inscription was chiseled we may read today in Farnham Churchyard. She left two daughters, only the one named for her surviving the father. Katharine Flood McCall never married.

The tiny fleet of Samuel McCall plied between Glasgow and the little town now called Tappahannock. There dwelt on the banks of the Rappahannock a tribe of Indians of that name numbering in 1608 about 400, their principal village being in Richmond County. This village became extinct in 1722 and the name was preserved only by the river. The Indian derivation, from Renape (meaning "true," "genuine" man) with the suffix, means people of the "alternating stream" (ebb and flow), that is tidewater; the tribal name signifying people of the tidewater. Upon the banks of this river the Scotchman built his home. It stands today, a witness alike to his ability and to his taste. As we so often find in houses of that period, this home on the banks of the Rappahannock is of brick construction, sheathed in weather boarding. The rooms are spacious, and while the paneling was fashioned from Virginia's forests by some long forgotten artisan, Archibald McCall undoubtedly saw brought from the hold of a little vessel the black marble mantels reminiscent of his native hills.

How little did he realize that through succeeding generations his daughter Katharine would descend that lovely stairway he fashioned with such care, clad in the shimmering robes in keeping with oft described "white satin slippers"!

" 'Tis an ill wind profits nobody"—Had not Archibald McCall been a Royalist, and sailed for England in 1775, possibly the lovely ghost of his daughter might not return to visit the home that was hers so many years ago.

Confiscation followed, and when at length, peace restored, the Scotchman came again to recover his estate, he found another reigned in his stead.

Katharine McCall found some other home, probably at "Cedar Grove," which she inherited from her grandfather,—but where she lies buried is unknown.

Mrs. B. B. Brockenbrough lived at this house of the Scotch pioneer for fifty years. To her the figure of Katharine McCall descending that stairway where perhaps linger her fondest earthly memories, was a quite natural and a quite frequent sight, "walking through the house from attic to cellar; coming down the beautiful stairway."

Miss Isabella Mason, who made frequent visits to her aunt, Mrs. Brockenbrough, writes me that years ago there was, leading to the garret, a stairway the ghost was seen to descend.

One day Mrs. Brockenbrough received a letter from another relative, also a frequent guest at this dwelling, once the home of Katharine McCall. This guest recalled seeing upon many occasions Miss McCall "dressed in white, and on her feet white satin slippers."

MOUNT CLEMENT

U PON the south bank of the Rappahannock from time im-
memorial has stood a little village called into being as a tiny
port. From its wharves sailing vessels spread their white wings
o'er a far reaching track, and in those early days, to a very uncertain destination. The name of the town has known several changes.
Before 1680 it was New Plymouth. In the time of Philip Fithian,
the young Princeton tutor at the home of Col. Carter at Nomini
Hall, Westmoreland County, it was Hobb's His Hole. Since that
day Tappahannock, a variant of the river's name, has been its portion.

Wonderfully well preserved old records dated earlier than 1656
chronicle for us the far-reaching importance of tobacco and rum in
the lives and the fortunes of America's Colonists. One old record
reads: "It having pleased Almighty God to bless His Royal Majesty
with the birth of a son This Court have ordered that Captain George
Taylor do provide and bring to the North Side Court House for
the County as much rum or strong liquor with sugar proportionable
as shall amount to six thousand five hundred pounds of tobacco, to
be distributed among the troops and others persons that shall be
present at the said solemnitie and bring to the South Side Court
House of this County as much rum or other strong liquor with
sugar proportionable as shall amount to thirty-five hundred pounds
of tobacco, to be distributed as above."

Huge hogsheads of tobacco were rolled down to the water's edge
opposite Hobb 's Hole from the great plantations of Sabine Hall
and Mt. Airy, and many an anxious eye scanned the horizon for
the cheering sight of a sail long overdue bearing to the great man-
sions silks and satins from London shops for the ladies; luxuries
for the table and casks of Madeira and Burgundy to gladden the
heart and loosen the tongue and befog the brain of man!

Two miles from Tappahannock, upon a high hill denuded of its
wealth of beautiful trees, etched against the flaming beauty of an
autumn sunset, its two tall chimneys pointing skyward, abandoned
and disintegrating, stands an old mansion bearing the charming
name Mount Clement. In the days when white sails dotted the

Mount Clement

Rappahannock and slaves worked the plantations, great coaches toiled slowly up the steep hill, over rough roads, to where awaited refreshment and repose for the elderly and all manner of merry-making for the young.

One evening a large party was given. A young girl stood in a lovely gown of stiff silk putting the finishing touches to her toilet. At length, satisfied with her appearance and taking from the dressing-table a beautiful fan, she turned towards the door. Doing so she chanced to glance into a long mirror hanging between the windows and saw in it, not her own lovely countenance, but the reflection of a man wearing a costume of one hundred years ago! She was horrified to see chains on his wrists and ankles! Frightened, the girl ran screaming down the long corridor, and tripping in her haste, fell headlong down the spiral stairway, receiving injuries from which she died the day following. Before death, she gave a vivid description of the image seen in the glass.

In the nighttime, through the passing years, when at Sabine Hall and Mt. Airy were heard sounds of music and of dancing, at Mount Clement down the long corridor leading to the spiral stair, could be heard the swish of a silken petticoat as if its wearer was in hasty flight.

Belle Ville

BELLE VILLE

BELLE VILLE, on the North River in Gloucester County, is an example of an old building fragrant with tradition, quaint rather than imposing, preserving to a remarkable degree in hoary old age those features essential to industry and to comfort on isolated plantations in the days of the Colonies.

Built by Thomas Booth in 1658 on an estuary of Chesapeake Bay, this picturesque dwelling has beheld the ebb and flow in the affairs of men and in the tide of North River for nearly three hundred years. Constructed of brick, but one-and-a-half stories in height, with dormer windows in the shingle roof, and a large frame addition of later date, as more room was required with the passing of time, Belle Ville suggests length of days.

Quaint window seats on either side of the chimney in the parlor afford an unbroken view of a sweep of water, while sail and rowboats at the end of a long wharf suggest the most profitable way of visiting in that locality.

In the distance at the water's edge stood the large icehouse with pointed roof; from it a long lane of cedars wound towards the creek far to the rear of the dwelling. An immense kitchen bespoke both large families and unbounded hospitality, while the Master's office afforded also shelter for guests.

Two great live oaks are conspicuous and beautiful, but beyond their shade a box-trimmed vegetable garden has been cultivated since those faroff Colonial days. The smoke-house and large brick dairy speak to us of prosperity.

Here and there stand cottonwood trees; a garden of old-fashioned flowers, and by the river side stood, in former days, a summer house, the color of its walls mellowed by the salt breeze to a pale pink. Beyond them all, the saw-pit where the logs for lumber were fashioned, the weaving room conveniently near the cabins of the house servants, and at a distance, in the shade of a dense grove of cedars, the slaves of the plantation were laid to rest when work was done.

Warner Taliaferro, of Church Hill, married the sole surviving daughter of George Wythe Booth, the last of the name to occupy Belle Ville. A coat is still owned by one of his descendants in which he is supposed to have been married; the sleeves are long and narrow, reaching to the knuckles, the collar would cover the ears.

They settled at Belle Ville—their son, later Major General Taliaferro, was a gallant soldier in two wars. Love could not stay the progress of a disease in the young mother's constitution and Belle Ville was once more visited by death.

Two years later the widower married Leah Seddon, of Fredericksburg, a girl fifteen years of age. Then war came, and desolation. The old house now for the first time felt the stress of poverty.

One summer evening, more than fifty years ago, Warner Taliaferro stretched his tall form upon a settle standing on a porch leading to the garden. The illness of a friend, the wife of Dr. Tabb, living just over a nearby inlet, was causing him much distress. Mrs. Taliaferro had retired. Having fallen asleep, late in the night he was awakened by a light touch, and starting up he saw the figure of Mrs. Tabb upon the steps leading down into the garden. There was no mistaking her identity. Believing she had eluded those who watched by her bedside, Mr. Taliaferro arose and followed, thinking she was wandering in delirium. From the steps the figure went swiftly down the box-bordered walk, over an intervening lawn. Stooping beneath a crêpe myrtle, she entered the summer-house. At the entrance Warner Taliaferro stopped in amazement. The little building was empty. His search was in vain. Retracing his steps to the house, he awakened his wife telling of his strange experience.

"You have been dreaming," she declared.

"Feel my clothes," he replied.

She found them drenched with dew from the tall grass through which he had walked.

The next morning a messenger brought news of Mrs. Tabb's death.

In later years Belle Ville was rented to Mrs. Richard Taliaferro, and a little child lived with her. One night a guest in the house Miss Nora Taliaferro, took the little girl to sleep in her room. Leaving the mother's chamber, they saw distinctly the figure of a woman in white ascend the stairway, proceed down the corridor and into the storeroom.

Another guest, the next morning at breakfast, declared she had awakened in the night to see a shadowy figure of a man in a dark coat and white stock stand at the foot of the bed.

Warner Taliaferro died suddenly away from Belle Ville. His wife grieved no farewell word between them had been possible. Strong in faith, she prayed often and fervently that he might appear and speak to her. The prayer was answered. The letter giving an account of the vision and of the words her husband had spoken was published in the *Southern Churchman*.

Midlothian

BELL, BOOK AND CANDLE

T HE Midlothian in Gloucester County, Virginia, of today was in Colonial times known as Middleway. It is a place of much interest, bearing to us from those faroff days a remarkable story. A comfortable homestead, with its inviting front porch, standing amid 1,200 acres of grain, yellow in the Autumn, and facing a cool green lawn sloping gently to North River.

This house was built by one of the earliest settlers in Gloucester County long before the Revolution. Iverson by name. A tragedy alone keeps them in remembrance today, where once they formed one family of the then sparsely settled countryside. Notwithstanding that oblivion, to which the passing of nearly two hundred years consigns most of the circumstances of this mortal pilgrimage, Love that Eternal Conqueror, preserves for us the names of Hubert Iverson and Jennie Bower, his sweetheart. She was of humble parentage and circumstance; a country girl whom he loved. Falling desperately ill of a fever, Hubert Iverson begs his parents to provide for her. This they refused to do, and we learn that before a great while Jennie Bower died of grief and privation.

Love was a light in their portals, and for them, sorrow as winds that passed. From the time of her death, the lovers were frequently seen. Always together; always walking hand in hand. In the garden, passing down the corridor or seated on a bench the members of the family, their guests, and the servants would meet the lovers at all times and in many places.

Frequently at night as the family slept they were awakened by the sound of moaning and of groans; pitiful and distressing. The Iversons were so harassed by these mournful sounds and apparitions, stirring ever within them painful memories, that they sold the property to a family by the name of Marable and left the county.

Of the Marable family, Gloucester chronicles can tell us little other than that they, too, experienced visitations and saw the lovers wandering amid the scenes of their earthly life. The Marables were much disturbed, and possibly zealous Christians. At any rate, they decided to call in consultation the rector of Petworth Parish, Rev.

Robert Yates; and in due season this clergyman undertook the order of Exorcism, it being an opinion held at that time to consign troubled Spirits to burial under water.

On a day appointed, the clergyman assembled the family, the neighbors and the servants, and with due solemnity, and as required, walking backward towards a well in a field adjacent, repeated the burial service according to the rites of the Anglican Church. The family and friends followed and gathered about the well. Some appropriate prayers and solemn rites of exorcism to lay the ghosts were said. This ceremony, according to tradition, was performed with "Bell, Book and Candle." Afterwards the well was filled in. The lovers were never seen again!

The flowing tide of Time swept the Marable family into the great sea of oblivion. There are no tombstones in the churchyard telling us that once they dwelt beneath the roof of Middleway.

Prior to 1790 this property was purchased by Josiah Deans, who made a fortune in the shipping business in Norfolk, and sought in Gloucester County a plantation, possibly for a summer home. He changed the name to Midlothian.

The following story of Midlothian was related by Mrs. Philip Yeatman, of Norfolk, who learned it from her grandmother. It is of well-established family history and county tradition.

Mrs. Yeatman's grandfather, Mr. Deans, was one summer day in the fields at harvest time. Quite accidently he came upon what was obviously a filled-in well. Mr. Deans remarked, "I have often wondered why there was no field well on this plantation. Here is evidence there was one; I wonder why it was filled in?" An aged negro among the servants stepped forward and said, "Master, I can explain it," and told the storying of the laying of the ghosts as he had heard it from the old negroes in the Quarters. At this moment Mrs. Deans was seated on the porch entertaining an aged relative of her husband, who remarked, "Do you see where Josiah is standing now? There is a well there in which, back in Colonial days, two ghosts were laid." She then related the same facts told to Mr. Deans by the old negro in the harvest field.

MORDECAI'S MOUNT

IN Gloucester County, Virginia, there stands an old house clothed in the interesting and unique history of not having had a mistress for more than a century, and of remaining in the same family for 270 years. A quaint structure, standing amid smiling fields and towering trees, it turns its back on a lovely vista of the river Ware. Even today traces of garden terraces planted when Sir William Berkeley was Governor may be seen. A place of memorial dinners, of fascinating balls, of high living and high thinking. A house so old that its earliest mistress is said to have been Joan Constable, wife of Mordecai Cook, one of the maids imported by the London Company; a house whose walls have heard whisperings of the gossip of Old World Courts, as well as rumors of Indian massacres; of uprisings and of rebellion; a house where many generations have seen names change and journeys end—it would be strange if no ghost should ever walk.

Thomas Cook was a son of Mordecai and of Joan of invincible and pioneering spirit, and a firm friend of Sir William Berkeley. The land grant taken up in 1650 included the present old house standing near Ware Church.

The ghost of Mordecai's Mount (now known as Church Hill) has never yet been seen, although frequently watched for. No white robed visitant has flitted from room to room to vanish when spoken to. Groans, if heard, were normally accounted for; yet that the place is haunted has been the belief of many living within its walls in succeeding generations.

A ghost so restrained as to be heard from but once a year, the reminder of a pitiful story, soon comes to hold rather a lovable place in the history of an old home. Certainly I have never heard of any member of the family standing in dread of the coming of the first snow, although it was then that the gentle spirit of a long-dead daughter of the house was supposed to manifest itself in an upper room by throwing wood on a ghostly fire. Neither maid nor fuel nor fire has ever yet been seen, but those now living will testify to the thud of falling wood and the crackle of flame, when, looking out of the window, they would see the first snow.

This was first heard so long ago that the full name of the young lady has been lost. She was a Throckmorton, her father a man of

Mordecai's Mount

substance, descended from people of position in the Old World. There were rings on her fingers as she walked in the terraced garden and romance in her heart. She herself was a romantic figure—

But the man of her choice did not please her Father and, according to the custom of the time, she yielded to his denial. She pined, however, and faded, and late on a blustering November afternoon they buried her in the graveyard at the foot of the garden. The stricken Father allowed her rings to be buried with her.

That night as he huddled over the fire, his heart heavy with grief, the first snow of the season fell. While he replenished the dying embers a faint scratching noise was heard at the door leading into the garden. "One of the dogs begging shelter from the storm," he told himself, and with the heedlessness of sorrow gave the matter no further thought. Far into the night he sat there and the sound ceased. In the morning servants opening the house found a mound of snow on the doorstep and under it the rigid figure of Miss Throckmorton. The rings were gone and a finger which had worn them was severed from her hand—probably the ghoulish act of colored servants, two of whom disappeared that night and were never seen again. It is supposed that they, knowing of her jewelry, opened her coffin. Her rings not slipping easily in their hurried grasp, they cut off a finger. This brought her to consciousness from a cataleptic condition. The terrified creature, hampered by her grave clothes, dragged her way slowly past the dead stalks of her summer garden; these also bent under a shroud of snow. At last she reached the doorstep and there strength failed her. She could only beat feebly upon the door. If she cried out the wind carried her voice away. Within she could hear her Father replenish the fire, but the door to rescue did not open. And so she died, and the grave in the garden once more received her.

The ghost at Church Hill throws wood on the fire no longer. A dozen years or more ago the room in which the sound had so long been heard was burned. Even the garden of Miss Throckmorton's last terrible experience has disappeared, but while the walls of Mordecai's Mount remain standing, she will be remembered.

"In the summer before his death in speaking to my cousin, Judge Taliaferro," said Mrs. Harriotte Lee Montague, "I asked him if he in his ownership of Church Hill had heard the sounds attributed to Miss Throckmorton." 'Not once, but many times,' was his answer. "My Father, Maj. Thos S. Taliaferro, who as a youth and in later years was frequently a visitor at Church Hill, told me he had heard the logs falling and looking out the window had seen the first snow."

Professor Warner Taliaferro, of the University of Maryland, resided for four years at Mordecai's Mount. One summer evening in 1879, he was passing the evening at the home of the Dabney's on North River, and a severe thunder storm breaking, remained for the night, leaving his home entirely unoccupied. The sisters of Junius Brutus Browne, Jr., residing at Roaring Spring, had earlier in the day left home in a buggy to make a visit on Ware Creek road. About 9 o'clock Mr. Browne rode along on horseback in order to meet them. Reaching a point on the highway from whence Mordecai's Mount could clearly be seen, he concluded his sisters had found shelter from the storm at Mr. Taliaferro's, inasmuch as every window in the house was ablaze with light. Riding up the lane and arriving at the front door, Mr. Browne shouted "Who's at home?" Receiving no response, he rode around the house and pounded on the rear door. No one answered his summons! Later it was ascertained the negro family living in the quarters also saw the lights and concluded Mr. Taliaferro had returned home.

In a few days Mr. Browne was told by Mr. Taliaferro, to whom he passed the remark, "You must have had a gay party Tuesday. What was going on?" "I was not at home, leaving early to make a visit, and on account of the storm, remained for the night."

Mr. Taliaferro adds his testimony to that of other members of the family. He heard the logs thrown upon the fire many times; also while sitting reading, would often hear the swish of a silk skirt, and would follow the sound up the stairs and along the corridor. He never saw the wearer thereof!

WHITE MARSH

GLOUCESTER COUNTY is one of the oldest and was in days gone by among the richest sections of Virginia. Memories of stirring events cluster around its broad acres. From the steps of the Court House Nathaniel Bacon made an impassioned appeal for sympathy and for support, and in its soil he was secretly buried lest Sir William Berkeley should endeavor to hang his body.

Gloucester County was the scene of bloodshed prior to the surrender at Yorktown, and beneath the shade of her trees foes sleep side by side, while today their descendants are comrades beneath the poppy fields of sunny France.

Through a long avenue of magnificent magnolias in the springtime perfuming the countryside stands an ancient brick dwelling; low wings to the east and west adding symmetry and grace; amid picturesque grounds and giant oaks smiling fields speaking of fertility and care, far off the silver line of Ware River.

In the Colonial period a branch of the Whiting family owned this extensive plantation, but after the Revolution a distinguished lawyer, Thomas Reade Rootes, made here his home. Through his second wife, a former Mrs. Prosser, her daughter the elegant Evelina Matilda Prosser became mistress of White Marsh. Miss Prosser gave her hand and large fortune to John Tabb, spoken of as "a man of lordly and ceremonious nature." The heiress is described as a notable housekeeper; a woman of great dignity and noted for her elegant costumes. She is still a tradition gowned in black "moire antique" seated at the head of her dinner table.

After the death of his parents, Philip Tabb, who lived in Baltimore, placed White Marsh in the care of Mr. James Sinclair, who among other duties engaged the servants necessary when the owner brought guests in fox hunting season.

Late one night Mr. Sinclair returning on horseback was astonished to find every window a blaze of light. He had received no word and wondered how he could possibly manage under the circumstances. After putting his horse in the stable, requiring some little time, Mr. Sinclair concluded every one had retired, inasmuch as when he reached the house all lights were out. Opening the

White Marsh

front door and expecting to find hats and coats in the hall, their absence led him to investigate. The house was untenanted!

The year following, Mr. Tabb engaged Mr. Franklin Dabney to take charge of the plantation. Mr. Dabney, a bachelor and fond of society, returned late one night and like Mr. Sinclair found a light in every window. He, hearing music and the sound of dancing, tied his horse at the post and ran up the porch steps in order to join the merrymaking. Standing at the door he could see the lights and hear the music. As soon as the door was opened darkness and silence prevailed!

One day Rev. William Byrd Lee, today rector emeritus of Ware Church, living in the rectory at the Court House, journeyed with Mrs. Lee to make a call at White Marsh. The lady of the mansion had been Catherine Tabb, granddaughter of Mrs. Prosser Tabb. The visit concluded Mr. Lee went to bring the buggy to the door and Mrs. Lee was seated alone in the hall. Chancing to glance up the long flight of stairs she saw an elderly lady of stately and distinguished appearance and carriage, dressed in an old fashioned costume of black moire antique, descending the stairs. A white fichu was around her shoulders, and on her arm hung a leather key basket, such as the mistress of a plantation carried. The figure, without pause or glance in her direction, crossed the hall and disappeared into the dining room. At the moment of disappearance, Mrs. Lee says, she suddenly realized this was not the figure of a mortal. She sprang to her feet and called "Catherine! Catherine!" Her friend appeared in haste from the drawing room. "Catherine, I have just seen an old lady with a key basket come down the stairs and go into the dining room." Catherine laughed and replied: "That is Mother Tabb; we see her very often. Usually she is seen only by members of the family."

Upon another occasion a member of the family awakened from an afternoon nap to see "Mother Tabb" enter the room, cross to the bureau, open the lowest drawer where some garments of an infant were kept, and removing each little article, shook it out before folding with care and replacing the clothing. The drawer was then closed, and the spirit of Evelina Matilda Prosser, the heiress of White

White Marsh, Gloucester County, Virginia

Courtesy of Mr. Swepson Earle

Marsh, left the room as quietly and as silently as she had entered.

A very peculiar psychic phenomenon occurred at White Marsh in Gloucester County a few years ago. It is called "the haunted rose bush." "White Marsh"—home of the Tabbs—passed to a Mr. Hughes of New York, and has had subsequent owners. It was early winter when the Hughes took possession of the property. In May the rose bushes were full of buds. On the second terrace of the falling garden was an especially luxuriant bush, whose blossoms were more backward than the rest. One bright morning in the last of May Mrs. Hughes found a blown rose upon it. Its creamy petals and golden heart filled her with joy and she put out her hand to pick it, but before her fingers touched the rose the bush swayed as if caught in the teeth of a mighty wind. Mrs. Hughes looked around —the landscape was peaceful—no storm was rising. Extremely puzzled, Mrs. Hughes again tried to pluck the rose; again the bush trembled. She grasped the stem firmly, but as if in wrath it snatched itself from her hand! The bush swayed violently again, and the very shutters of the house banged sharply. Mrs. Hughes was frightened at this phenomenon and left the rose bush.

She spoke of the occurrence and when her husband tried to pluck the rose the same thing happened, and he had the conviction that if he did pick it something tremendously disagreeable would occur.

The servants alleged solemnly that "Ole Miss ain't never 'lowed nobody to pull dat rose." The incident puzzled the whole countryside and many came to witness the antics of the "haunted bush."

Mrs. Hughes became nervous over the inexplicable performance and decided to have the bush destroyed. She was sick of its frantic twirling, the spontaneous banging of shutters and banging of doors. One morning as she was making her rounds of the garden the rosebush was gone, roots and all—the place thereof knew it no more. Did the gardener take it up? He says not.

The Haunted Woods

THE HAUNTED WOODS

A BOUT five miles from the village of Mathews Court House, Mathews County, Virginia, less than a quarter of a mile from Chesapeake Bay, stands today, as in Colonial times, an old pine woods some sixty acres in extent. These woods are, far and near, reputed to be haunted. They border the Bay Shore road on one side for half a mile.

In Revolutionary times a large frame house stood in the forest where today may be found a delapidated cottage, unoccupied for many years, known as "the Old House." As long ago as 1798 residents living near "Old House" woods declared ghosts had been seen there. Today, according to reputable witnesses, a ghostly threefold vigil is maintained over the gloomy pine woods. The ghosts of murdered royalists, of pirates who were killed in a drunken brawl over their plunder, and two officers and four men of Cornwallis' army have been seen.

White's Creek, wide and deep, separates Gwynn Island from the mainland, and its wooded shores offer an inviting haven for the hiding of treasure. The story runs that Cornwallis' army buried money and treasure, after slipping through the French and American cordon drawn around Yorktown and Gloucester Point in the summer of 1781. The six men were either killed by the fleet of the French Commander De Grasse or in an attempt to escape overland with their treasure.

It is recorded in the history of Virginia that when Sir William Berkeley, Philip Ludwell and others in his Company, made their escape to the Eastern Shore at the time of Bacon's Rebellion, they passed these haunted woods to refugee on Gwynn Island and met at Milford Haven, the King's vessel which carried them across the Chesapeake to safety.

That Milford Haven and Gwynn Island were much better known at former times than now is shown by the additional fact that Lord Dunmore, Royal Governor of Virginia at the time of the Revolution, made his escape at the same place and in the same manner.

Charles II is reputed to have, contemplating flight, sent treasure, not to Jamestown, but the Agents sailed up Chesapeake Bay to the mouth of White's Creek. The ghosts seen in armor are the aftermath of that adventure.

Tradition tells us the Royalists, after burying their treasure in the forest near the creek, were said to have been ambushed and murdered by white bondsmen captured at the battle of Worcester, and sent to the Colony.

"I am not apologetic nor ashamed to say I have seen ghosts in that woods," declared Mr. Jesse V. Hudgins, a merchant of Mathews Courthouse, Virginia.

"I do not care whether I am believed or not, I have seen ghosts not once, but a dozen times. I was seventeen when I first actually saw a ghost, or spirit, in 'Old House' woods. One October night I sat by the lamp, reading, bedtime two hours off. I was not sleepy. A neighbor whose child was very ill came asking me to drive to Mathews for the doctor. We had no telephone in those days. I hitched up and started for town. The night was gusty, clouds drifting now and then over the moon, but I could see perfectly, and whistled as I drove along. Nearing 'Old House' itself, I saw a light about fifty yards ahead moving along the road in the direction I was going. My horse, usually afraid of nothing, cowered and trembled violently. I felt rather uneasy myself. I have seen lights on the road at night, shining lanterns carried by men, but this light was different. There was something unearthly about it. The rays seemed to come from nowhere, and yet they moved with the bearer.

"I gained on the traveler," Mr. Hudgins said, "and as I stand here before you, what I saw was a big man wearing a suit of armor. Over his shoulder was a gun, the muzzle end of which looked like a fish horn. As he strode, or floated along, he made no noise. My horse stopped still. I was weak with terror and horror. I wasn't twenty feet from the thing, whatever it was, when it too, stopped and faced me.

"At the same time the woods about one hundred feet from the wayfarer became alive with lights and moving forms. Some carried guns like the one borne by the man or thing in the road, others carried shovels of an outlandish type, while still others dug furiously near a dead pine tree.

"As my gaze returned to the first shadowy figure, what I saw was not a man in armor, but a skeleton, and every bone of it was visible through the iron of the armor, as though it were made of glass. The skull, which seemed to be illuminated from within, grinned at me horribly. Then, raising aloft a sword, which I had not hitherto noticed, the awful specter started towards me menacingly. I could stand no more. Reason left me. When I came to it was broad daylight and I lay upon my bed at home.

"Members of my family said the horse had run away. They found me at the turn of the road beyond 'Old House' woods. They thought I had fallen asleep. The best proof that this was not so was we could not even lead Tom by the 'Old House' woods for months afterwards, and to the day he died whenever he approached the woods, he would tremble violently and cower. It was pitiful to see that fine animal become such a victim of terror."

In company with another man, Mr. Hudgins was making his way towards Haven Beach one summer day. "What's that?" his companion asked in alarm, pointing to "Old House" woods. In the low growth along the roadway they saw a white object moving farther into the thicket. Both men immediately left their carriage and entered the woods.

"About thirty yards ahead of us we saw a woman in a white nightgown, her long fair hair flying back from her shoulders," said Hudgins. "She was half floating and half walking along. Without exhibiting any haste or alarm, the apparition proceeded leisurely, keeping the same distance from us as she neared the low trees on the edge of the woods on White's Creek side. She arose in the air and slowly floated out over the tops of the trees and disappeared. The storm and ghosts held high revel in 'Old House' woods that night," concluded Hudgins.

Harry Forrest, who both farms the land and is a fisherman,

lives within six hundred feet of "Old House" woods on the Milford Haven, or White's Creek, side, probably is more familiar with the true state of ghostly hauntings than is any other person residing in those parts.

"I've seen more strange things in there and in this Haven section than I could relate in a whole day," declared Forrest. "I've seen armies of marching British red coats; I've seen the 'storm woman' and heard her dismal wailings, and my mother and I have sat here all hours of the night and have seen lights in the woods. We have sat here on our porch, overlooking Chesapeake Bay and have seen ships anchor off the beach and boats would put to shore, and bodies of men go to the woods. I would see lights over there and hear the sound of digging.

"Once, over there at Rigney Point, I went to shoot ducks. I found a flock asleep on a little inlet where pine trees come down to the edge of the water. As I raised my gun to fire, instead of them being ducks, I saw they were soldiers of the olden time, as sure as you were born. Headed by an officer, company after company of them formed and marched out to the water. Recovering from my astonishment, I ran to my skiff. Arriving there, I found a man in uniform, his red coat showing brilliantly in the bright moonlight, sitting upright and very rigid in the stern. I was scared, but mad too. So I yelled to him, 'Get out of that skiff or I'll shoot.' 'Shoot and the devil's curse to you and your traitor's breed,' he answered, and made as if to strike me with the sword he carried. Then I drew my gun on him and pulled. It didn't go off. I pulled the trigger again. No better result. I dropped the gun and ran home, and I am not ashamed to say I swam the creek in doing it, too.

"One night I saw a white ox lying in my corn pasture," continued Forrest. "I went out to drive him away. When I reached the spot where the animal was lying, I saw it was a coffin covered with a sheet and borne along by invisible hands, just at the height pallbearers would carry a corpse. I followed until it entered the woods by the old pine tree over there. The sheet only partly covered the coffin. Well, sir, the following Wednesday they brought the body of Harry Daniels ashore from Wolf Trap lightship. Harry was killed when the boiler blew up aboard the lightship. As the men carried him up the beach to the waiting hearse, I recognized instantly the coffin I had seen borne into 'Old House' woods. The men were carrying it in the selfsame manner in every particular, even to the peculiar, somewhat clumsy, swaying motion I had observed in my cornfield."

———

Ben Ferbee, an intelligent negro fisherman, lived along the Bay Shore some years ago. One experience with the ghosts of "Old House" woods was enough, and as a result he took his family away to the city.

"One starry night I was fishing off the mouth of White's Creek, well out in the bay," related Ferbee. "As the flood tide would not set in for some time, I decided to get the good fishing and come home with the early moon. It must have been after midnight, when, as I turned to bait up a line in the stern of my boat, I saw a full-rigged ship in the bay, standing pretty well in. I was quite surprised, I tell you. Full-rigged ships were mighty scarce then; besides that, I knew she was in for it if she kept that course. On the ship came, with lights at every masthead and spar, and I was plumb scared. They'll run me down and sink me, I thought. I shouted to sailors leaning over her rails forward, but they paid no heed to me. Just as I thought she would strike me, the helmsman put her hard aport and she passed so close that I almost swamped by the wash. She was a beautiful ship, but different from any I had ever seen. There are no ships like her on any ocean. She made no noise at all, and when she had gone by the most beautiful harp and organ music I ever heard came back to me. The ship sailed right up to the beach and never stopped, but kept right on. Over the sandy beach she swept, floating through the air and up to the Bay Shore road, her keel about twenty feet from the ground. I could still hear the music. But I was scared out of my wits. I knew it was not a real ship. It was a ghost ship.

"Well, sir, I pulled up my anchor and started for home up White's Creek. I could see that ship hanging over 'Old House' woods, just as though she was anchored in the sea. And running down to the woods was a rope-ladder, lined with the forms of men carrying tools and other contraptions.

"When I got home my wife was up, but had no supper for me. Instead she and the children were praying. I knew what was the matter. Without speaking a word she pointed to 'Old House' woods, a scared look on her face. She and the children had seen the ship standing over the woods. I didn't need to ask her—I started praying too."

On one occasion a farmer's wife living on a place adjacent to the haunted woods went to a pasture to bring home their work-horses. She drove them down a lane towards the barn. Arriving at the gate, she called to her husband to open it. He did not respond at once, and she opened it herself. As she did so, her husband came out of the barn and laughed at her, saying he had put the team in the stable two hours before.

"Don't be foolish," said the woman. When she turned to let the team pass through the gate, instead of two horses standing there she saw two headless black dogs scampering off towards 'Old House' woods.

All attempts to dig for buried treasure in the ghost-woods have met with tragedy and failure, persons living in the neighborhood declare. Tom Pipkin, a fisherman who lived in the vicinity more than half a century ago, disappeared after a treasure hunting trip. His boat was found in the bay. Two gold coins of unknown age, and a battered silver cup all covered with slime and mud, were found in Pipkin's boat. One coin bore a Roman head and the letters "I V V S" were distinguishable. No one would take Pipkin's boat as a gift, and it rotted away on Gwynn Island. Pipkin never again was heard of.

A Richmond youth had tire trouble at a lonely spot along the road near the haunted woods one night very late. As he knelt in the road, a voice behind him asked, "Is this the King's highway? I have lost my ship." When the boy turned to look he beheld a skeleton in armor within a few feet of him. Yelling, the frightened autoist ran from the spot, and did not return for his car until the next day. Farmers and fishermen living along the Bay Shore road say he saw a member of the ghostly watch that guards the buried treasure of Charles Stuart.

On September 26, 1926, *The Baltimore Sun* contained an article recording many of the facts here presented.

Woodlawn, King and Queen County, Virginia

WOODLAWN

IN an isolated spot in King and Queen County, Virginia, twenty miles from the little town of Tappahannock stands a great water oak six feet in diameter two feet from the ground. Beneath its shade, about two hundred years ago, someone built a commodious frame dwelling, now soon to pass from the memory. Great plastered vestibules twelve feet square, lighted by large windows and topped by tiny chimneys, present an unusual entrance feature at either end of an eighteen foot hallway; while nearby, a sapling in the days of the Revolution, now a twisted and gnarled old relic, still puts forth green leaves in the spring.

Woodlawn was bought by Thomas Gresham, Commonwealth Attorney of Essex County, from "a General Gaines" about 1821. On account of burned records the name of the original owner is unknown, but builders estimate the age of the house to be two hundred years. The property now belongs to Mrs. Ella Haile of Tappahannock, granddaughter of Thomas Gresham, whose excellent memory carries her back eighty-three years, and to whose courtesy I am indebted for these interesting and valuable reminiscences.

It was feared in 1812 Tappahannock might be burned, consequently Mr. Gresham moved his household effects to his plantation "Pigeon Hill," and ten years later the household took up residence at Woodlawn, seeking a locality free from malaria. Mrs. Gresham did not long survive, and for a time after her death the house stood vacant. During this period the tenant from his home, and the slaves from their cabins, frequently saw lights at night in "the big house." Among the furnishings taken from "Pigeon Hill" was an interesting clock which Mrs. Gresham hung in the front hall; but unfortunately owing to the rough roads, after the journey the clock would not run. This clock was set in an oblong case about four feet high and one and one-half feet wide. The gold leaf of those days is now tarnished almost black. The front is divided into three sections; a large mirror has openings at the top for the face, and at the bottom to show the pendulum. Around the face and the lozenge shaped opening colored pictures of houses and trees were painted. Sometime after Mrs. Gresham's death and "Woodlawn"

Kitchen and Well, Woodlawn, Virginia

once more became the family home, a strange phenomenon was observed. Just before a death the clock mute at all other times would strike! Mrs. Haile herself recalls vividly three of these happenings. The first time she was four years old. Her mother's brother was ill of consumption; as he was brought into the house the clock struck! His death occurred shortly. Again six years later the clock struck foretelling her grandmother's death only a few hours before her passing. The third time Mrs. Haile heard the ominous sound the clock struck "one." She was twelve years old, and at this time the creeping child of her colored "mammy" playing about the kitchen floor was scalded to death.

Finally the clock proved such an annoyance, and as Mrs. Haile's father said, "Such a source of superstitious dread," that he had the works removed. These were thrown into the woodshed where the children often used them as playthings. The case of the clock was moved upstairs into what was known as "the haunted room."

Wythe House

WYTHE HOUSE

Lady Skipwith Revisits Williamsburg

THE George Wythe House, built in Williamsburg in 1755 by Richard Taliaferro, who gave it as a wedding present to his daughter, when, in 1775, she married George Wythe, is of massive and solid construction, designed to furnish its owner such comforts as that day afforded the affluent, and to withstand the corroding influence of time. The traveller of understanding heart perceives here, how enduring is honest masonry and how "soon are forgotten both the praiser and the praised." The huge fireplace still affords cheer and comfort to those who gather around it in our day, but the aristocrats who warmed their cold feet before the cheerful blaze, and the slaves who piled on the logs, are alike forgotten.

We learn that Washington made here his headquarters, and with Lafayette planned the discomfiture of Cornwallis.

We do not know—life's fitful fever ended—to what spot in Bruton Churchyard, and just where, into the keeping of the Great Mother of us all, was consigned all that was mortal of her whom men called Lady Skipwith. From the musty pages of an old prayer book, still treasured by the Randolphs, may be learned that in 1791, at Corotoman, her daughter, Lelia Skipwith, born in 1767, married St. George Tucker. It comes to us that her husband was Sir Peyton Skipwith, Bart., of Prestwould, Mecklenburg County. He married Ann, daughter of Hugh Miller, and secondly her sister Jean. The record of his faithfulness does not reach us entirely without blemish. The marriage service shortly after the burial beneath the shadow of Bruton Church occasions ground for belief that jealousy was the cause of Lady Skipwith's suicide.

Her home was in the Wythe House upon the palace green. From generation to generation is told the story that one night a ball was given at the palace, and that Lady Skipwith danced in tiny red slippers, upon which shone buckles of brilliants. While long, long years ago the feet of those Colonial belles and beaux of the dances grew weary, and the music dropped from their song, we may still in the night-time hear the music of the little red slippers upon the stairway, and some few favored of the gods have seen their glorious color! From "some sphere, we know not where, but we shall know e'er long," Lady Skipwith returns to Williamsburg! She is most frequently seen—"a beautiful woman, fully gowned in Colonial ball costume, to come out of a closet in a certain room, look at herself in a mirror and finally pass out of the door."

A stranger once staying in the room described accurately the dress of which she had never heard and had never seen, for it is hidden away from view in a Williamsburg attic, perfumed with lavender gathered from the garden below.

In this dress of cream satin, Lady Skipwith is said to have danced her last minuet, and then to have hastily left the palace long before the ball was over. What tragedy in life was responsible for this sudden and mysterious leavetaking When the swish of her silken petticoats are heard in the twilight does she long to reveal to us the sorry tale?

Lady Skipwith alone of all that merry crowd of revellers returns again and again to remind us by the sound of her dainty slippers on the steps that one night 150 years ago she tripped lightly

down the same stairway, and across the green, wearing her little red slippers trimmed with sparkling buckles.

YORK HALL

UPON a bluff facing the river stands "York Hall," the old Nelson House, Yorktown's most interesting relic. Built on a terrace and surrounded by a garden and its protecting wall, the ancient dwelling survives many generations. Tall box-trees guard the gate leading to this spacious and dignified old mansion with its high pitched roof and unique chimneys; a dwelling filled with the memories of America's Colonial history; and here, in their day, many of her most distinguished sons found the latch string ever out. Many a cheering cup was filled to the brim in the dining-room where candles gleamed, while shadows danced on the lovely pine wainscot, now mellowed by age to a beautiful brown. Deep window seats suggest whispered conversations and, crowning all, the mysterious stairway hidden behind a panel in the dining-room wall and leading to a garret. It has always been said that behind this panel a British soldier was killed at the bombardment of Yorktown.

When but one year old, Thomas Nelson's Father put a brick in his hand to lay at the setting of the cornerstone, so young Thomas, born in 1739, might claim in after years to have participated in the building of his home.

Thomas Nelson was Governor of Virginia, signer of the Declaration of Independence, and a Major-General in the Revolutionary Army.

During the siege of Yorktown Lord Cornwallis made his headquarters in "York Hall," and a cannonball imbedded in the massive wall remains, testifying to the damaging fire to which the house was exposed. General Nelson directed General Lafayette not to spare his property in the effort to dislodge the enemy.

It is not strange that the last owner of "York Hall" should have had a remarkable experience in a house surviving the many tragic dramas staged beneath its roof. This property belonged to the late Mr. and Mrs. George Preston Blow. Mrs. William Jeffries Chewning, of Fredericksburg, visited "York Hall" more than a year ago, attending a tea with some members of the Garden Club of Virginia.

Mrs. Chewning writes: "I asked Mrs. Blow if the house was haunted. She said that when they bought it, it was said to be

York Hall

haunted by a British soldier who had been killed in the secret stairway when General Nelson turned the guns on his own house." "Mrs. Blow told me," continued Mrs. Chewning, "she had several ladies to luncheon a short time before, and one of them, much interested in ghosts, asked concerning the story of the British soldier and the panel. Mrs. Blow admitted that story was told of York Hall, but said throughout their stay, nothing had 'been seen or heard.'

"No sooner had Mrs. Blow ceased talking than the secret door burst open with terrific force, knocking with such violence against the sideboard that several dishes crashed to the floor, shattered beyond repair! Absolute silence ensued. The faces of the guests blanched! Mrs. Blow, with admirable presence of mind, attributed the catastrophe to a sudden draught from above, and skillfully turned the conversation into other channels.

Mrs. Blow stated to Mrs. Chewning that she afterwards assured herself there had been "no draught whatsoever; no normal explanation of the opening of the door possible."

A CONFEDERATE SOLDIER

"MRS. RICHARD MASON and her husband the Rev. Mr. Mason, came from Virginia directly after the Civil War. He became the Rector of St. James Church on 'My Lady's Manor,' Baltimore County, Maryland. Later he left that church and became Rector of Emmanuel Church near Glencoe, Baltimore County, Maryland.

"I attended that church and became very much attached to both of them. They are buried in the graveyard at the church.

"On one occasion when Mrs. Mason and I were talking about various things she told me the following story. She said just after General Lee surrendered she had been very ill in Richmond, in a house that had been used as a hospital for wounded Confederate soldiers. She was getting better but was still in bed. One night she was lying with her eyes closed. Her sister who had been nursing her had gone out of the room. The door was open—with the light on a table in the hall. Mrs. Mason said she happened to open her eyes, and there a Confederate soldier was standing with his back against a wardrobe, and the light from the hall shone directly upon him. She said she was very much startled and at first thought she was dreaming. As she stared at him he faded away. Mrs. Mason told me she immediately thought of having heard of Dr. Charles Frick's experience in Baltimore and when her sister Julia came in the room she said: 'Julia, I have had an optical illusion like Charles Frick had.' I laughed and told her I had heard that story long ago.

"Mrs. Mason was Nannie Johns, daughter of Bishop Johns of Virginia. Before he was made Bishop he was the Rector of Emmanuel Church in Baltimore, so that is how she heard that old story. Mr. Mason was a Virginian. He had been in the Confederate Army."

—*Louisa Tilghman Carroll.*

The Governor's Mansion, Richmond

THE GOVERNOR'S MANSION

IN one corner of Capitol Square has stood for 120 years the Governor's Mansion. First named "The Palace," it was erected in 1779 when Thomas Jefferson was Governor. A two story frame building of but four rooms, never painted, and only partly inclosed by a cheap wooden fence. Governor Tyler in his message in 1810 called attention to the dilapidated condition of the Governor's house and asked that improvements be made. An act in 1811 appropriated $12,000 to build a new mansion. A large two story building now occupies the site. Today the brick is painted white, the low roof remains unaltered, and a tall iron fence encircles a box-trimmed garden, at the same time affording privacy from the adjoining street.

The fine Mansion was built in 1812 when James Barbour was Governor, and an old colored butler named Winston has been in service since 1886 when General Fitzhugh Lee was elected.

Andrew J. Montague was Governor of Virginia for four years from 1902. Mrs. Montague tells me she had several small children, and that Mr. Robert Lynch and Dr. Horace Hoskins were also of the household. These two young men occupied beds in a very large room with bath adjoining. One morning Mrs. Montague was told that during the night they were both awakened by unmistakable sound of footsteps in their room accompanied by the swish of a silk skirt. The young men jumped up and followed the sound along the corridor and down the hallway below the stairs, where the sound could no longer be heard.

Mrs. Montague, careful not to alarm the children, took Winston aside and asked if he had ever heard of any apparitions seen in the house. After having the word explained Winston said, "Yes, during Governor McKinny's day." One hot August afternoon the Governor came in from the Capitol and going upstairs took off his coat in the bathroom before going into the room where Mr. Lynch and Mr. Hoskins slept. There he saw a young lady sitting by the window. Much astonished the Governor backed into the bathroom, put on his coat, and finding Mrs. McKinny asked who the young lady was. "There was no young lady visitor," and so far as Winston knew, the ghost was never seen again.

THE LITTLE GRAY LADY

THE old brick homestead of the Hawes family, 506 east Leigh Street, Richmond, Virginia, was a big square Colonial house of many large rooms and long passages. It stood in grounds once extensive and beautiful, but year by year the encroaching city and its streets removed much of its gardens and many of its large shade-trees.

The well-known writer, "Marion Harland," tells us in her "Story of a Long Life" that many years ago, one stormy night, she extinguished the hanging lamp in the front hall, and with one from the parlor table to light her to her bedroom up a broad easy stairway, ascending by a succession of landings from the lower to the upper story; she passed through a small archway in the hall, closing the door behind her, the lamp throwing a bright light across the passage here, a little over six feet wide.

She said, as the door behind her closed she saw, as distinctly as if by daylight, a small woman start out of the opposite door, glide noiselessly along the wall, and disappear at the Venetian blinds hanging at the end of the front hall. She was dressed in gray; she was small and lithe; her head was bowed upon her hands; and in her hair was a tortoise shell comb. She glided away along the wall as if in flight, vanishing, the door not opening as she passed through. The house, as usual, had been locked at ten o'clock. Up to that moment, Marion Harland declares she had never known one moment of fear.

Turning and entering mother's room, she placed the lamp on the table, and said: "If there is any such thing as a ghost, I have seen one."

Her Father wheeled sharply about! "What?"

"I have seen a ghost!"

"Putting his hand on her head, he said: "I know it, my child, but we will talk no more of it tonight. I will go to your room with you."

The next morning after breakfast he took her aside and told her to keep what she had seen to herself.

About a month after her experience, at about nine o'clock one night, her mother entered the room in which she and her Father were sitting and, hurridly glancing behind her, said: "I have seen Virginia's ghost!"

She saw it just as had her daughter, issuing from the closed door and gliding close to the wall, vanishing at the Venetian door.

"It was all in gray," she reported, "but with something white wrapped about its head."

Again the Father cautioned them not to mention the apparition to anyone.

Before a great while a younger daughter had to be taken into their confidence. She burst into the drawing-room at twilight one evening, shut the door, and with her back against it, trembling from head to foot, and white as a sheet, declared something chased her down the stairs! Somebody in high heel shoes went tap, tap, tap on the oak stairs behind her, from the time she left the upper chamber, where she had been dressing, until she reached the parlor door.

One night Alice, a girl of fourteen, and a young cousin, were sent to bed at nine o'clock. Seeing the bright coal-fire in the parlor, the door of which was ajar, they entered and sat down in the dark for a talk. Suddenly the call of the sentinel at the barracks on Capitol Square told them it was ten o'clock. Going into the hall, they were surprised to find it dark. The lamp had burned out.

It was a brilliant moonlight night, and the great window on the lower staircase was unshuttered. From the doorway of the parlor the girls had a full view of the stairs. The moonbeams flooded it halfway up to the upper landing, and from the dark hall they saw a white figure moving slowly down the steps. The girls jumped to the conclusion that one of the boys was on his way *en dishabille* to get a drink of water from the pitcher always standing on the table in the main hall. To get to it he must pass within a few feet of them. Down the stairs the figure moved without sound, and slowly.

The Hawes House

The girls said afterwards that the nightgown trailed on the stairs and something white was cast over the figures' head. The apparition crossed the moonlit landing—an unbroken sheet of light—and stepped yet more slowly from stair to stair of the four that composed the lowermost flight. It was on the floor, and almost within the archway, when the front door opened suddenly and in walked all the boys!

In an instant the apparition was gone! As Alice phrased it, "It did not go backward or forward. It did not sink into the floor. It just was not!"

In the morning the Father summoned his wife and children to a private conference. He began the business without preliminaries. "It is useless to try to hide from ourselves any longer that there is something wrong with this house. I have known it for a year or more. In fact, we had not lived here three months before I was made aware that some mystery hung about it. One windy November night I had gone to bed as usual before your mother. I lay with closed eyes listening to wind and rain when somebody touched my feet. Somebody—not something. Hands were laid lightly upon them; were lifted and laid in the same way on my knees, and so on until they lay more heavily upon my chest and I felt someone was looking in my face. Up to that moment I had not a doubt but that it was your mother arranging the covers to keep out draughts. I opened my eyes to thank her. She was not there! I raised myself on my elbow and looked towards the fireplace. Your mother was deep in her book!

I have never spoken of this even to your mother until this moment. But it has happened to me not twenty, but fifty times or more. It is always the same thing. The hands, I have settled in my mind, are those of a small woman, or child. Sometimes the hands rest on my chest a whole minute. Something looks into my face and is gone. You can see, my daughter, why I was not incredulous when you brought your ghost upon the scene. I have been on the lookout for further manifestations. By all means do not let the servants hear of this. You girls are old enough to understand that the value of this property would be destroyed were this story to creep abroad. Better burn the house down than attempt to sell it at any time within the next fifty years with a ghost story tagged to it."

They kept their pledge of silence.

The one comic element connected with the ghost was introduced by a sanctimonious clerical uncle-in-law who now and then paid them a visit.

On one occasion his appearance caused dismay. They were expecting a household of younger friends and needed a guest room he must occupy. He was good for a week at the shortest. It was much of a surprise when he announced the morning after his arrival his intention of going to Olney that day and remain perhaps a week.

Sometime after the close of his visit in Olney, their aunt drove into town to spend the day with them. "Did any of you ever suspect that your house is haunted?" she asked. "How ridiculous," laughed her sister. "Why do you ask?"

"Well, the old clergyman had an awful scare the night he was here. He declared he was standing at his window looking out into the moonlight in the garden when somebody came up behind him and took him by the elbow and turned him clear around! He felt plainly the two hands that grabbed hold of him. He looked under the bed and in the closet. There was nobody in the room but himself, and the door was locked. He said he would not sleep in that room again for one thousand dollars!

After the death of her husband, twelve years later, and the marriage of sons and daughters, Marion Harland's mother was left alone in the old Colonial homestead. She decided to sell it and live with one of her daughters.

The property was bought as an orphanage by a prominent Episcopal parish. In digging an areaway in front of the premises to adapt the building to the new uses, the workmen came upon—about four feet below the surface of the front yard—the skeleton of a small woman. She lay less than six feet away from the wall of the house and directly under the drawing-room window. There was no sign of coffin or of coffin-plate. Under her head was a richly carved tortoise shell comb.

The oldest inhabitant of a city, tenacious of domestic legends, had never heard of an interment in that residential district. The grave was dug in the front garden, and so close to the house as to render untenable the theory that the plot was ever part of a family burying-ground.

Marion Harland concludes, "I have talked with a grandson of our former next-door neighbor, and had from him an account of the disinterment of the nameless remains. They must have lain nearer the turf above them a century back, than when they were found. He verified the story of the high carved comb. He told me of a midnight alarm, of screaming children at the occasion of a little gray lady walking between the double row of beds in the dormitory, adding, 'I told those who asked if any story was attached to the house that I had lived next door ever since I was born and never heard that the house was haunted.'"

We had kept our pledge of silence.

AN ARMY VISITOR

A YOUNG lieutenant in the United States Army, a member of a prominent family of Richmond, Virginia, was an officer in the Mexican War. No news had come from him for some time, when at 5 o'clock one morning his younger brother awakened and saw the young officer standing at the foot of the bed.

Astonished to see him, the brother exclaimed, "Why, James, when did you get back?"

"Major Smith will see you later and tell you all about it."

After this remark the officer turned, and walking to the door, passed through into the hall.

Startled and amazed, the brother sprang from the bed and rushing into the passage found nobody there. He ran downstairs and into the garden, but never found his brother.

The apparition, for such it was, was clad in his uniform; spoke in a natural voice and looked as material as he had looked in life.

In due time Major Smith arrived and informed the family of the young officer's death, which occurred on that day and at that hour of his appearing.

THE EXPERIENCE OF A UNITED STATES
ARMY OFFICER

IN 1908 Captain Jeffry Montague, an infantry officer in the regular army, and Mrs. Montague, were occupying a rented house, an old brick residence on Franklin Street, Richmond, Virginia. It was afterwards learned that some years before a Mrs. Charles O'Brien Cawardin, formerly Miss Jessie Evans, had died in the room in which Captain Montague had the very remarkable and interesting experience he relates.

At the particular time of this ghostly appearance Captain Montague was city editor on the staff of the *News-Leader,* then as now, one of the leading newspapers in Richmond. He had had no personal experience in matters of a supernormal nature nor was he interested in such happenings.

At the Westmoreland Club the experience was received in a spirit of universal unbelief, other than by Dr. Gildersleeve, a leading physician of the city, and a brother of Dr. Basil Gildersleeve, the noted Greek scholar of Johns Hopkins. Dr. Gildersleeve was willing to concede that Captain Montague saw what he claimed he had seen. Dr. Gildersleeve explained in professional terms that what he saw was an image in that remarkable camera—the eye— which lingered there after he was awakened suddenly by the noise. On the particular evening of which Captain Montague writes, he ate a light supper, smoked a cigar, played a while with his son, and about 10 P. M. went to bed. He was in a perfectly commonplace, comfortable frame of mind and body, and being tired after a hard day's work, was soon sound asleep.

"My wife slept in the back room and I at the front of the house, in the top story. The door in the partition wall between the two rooms was open; doors of both rooms into the hall were open; the windows both front and rear were open.

"I was awakened sometime between 2:30 and 3 o'clock in the morning by a roaring sound, which, as I became conscious, resolved itself into the noise of an automobile going east on Franklin Street at high speed. I had not moved as I listened to this noise.

Suddenly I felt sharply aware that someone else was in the room. The natural thought 'burglar' sprang into my mind. I opened my eyes just enough for vision. Standing about a yard from the foot of my bed was the figure of a woman. The head and shoulders were distinctly outlined, but the rest of the figure was a white blur. I really do not know how to describe accurately the surface appearance of this figure. It seemed like a million tiny, dull, unpolished pearls laid together. I thought of course it was my wife, awakened by the noise and come into my room to look out of the window. In her childhood she had sometimes walked in her sleep. I had always heard it was dangerous to awaken a sleep-walker suddenly, therefore I kept perfectly still and watched the figure through eyelids almost closed. The figure stood another five or ten seconds apparently looking at me and then turned and moved towards one of the two front windows, the one farthest from my bed.

"I thought nothing of it at the time, but recalled later that it did not walk as a living person would. It seemed to float to the window. This latter impressed me as strange, however, because my wife was of a substantial mould and walked with a distinct characteristic motion.

"The figure, upon reaching the window, inclined its head and looked down into the street. Now for the first time features were recognizable. They were the nose and chin. The nose, well shaped and of good size, clearly topped the lower indoor blinds, which were closed and latched. The upper indoor blinds were open and so were the upper sash. There were no outside blinds.

"I had risen cautiously upon my elbow while this was going on. I watched the figure while it gazed into the street, wondering what I should do, if anything.

"The figure now turned and came back to the foot of my bed, where it stood facing me. Still thinking it was my wife, I was convinced now that she was sleep-walking, because if she were awake, she would speak, seeing me raised up on my elbow looking at her.

"Very gently, so as not to alarm her, I murmured her name, 'Hally.' Instantly the figure sank to the floor, disappearing in the blackness at the foot of my bed. The fall or disappearance was noiseless, but I did not notice that at the moment.

Shocked and anxious, fearing a serious consequence to my wife, I sprang up, hurried to the mantel over the fireplace opposite my bed, groped for a match and lighted the gas. *There was no one on the floor.* I looked hastily around the room: No one was there.

In another moment I was in my wife's room, and there she was in her bed, apparently just awakened by the flash of light and the commotion I was making in my search.

"Hally! You here? I exclaimed incredulously; a silly enough question, of course, for there she was.

" 'Where else should I be at this time of night?' she responded.

"Weren't you in my room just now looking out of the window?"

" 'I certainly was not. Your light waked me up. What is the matter with you?'

"For the first time it dawned upon me that I had seen a 'ghost.' I told her what had happened and asked her if she would get up, come into my room and do exactly what I told her to do. She agreed, with the idea of humoring a harmless lunatic. She was in a long plain white nightgown. I placed her standing where I had first seen the ghost, turned out the light and got back into bed. *She was invisible.* The white of her nightgown did not show at all. I could hardly discern the dark outline of her figure. The ghostly substance, therefore, while not radiant, had been *luminous.*

I asked her to go to the far window and look out. She turned towards the window and was stopped by a large Morris chair, and asked me facetiously what she should do—climb over the chair or walk around it. I told her to go around it. Arrived at the window, she was unable to look out over the lower blind, the top of which was above her head!

"I remained awake for some time, hoping that the Spirit would reappear, but it did not. I never saw it again. I believe firmly that that night I saw the ghost which haunts that old brick house on Franklin Street, Richmond, Virginia."

EDGEWOOD

FOR his own use, and for that of his neighbors on the James River, two hundred years ago, Benjamin Harrison, Signer of the Declaration of Independence, owned and operated a grist-mill for grinding corn and wheat on his plantation of 17,000 acres, "Berkeley" in Charles City County. Today, as at that time, a canal more than one mile in length, dug by slaves, supplies water from a large lake, and in Colonial times there were in connection with the mill immense bakeovens in which sea-bread was baked for use on the return voyage to England, after the sailors had discharged their cargo for the settlers.

The great stones which ground the grain came from Italy, and are the hardest and finest grained rock of the Alps. These stones, probably the original, over two hundred years old and very valuable, were bequeathed to his wife by Benjamin Harrison in his will.

The present mill, more than a century old, contains some of the massive handhewn timbers built into the original Berkeley mill.

On part of the Berkeley plantation, amid great oaks at that time very old, Edgewood was erected by Spencer Rowland, more than one hundred years ago, on a gentle eminence beside the road and on the bank of Herring Lake.

Large and substantially built, Edgewood's atmosphere is that of comfort and of cheer. Tall chimneys suggest hospitable fires when the winds of winter blow, and the great oaks speak of grateful shade in summertime.

Edgewood stands within the sound of the old wheel turning, and ever at hand the same inspiring stream, fed by countless age-old springs, beside which the pioneer tarried a few brief years.

Mrs. Grace D. Harrison very kindly tells me of the ghost whose name, Lizzie Rowland, is etched upon the windowpane in the room in which she died, and upon a tombstone in Westover churchyard may be read the inscription:

> "ELIZABETH ROWLAND,
> BORN MAY 20 1823
> DIED FEB. 6 1870
> DEAR SISTER HOW WE LOVE THEE."

Lizzie was the only daughter, and her lover, living on one of

Edgewood

the adjacent plantations, could always be heard from quite a distance approaching Edgewood, as he rode a very spirited horse. Throughout the years her Spirit has been seen roaming about the house and looking out the windows along the road in the direction from which her lover was accustomed to come.

Mrs. Harrison says: "As one drives or walks on a moonlight night it is at times quite startling to see 'Miss Lizzie' standing at the side door or peering out of one of the windows. Sometimes if you stand still for a time this figure in white, which seems to have a light in her hand, will pass from one window to another. She has been seen a good many times in past years and by quite a few people. I have heard my uncle, William Harrison, tell that on several occasions he was so certain someone was in the house he went all over it after entering searching and calling. The ghost never roams when anyone is at home, but only when she has the place to herself. Possibly her Spirit is awakened by the hoofbeats on the road of some passing traveller."

Greenway Court, Charles City County, Virginia

GREENWAY COURT

S EPT. 28, 1930, Dr. Lyon G. Tyler, son of President John Tyler, writes as follows:

"Greenway was the residence of General John Tyler, Sr., and birthplace of President John Tyler. Maria Henry Tyler married John B. Seawell of Gloucester County and had two distinguished sons, John Tyler Seawell, father of Molly Elliot Seawell the novelist, and Machen B. Seawell, a well known lawyer of Gloucester County.

"Greenway is still standing. It is a frame building one and one-half stories high. It stands half a mile from the Court House in this county. No one knows who built the house, though it is believed to have been built by General Tyler about 1776. He certainly resided there throughout the Revolution.

"Maria Henry Tyler was named for the wife of Patrick Henry. She had a sister Martha Jefferson Tyler named for Thomas Jefferson's wife. Maria Tyler's granddaughters might recall the story of the apparitions."

A discarnate phantasm was witnessed at "Greenway Court" during the lifetime of Governor Tyler, the father of the President of the United States. The wife of Governor Tyler was dead, and his daughter the namesake of Patrick Henry's wife and the pet of Jefferson was sleeping in a double bed with a girl friend. The little sister lay in a smaller bed on the other side of the room. Long past midnight Maria Henry Tyler awoke. The moonlight made her chamber almost as bright as day. Something drew her gaze toward the other bed and her little sister, and bending over the child was the discarnate image of her beautiful mother! She did not dare to speak lest the vision vanish. "Maria!" her friend lying beside her called suddenly. "There is your mother!" The vision vanished.

This strange experience was often related by both women, and the chamber is called the haunted chamber to this day.

Maria Tyler married, and many years after this vision she was at Greenway Court. Her brother the future President then owned it. Upon a certain night one of the young Tylers was taken very ill, and Maria who was helping to nurse him needed something from the very room in which the apparition of her mother had appeared.

As she entered the chamber the phantasm of her father stood before her. He wore a suit of brown clothes which she well remembered, and as her eyes darted to his forehead she saw his birthmark, a large mole. He was motionless and silent as well as herself. "Maria! Maria!" her sister-in-law called from below, and the phantasm vanished. This is on record.

SHIRLEY

IN 1611 Sir Thomas Dale, Governor of the Colony, gave title to the plantation of West Shirley, named in honor of Sir Thos. Shirley, of Whiston, England. The estate comes into prominence as the seat of the Hon. Edward Hill, "a member of His Majesty's Council in Virginia, Colonel and Commander-in-Chief of the counties of Charles City and Surry, Judge of His Majesty's High Court of Admiralty, and Treasurer of Virginia." He was Speaker of the Assembly of Burgesses in November, 1654.

The date of the building of the present mansion is uncertain. It was erected by Col. Edward Hill, a man of prominence in his day and generation in the Colony, about 1675, or prior to that date. On a gentle eminence above the river, in a bend of the stream, Shirley commands a far-reaching view of water and of the countryside. Compact in design, of great age, and finished with a superbly designed roof bearing sixteen large dormer windows glazed with many panes. Above all, great massive chimneys towering, Shirley was fashioned for length of days and to endure from generation to generation.

Beneath a massive tomb in the little burial-ground quite close at hand, Colonel Hill sleeps among his descendants as the years gather into centuries, while the slips of box become marvelous bushes, and the James ceaselessly bears upon its bosom the tiny streams from far-distant sources, onward to the sea. In the Springtime the scent of the flowering box at Shirley edging its garden squares and gracing the landscape, the wealth of golden daffodils heralding the approach of dainty lavender, glorious roses, and green mignonette, call from afar to their fragrance the honey-loving bee.

This splendid mansion is preëminently noted for its superb collection of portraits, immensely valuable and greatly valued. Strangely enough, a portrait little cared for, and for more than fifty years consigned to an attic closet, proves the magnet attracting to her former home the Spirit of the woman whose features were delineated upon the canvas, and enabling her to make her presence heard and understood after the passing of possibly 150 years!

Mrs. Marion Carter Oliver, now mistress of Shirley, and her sis-

Shirley

ter, the late Mrs. Alice Carter Bransford, were not unmindful of the sound of the rocking-chair on the bare floor of an attic room. Mrs. Grace Harrison, of "Edgewood," writes me: "Of course you have heard the little stories connected with Westover and Shirley.

"At Shirley one night while sleeping in the big four-poster bed in the guest-room, I was quite sure I heard the lady—I forget which one of the Carter women Mrs. Bransford told me it was—who rocks back and forth incessantly in the room overhead on certain nights. I believe she started to have these nights of unrest and disquiet when some later generation took her portrait down from where it had always hung and put it in the attic. Indeed, I am told she was so upset about it, and made such a mighty disturbance, that they were forced to bring it back and hang it again.

"All this was told me about twenty-five years ago by Mrs. Bransford."

Mrs. Oliver, whose letter I quote in part, adds the following interesting notes:

"I have your letter today about 'Aunt Pratt.' My earliest recollection of the portrait was up in the attic with all sorts of rubbish, perhaps half the paint had gone from face and figure. We were told as children that it was a picture of 'Aunt Pratt,' a sister of Edward Hill, whose daughter, Elizabeth Hill, married John Carter in 1723. We never heard her history nor why she was banished to the attic, but there did seem to be some sort of mystery about her, so when we used to wonder why there was a sound in one of the upstairs rooms like the rocking of a chair on a bare floor, we always said it must be Aunt Pratt."

Some years ago a lady asked to restore the portrait, and later it was hung in the second floor hall. Mrs. Oliver adds, "Also it is perfectly true that the sound of the rocking-chair is heard no more."

William Byrd III of Westover

COLONEL WILLIAM BYRD III OF WESTOVER

B ORN September 6, 1728, the third William Byrd of Westover inherited most of his father's property at the age of sixteen.

Virginia Gazette, Jan. 12, 1749.
William and Mary, 20, 17.
"On Saturday night last (7th) the house of Wm. Byrd, Esq. at Westover, Charles City County took fire and was burned to the ground with the loss of all the furniture, clothes, plate, liquor."

We are told that at great personal risk Colonel Byrd rescued his wife's brothers from a third story room.

"We are assured that the third William Byrd built 'Belvidere' after his marriage to Elizabeth Hill Carter in 1748." (Letters of the Byrd family.)

A prominent officer in the Colony, William Byrd III, was given command of two Virginia regiments, raised after Braddock's defeat in 1775, to protect the frontiers against the French and Indians. Still under age, he involved himself in a debt gaming with the no-bility while abroad; heedless that "punishment is a fruit which ripens unsuspected within the flower of the pleasure which conceals it." We read in his will of an estate heavily encumbered with debt. The vision of the harvest his children must reap of his sowing he declares, "Embitters every moment of my life." In this will, dated 1774, he says: "Next I desire My Body may be privately buried by the tomb of my sister Evelyn in the old church yard." There, in an unmarked grave, he doubtless rests.

William Byrd married, April 14, 1748, Elizabeth Carter of Shirley, a girl not yet seventeen years of age. Letters in possession of the Byrd family state that their home was "Belvidere," now a for-

Elizabeth Hill Carter, Wife of William Byrd III of Westover

gotten spot traversed by the thoroughfares of Richmond. The two children lived unhappily. Betty, during her short married life of eleven years, bore five children; bore with an unkind mother-in-law, and grieved bitterly for her two little boys sent to England, and whom she never saw again. It is said she entertained serious doubts of her husband's faithfulness. Was it jealousy prompted a search for letters on the high wardrobe, when it careened and crushed out her life, or was she searching for some of her precious trinkets, word comes to us down the years, her mother-in-law would hide? We have no word that poor Betty has ever been seen walking amid the ever fading flowers in any garden planted by man. The tragedy of her life is ever a dark thread woven in and out among the faintly tinted warp and weft of the fragmentary history of that old mansion.

Six months after he was called from the card table by learning of the death of his wife, Colonel Byrd married Mary Willing of Philadelphia, a woman of great ability. They were devotedly attached. Although "Such harmony is in immortal souls," love is powerless to alter life's great decree: He who dances must pay the music's price. We read that "January 1, 1777 he died by his own hand."

The late Mrs. Parke Chamberlayne Bagby stated some years ago that a young man told her he went to spend the night at Westover. Sitting around the fire before bedtime several interesting ghost stories were told, the host declaring that William Byrd III went to a certain chamber every night and sat in an armchair before the fire. The visitor expressed great interest and requested to occupy this room. He told Mrs. Bagby that as midnight approached he was standing in the silent chamber gazing at the door. The great clock in the hall girded its loins with a rattling resolution for the stroke and then pealed slowly twelve times. Was the door opening? Yes—yes—before he could decide what to do an awful crash re-

Evelyn Byrd

sounded through the house. The youth's emotions were indescribable! He recalled William Byrd III had killed himself in this room. Could poor Betty have been on a visit; and was it in this room the ponderous wardrobe had fallen on her? The door opened slowly, deliberately, and a shadowy, icy presence seemed to glide past the great bedstead and then to the chintz covered chair. Its vapory unreality filled not only the chair, but the room, and turned the atmosphere into the chill of death. He crept into bed and pulled the covers over his head.

"Did you see William Byrd?" his host asked him at breakfast.

"Yes."

"Did you hear him?"

"What was it?" he replied.

"Ah! Who can say? The maid found your umbrella on the middle of the hall floor this morning."

Evelyn Byrd of Westover

THE site of Westover, a splendid relic of Colonial life, is the most desirable on the entire length of Virginia's famous river.

Too well known to warrant in these few pages other than passing mention, it stands today almost as when built in 1726 by William Evelyn Byrd, son of the emigrant.

Handsome, well educated, courtly and possessing a keen wit abiding with him even into the shadow of death, his journey's end is marked by a handsome monument in the garden at Westover.

In life, among his acquaintances, they tell us, Col. Byrd had one Patrick Coutts, a man of substance, coming from above the Tweed, and operating a profitable ferry near Richmond. Coutts was also about to die. With an ever-abiding sense of humor, Col. Byrd dispatched a courier to beg the Scot to delay his exit from this mortal strife and wait for him. About to expire, Coutts delivered himself of a pithy message, surviving long after all other

Westover

memory of its author had vanished. "Tell Col. Byrd that when Patrick Coutts makes up his mind to die, he waits for no man!"

Through the long vista of the years we see the handsome, magnetic and sparkling personality of the Colonel, the most picturesque figure of his line, standing in the finest library in the Colonies, and dispensing a generous hospitality. His mansion, filled with treasures brought from beyond the seas, a gilded cage in which the greatest treasure of them all, Evelyn, died early of a broken heart. William Byrd is described as having "vision when he built his domicile," but he certainly had none when dealing with his daughter's life and happiness. A staunch Protestant, he strenuously objected to her love for Charles Mordaunt, grandson of the Earl of Peterborough, an ardent Roman Catholic, who crossed her path in London, where, when eighteen years old, she was presented at the Court of George I.

We learn the girl was hastily returned to a monotonous life in the woods on an isolated Colonial plantation. Her portrait by Kneller is still in the keeping of her family, and above and beyond the lovely skin, mouth, and brow, can be read in the eyes the power of endurance and a certain wistful foreboding of that sorrow to come.

It is recorded suitors came and went. The Master of the house expressed himself as not knowing whether they were too smart for her or she too smart for them.

In a grove of fine old trees a quarter of a mile north of her home, near the river, Evelyn's tomb with that of her grandparents may be found.

One afternoon, some weeks before her death, she and her dearest friend, Anne Harrison, of Berkeley, were slowly climbing a slight ascent. The girl, feeling confident her days were numbered, promised to appear sometimes after she had passed from sight. Accordingly, on an evening the following Spring, as Mrs. Harrison walked slowly and sadly down the hill, she "saw her friend dressed in white, dazzling in ethereal loveliness, standing beside her own grave. She drifted forward a few steps, kissed her hand to the beholder, smiling happily, and vanished."

By great good fortune Westover is once more—after many days —the scene of generous hospitality and cordial greetings. The daughter of one of Virginia's foremost families is its Chatelaine, Miss Ellen Bruce, now Mrs. Richard H. Crane. Mr. and Mrs. Crane create the delightful atmosphere of cordiality and gracious welcome for which the famous old mansion was noted in the heyday of Col. Byrd's prosperity.

From beside the cheerful blaze of oak logs, where the Colonel once sat at ease, while Evelyn looked from her window upon the falling snow, comes the interesting information that "her ghost has reappeared from time to time and has been seen by numerous people, generally walking in the garden. She is a gentle ghost, keeping her promise to return, but in such a manner as to frighten no one. "

Mrs. Crane tells me that one night her daughter and a pupil from Foxcroft School were sleeping in a large bed. The visitor awoke in the middle of the night to find a woman in white standing at the foot of the bed. For a moment she concluded her friend had arisen, until a glance assured her she was sound asleep. A very reliable servant long in Mrs. Crane's family speaks of seeing the woman in white on the steps leading from the kitchen to the pantry.

On December 11, 1929, a party of three journeyed from Washington to Westover to spend a few days with Mr. and Mrs. Crane. On the evening of their arrival the talk was entirely of ghosts— the ghosts that haunt so many of the famous old houses of Virginia. In speaking of Evelyn Byrd it was brought out that although many guests coming to Westover have seen her, such has not been the experience of the present owners.

Towards eleven o'clock the party broke up. One of the guests was given the bedroom on the side of the house overlooking the great gates from which room there is also a view of the garden. Sometime during the course of the night she awoke and went to the window. She does not recall her reason for doing so. The night was very dark. While looking out Evelyn Byrd appeared upon the lawn below! This lady describes the apparition as "the filmy, nebulous and cloudy figure of a woman, so transparent no features could be distinguished, only the gauzy texture of a woman's form. It seemed to be floating a little above the lawn, almost on a level with the window itself."

As she gazed the apparition raised its head and arm and beckoned to her to go back into the room and away from the window. She did so, for the gesture was imperative!—feeling no fear, but only distinctly aware of having seen Evelyn Byrd and that she desired her to retire from before the window.

It seems to me well for purpose of preservation, to record here additional evidence of the reappearing of Evelyn Byrd at Westover.

Mr. John Selden was the owner of this property for a period of thirty years prior to and during the Civil War. Mr. Selden had fifteen sons and three daughters. A governess having been engaged to teach the Selden girls, their cousin Elizabeth Saunders came to stay at Westover and share the instruction. Her parents, John Loyall Saunders and Martha Bland Selden, were married at Westover in 1834.

Miss Bland Taylor tells me that the morning following her arrival at Westover, she believes in the year 1856, her mother said at the breakfast table she had awakened in the night and found a young lady standing in the room who quickly went out the door. Elizabeth was asked to, and described the lady and her dress. Mr. Selden then said: "Oh, yes, that was Evelyn Byrd."

This appearing of Evelyn Byrd, Miss Taylor says, has always been known in this branch of the Selden family.

Marguerite du Pont Lee.

THE CHILES PLACE

ABOUT six miles from Richmond stands one of the oldest homes in Chesterfield County. The date of its building is not known, but certainly prior to 1800. The fact that the doors are guarded by heavy oak bars gives assurance that the old homestead has sheltered many generations of the children of men. Of frame construction, two stories in height, we may be sure a fine spring decided the builder, whose name has long been forgotten, seeking an abiding place for his children's children, to wander no farther.

The old office, little school house, and other buildings once standing here and there beneath the trees; the garden in other days gay with roses, mock-orange and crepe myrtle, have vanished; while the spring still flows, and the generations gathered one by one into the little burial ground guarded by the stout rail fence sleep unmindful of the changes and chances of life as we live it today.

About 55 years ago a member of the Chiles family again obtained possession of the property which had long been in alien hands, moved in and made it his permanent home.

Mrs. E. L. Gibbon of Richmond writes me her grandmother Virginia Elliott Chiles Snellings told her that the family had not long been established before they were disturbed by strange noises. Doors which had been carefully locked would open; shutters to windows could not be kept shut, and windows would be raised that had been carefully fastened. Whisperings and soft step movements could be heard over the house where no one should have been.

"The mother of the owner, my grandmother's sister, and my grandmother, decided to make a lengthy visit to the place and ascertain if indeed the strange visitors were mortals or visitants from another sphere.

"The house had a broad hall through the center with double doors front and back. These doors were locked with the old fashioned heavy locks of the early days which held a key five inches long. Besides the locks the doors were held in place by an oak bar which was placed across after they were closed at night. The bar fell into wrought iron brackets and made a very formidable fastening. To the right was the living room which ran the entire length of the house with a window back and front. A stairway extended from the hall to the second floor where were the bedrooms generally used for guests. A very winding stair led from the dining room which was across the hall from the living room to that part of the upstairs occupied by the family.

"One evening several days after the arrival of the two investigators, as the family sat before the large fireplace in the living room they heard the tip, tip, tipping of some one coming down the front stairs. The man of the family went out into the hall, but no one was there. His wife remarked it must have been the nurse who had come down to get a drink for one of the children; and wondered why she came down that stairway. Upon investigation the nurse was found sleeping and the children all asleep in the nursery. The man went over the entire house with other members of the family stationed at places which would cut off any intruder trying to escape. No one was in sight and all doors were locked and barred. Again seated, the conversation was resumed where it had been left off and all seemed quiet for a while, but soon came the tip, tip, tipping as before, and whispering on the stair. Once more the entire house was looked over without results. Coming back to the living room the owner said: 'Well, it is bedtime anyway, so we will have our evening prayers and go to bed. If our visitor wishes to join in this worship we shall not object.' Having read the scripture he placed the Bible on the lamp stand, when suddenly the oak bars were heard to fall, and both back and front doors flew open! The doors were closed and locked and the bars put in place, while the family could only look at each other and wonder just how this could happen. My grandmother took her place at one window with her hand on the shutter with window raised; her sister at the back window did likewise, and the son with hand on the living room door waited. His wife put out the light and only the glow from the fire remained. In a few minutes the tip, tip, tipping was heard on the stair, and suddenly followed the falling of the bars and both doors flew open! The son went immediately into the hall, and both sisters threw open the shutters to see if anyone was outside the doors.

"Often when the tipping would be heard it would be accompanied by a soft sobbing cry at the foot of the winding stairs leading to the dining room. These strange manifestations were observed by other members of the family before my grandmother's day.

"After several months of this the place was again sold to strangers who were frankly told of this experience. No manifestations came to the strangers except on two occasions while entertaining a member of the Chiles family. They with their guests heard strange sobbing cries, and the tipping. These phenomena have never been explained. One member of the Chiles family offered $1000 to any of the connection who would spend a night there and unravel the mystery."

RECESS-BREMO

RECESS-BREMO, on the James River in Fluvanna County, was built in 1803 by Gen. John Hartwell Cocke, who occupied it while building his more pretentious mansion, Upper Bremo, one mile away. A tall sloping roof lighted by dormer windows, forms the second story of this, by no means large, but picturesque and quaint old brick dwelling, portraying that Jacobean influence so marked in the architecture of Bacon's Castle, one of Virginia's oldest relics. There may be, and doubtless is, a wing beyond the reach of the eye of the camera. That primitive device, a lightning rod, pointing to heaven beyond the three chimney pots, descends over the roof into the ground! Dense shade beneath magnificent trees, a beautiful lawn, and long rough ivy-decked stone walls surrounds a garden, the photograph leaves one's imagination to picture.

An atmosphere of remoteness suggests that those who abide beneath this roof-tree dwell "far from gay cities and the ways of men." Doubtless many visitors are cordially received, but one, a ghost, is neither welcomed to her former home, where from time to time she endeavors to make herself known, nor will any tell her history or the account of occasional reappearings.

It comes to us, a mysterious green dress lies in a trunk upstairs. In March, 1930, a dinner was given at the Willard Hotel in Washington in behalf of the fund destined for the purchase of Stratford, the birthplace of Gen. Robert E. Lee. An absentee subscriber's table was surrounded by a group of guests, among them Dr. Lewis Greene, formerly of Alexandria. Before the orators arose to eulogize the General, the conversation drifted to the subject of ghosts, and I am told Dr. Greene announced he had seen one. Twenty years ago it seems he found himself a visitor at Recess. One night the family went to a party. Before sitting down to his book, Dr. Greene placed a bottle of wine and some crackers on the dining-room table as refreshments for the returning family. The house was locked up—he was alone.

After reading a while Dr. Greene noticed a shadow pass over his book. Looking up, a woman stood before him wearing a green

Recess-Bremo

skirt! Astonished, he followed her into the dining-room, but there she was not!

In due time the family returned and went into the dining-room, followed by the Doctor. There was no bottle on the table! Astonished, he exclaimed, "Why, I put the bottle there. The ghost must have taken it." At this saying the face of one of those present "blanched," and at this period Mr. Walton Moore interrupted the story with the opening sentences of his eulogy.

Tuckahoe

TUCKAHOE

AN old vault on this plantation bears the date 1689. Prior to that time William Randolph, of Turkey Island, gave to his son Thomas Randolph the land on which he built his home and where it may still be seen after the passing of 240 years.

Simple and unpretentious without, a lovely wisteria trailing over the small porch, approached by a long flight of stone steps fashioned by hand, in their old age here and there clamped together with iron bands, bearing silent witness to the great age of the dwelling to which they lead.

Through a vista of old cedars long past their prime one perceives from a distance a two-story white frame building, its simple lines giving little suggestion of the lovely paneling and splendid carving within.

A narrow brick walk from the dining-room leads to the kitchen, low of ceiling, with a brick floor and tiny windows, and the great fireplace tended so faithfully by innumerable hands·long since forgotten.

The little schoolhouse where Thomas Jefferson was taught calls up visions of weary tasks, hard benches and long hours; faces of little children whose lessons have all been learned, and they far beyond the unwelcome sound of the recalling bell.

Boxwood was planted and took root in a day when great logs sufficed for heating, and candles for light, even as they do at Tuckahoe today, when the great bushes frame in beautiful green the old white mansion, bringing to us from along the years a lesson of simplicity, sincerity and serenity.

Thomas Mann Randolph, grandson of the builder of Tuckahoe, was the last of the name to own this home. He married Harriet Wilson, of Richmond. After her death Mr. Randolph was ill for sometime. One night he dreamed that a young lady opened the closet door and brought him a glass of water. The next day he spoke of the dream and said the face was so clear that he would recognize her, and if they ever met he would ask her to marry him. They met in afteryears and were married—a Miss Patterson, of New Jersey.

In 1830 Tuckahoe was purchased by Edwin Wight and in 1850 by Joseph Allen. Mrs. Richard S. Allen relates that upon one occasion she and her friend, Miss Mary Brooks, were standing in the dining-room at Tuckahoe and both of them saw distinctly the figure of a small woman in gray enter through the hall door and pass out the little entry door leading to the outer kitchen.

One day Mrs. Allen was sitting in the upstairs hall unpacking a box. There was no one around other than the maid washing windows. Presently Mrs. Allen heard someone call her name, "Jennie!" Her thoughts were engaged elsewhere, so merely glancing around and seeing no one, she went on with her work. Soon the call was repeated in loud and anxious tones, "Jennie! Jennie!" Fearing the maid must be in dire distress to so forget her manners, Mrs. Allen tumbled the things off her lap and ran to the room where she knew the maid to be. Annette was quietly washing a window. At that moment a loud crash startled them both. A large portion of the ceiling had fallen and completely demolished the chair upon which Mrs. Allen had been sitting!

Upon one occasion the family and guests were amusing themselves with a Planchette. Someone asked, "Who is your master?" The pencil wrote plainly, "the devil." They then asked, "Is Tuckahoe haunted?" The answer came "Yes, the red room upstairs, and it has an odd panel in the wall." Everybody ran upstairs and they found an odd panel that had never before been noticed.

Years before, a traveling man who spent the night in that room had been awakened in the middle of the night by a rocking-chair rocking violently back and forth. He got up, lit the lamp, and saw the chair rocking. Searching, but discovering no draught, he concluded all would be well, so returned to bed and to sleep. Again he was aroused by the rocking, and, day breaking, dressed and left the house. Meeting one of the servants, the man related his experience, declaring nothing on earth would induce him to stay in that room again.

ASH LAWN

JAMES MONROE, fifth President of the United States, was born in 1758. Very shortly after the Revolution, generally supposed at the desire of Thomas Jefferson, he bought a tract of land and built a house on the east side of Carter's Mountain, near Charlottesville, Virginia. He called his home "Ash Lawn." According to Rawling's "Albemarle and Other Days," here he spent "the working years of his life."

Monroe moved to Loudoun County in 1825, after retiring from the Presidency, and died in 1831. From the fireside at Ash Lawn he went three times to the Governor's home at Richmond, and also to represent his country as Minister to France and to England. From the borders of that garden, giving then but faint promise of its wonderful beauty today, from beneath the shadow of a Norwegian pine brought from Europe, and which today rears itself as a mighty sentinel, visible to the traveler for many miles around, mounting his horse from a block still shown to visitors, he rode to Washington for his inauguration. The many splendid borders and bushes of box were probably planted nearly, if not quite 150 years ago. The garden is full of a charm only great age can impart. By great good fortune the house has had restored its original aristocratic outlines.

Mr. Joseph Massey, connected with the offices of the Chesapeake and Ohio Railroad at Charlottesville, and whose mother owns Ash Lawn, declares, "I will tell anybody, and have no objection to its being known—I have seen, not once but time and time again—the rocking-chair in my bedroom rocking exactly as though someone were in it. I have awakened my brother John to watch it rocking. We both have taken pains to observe and make sure there is no draft by closing the bedroom door and windows. Still the chair rocks on. We have gotten up and gone to the chair to feel and see who was sitting in it while the chair was rocking, but found nothing. So long as we did not touch the chair it continued to rock violently. If we touched it, it stopped!"

Ash Lawn

Castle Hill

CASTLE HILL

CASTLE HILL has, for 165 years, been one of the beautiful manor houses of Albemarle County. Today this historic mansion is the home of Prince Pierre Troubetzkoy, whose beautiful portraits of the nobility of England are famous, and many from his brush add beauty to American homes. The Princess, known far and near as Amelie Rives, author of many charming stories and plays, requires no introduction where she is so justly popular.

Dr. Thomas Walker, who built Castle Hill, was the son of Captain Thomas Walker, emigrating to Gloucester County, Virginia, from Staffordshire, England, in 1650. Dr. Walker was a celebrated physician in his day; the guardian of Thomas Jefferson; and he introduced the famous Albemarle pippin into his native state from New York. That famous British Cavalryman Tarleton, his appetite whetted by a long ride, stopped at Castle Hill one day for breakfast, lingering it seems, over long. Owing to this delay news of his coming visit reached the ears of the Legislature in session at Charlottesville. The spot near Castle Hill where the British troops rested is still known as "Tarleton's Woods."

Princess Troubetzkoy writes me, "The original house was reputed destroyed by Indians. The old porch at the back is laid with large square stones, evidently once used for the walls of a house, as they have in them the sockets and the remains of iron clamps such as were long ago used in the construction of stone buildings. It is a lovely rambling old house, the front brick imported from England, with Tuscan Doric columns of white stucco running all across the front." The small panes of glass and brass doorlocks, still in this ancient mansion, came from London.

The passing years have left a legacy of immense hedges of treebox, standing at a height of thirty feet at the end of a lawn of six hundred feet, gracing the landscape near the house with a marvelous growth of verdure fifty feet in height! Time, so destructive in many places, has proved a beneficient husbandman at Castle Hill.

A mansion filled with delightful memories of the lavish hospitality of days when life was leisurely, and visitors lingered long over the crackling logs and the fine old Madeira. Days when in the great hall, one hundred feet in length, the music-loving Jefferson played his fiddle and the more youthful Madison danced. Little wonder that in memory of so much beauty the laughter and song of joyous living in the long ago, some ancestress in satin gown and with powder in her hair should in benediction flood with a marvelous psychic perfume of roses the atmosphere of the room where her charming descendant reigns in her stead. Two friends on different occasions perceived the scent when Princess Troubetzkoy was present. This well-known psychic phenomenon seems rare in Virginia.

Castle Hill presents a most interesting record of haunting. Shall we give it in the words of the Chatelaine of the mansion?

"Many people visiting here have declared that they heard footsteps, noises of furniture being moved at night, and even voices. Some of the old servants have declared that they saw my grandfather on different occasions.

"The most interesting apparition is connected with a very distinguished writer who visited Castle Hill about five or more years ago. He came from the University with a young friend of ours who was also a student there at that time, to stop over Saturday night and return to the University late Sunday afternoon. The young friend who brought him was Edmund Archer, the son of a dear friend of ours who lived in Richmond. Mr. X was so happy at Castle Hill he decided to remain over Sunday and let Edmund Archer return to the University alone. That was on Saturday evening before he had spent a night in one of the old panelled rooms in the more ancient part of the house. This is said to be an especially haunted room, but many people have slept in it without being disturbed in any way. It is on the northwest side on the lower floor of the older part of the house.

"On Sunday morning I noticed that he looked pale and had

very little to say. Later on he explained that after all he would have to return to the University that afternoon and so could not remain for Sunday night.

"I was troubled, fearing that in some way we might have offended him, or hurt his feelings—he was so entirely different from the evening before. It wasn't until about a month later, that Ned, coming again to visit us, gave me the solution. I mentioned the thing to him, and he exclaimed:

" 'Oh, don't you *know* why X left so suddenly?'

" 'I certainly do not,' I said.

"Then he told me that Mr. X had told him (Ned) that during the night of that Saturday which he had spent in the room called 'the old Chamber' he was wakened by a charming looking woman dressed in the fashion of long ago, and carrying a tiny fan. She had gazed at him steadily while saying over and over: 'You must please go. You must go away. You must not stay here.'

"X told Ned that he would not spend another night in that room for anything, and that he went away as soon as possible.

"A cousin of mine, a Mrs. Frederick Page, of the University, who knew X well told me only this summer that X had also told her that he would not sleep in that room again for worlds. When she asked him to explain however, he would only—as she described it—'wave his hands in a gesture as if words were inadequate—.'

"The legend is the ghost of one of my great-great-great-grand-mothers appears in that room to people she does not consider suitable visitors to Castle Hill. Not necessarily unsuitable because of anything derogatory about them, but merely that they are out of touch with its atmosphere in one way or another. Three other people have been, as it were, pushed out of the house by a sensation of its 'not wanting them,' as they expressed it. One of these said that a lovely woman had appeared to her and asked her not to remain 'in her room.' (This was not the 'old panelled chamber' however, but one on the second floor.)"

SUNNY BANK

IN the home of yet another Scotchman seeking an abiding place in Virginia do we learn of most interesting evidence of Spirit return. Before the Revolution, Andrew Hart stepped ashore from some now long-forgotten vessel and, finding his way to Albemarle County, built "Sunny Bank" in 1797, about eighteen miles from Charlottesville.

Today, well-shaded, one may find an old mansion of a delicate yellow color; the large shutters painted a cool deep green. It stands upon an eminence; while Andrew Hart found springs of water winding their course through the tall grasses at the foot of the hill. "Sunny Bank," mellowed by the passing of 135 years, has never left the possession of the Hart family. This fact makes it at least reasonable to suppose the two ghosts of youthful appearance, seen in the rooms in which each died, may be the apparitions of certain young women.

Mrs. Andrew De Jarnette Hart writes me: "Sunny Bank was the scene of cordial hospitality to refugees during the Civil War." Inasmuch as a little girl was welcomed throughout those precarious times, that she may possibly return to be seen once more after many days brushing her beautiful hair before a mirror, makes the following story worthy of preservation here.

The two little children of Mr. William Cazenove of Alexandria, Virginia, with their nurse, were enjoying the shelter of the Hart home. Mrs. Hart writes that one day two Yankee officers galloped up at great speed, searching for two Confederates they declared had murdered a couple of Federal soldiers. After tramping over the garden, and through the house, there remained the attic; but the very steep and narrow stairway caused the invaders to pause.

The nurse, Sarah Stiddolph by name, probably suspecting the attic to be occupied, decided the time had arrived for her to take part in the exciting drama. Advancing upon the officers with uplifted arm and waving a large paper to and fro, she exclaimed in a loud voice: "I am a British subject! I claim the protection of my country! Here are my credentials!" At this highly dramatic moment,

Sunny Bank, Albemarle County, Virginia

Mrs. Hart declares the officer sprang forward, tore the paper from the hand of Queen Victoria's dependent, and stamping upon it, shouted: "Your British protection be damned!"

Many remarkable happenings at "Sunny Bank" are recorded. In the dead of night, in two rooms, the sound as of the pouring of water into a basin has been heard. Footsteps on the stair; thence across the hall and into a room in which one of the ghosts has been seen. The sound of a horse and buggy being driven up to the front door is heard from time to time; the rocking of chairs in vacant rooms.

Mrs. Hart writes me: "My son, Dr. Hart, and other members of the family, can vouch for the violent shaking of the front door when no one is near by. We believe this visitant to be the Spirit of an old lady who persisted in roaming out of doors, so we kept the door locked in order to safeguard her. Several of our guests have seen a woman dressed in black, and wearing white stockings, going upstairs, her costume recalling fashions of an early period."

Mrs. Hart had a very interesting experience herself years ago. She woke one morning to see in profile a young woman dressed in white and of a lovely ethereal appearance sitting on the edge of her bed.

Presently the vision vanished! Mrs. Hart believes this to have been the Spirit of her husband's sister, Betty Dew, who died in that room.

While occupying the room in which Constance Cazenove died, the child of Civil War days and friend of Betty Dew, Miss Anne Byrd, saw a woman standing before the bureau combing—

" 'The most resplendent hair'!

Mrs. Hart adds:

"I failed to tell you of another very strange thing, to which several members of my family can attest. My sister, Miss Evelyn Byrd, had a pretty striped silk dress. One afternoon she chose to wear this dress—it had been put away in her wardrobe for awhile—and found that it had been cut and made over ridiculously small so she could never wear it again! The passementerie had been sewn on exquisitely; the daintiest of stitches. No one here did it, and it has ever been a mystery."

A MOTHER'S WARNING

AT Amherst Courthouse, Virginia, Judge Samuel Hugh Henry lived years ago with his children—Miss Mildred Henry, who related the following facts, and four sons. Three of the sons were well behaved and studious boys who gave no trouble to their family or teachers, but Edmund, a lad of fifteen, the best looking and brightest of the group, while goodhearted and helpful around the home, had an incorrigible love of mischief and often engaged in fighting with the village boys and could not be induced to take an interest in his studies. So bad were his monthly reports that his Father had finally adopted the plan of making the boy study in his library every night and of occasionally hearing his recitations before permitting him to quit the room.

On one occasion there was company to tea and the Father told the boy to take his books into the parlor that night, as he wished to take the visitors into the library to show them some engravings he had bought and they would probably spend the evening there. Edmund did as his Father had directed, and after a time the housemaid came to the library door and informed her young mistress that she had heard peculiar noises in the parlor and thought it would be well for her to go into the room and see if anything was wrong with Edmund, as she had opened the door and saw him standing on the floor looking very frightened, and he would not answer when she spoke to him.

Miss Henry went to the room and found that the maid had not at all exaggerated her brother's condition. He appeared terrified, was deathly pale and seemed not to be able to speak.

She ran to the library and begged her Father to go immediately to Edmund as she thought he must be ill. The old gentleman could be very stern on occasion, and had but little faith in the boy's supposed illness.

"Pooh, pooh," said he, "Edmund's not ill; it is just a trick to get rid of his books," and resumed conversation with his guests.

"O, but Father," said his daughter, "please do go and see Edmund; I know he is ill. He never could look as he does if he were not. I spoke to him and he did not notice me, and his hands and face were as cold as ice." Then she commenced to cry.

"Well, well, daughter, I will go," said her Father, "but depend upon it, Edmund is just up to one of his tricks. There is nothing the matter with him, but to satisfy you I will go and straighten him out and show you that I am right."

So, excusing himself to his guests, he went to the parlor where he found the boy standing with his back to the fire, looking deathly white and staring intently at one corner of the room. He seemed utterly oblivious of his Father's presence; his jaw had dropped, he did not answer, and seemed as if frozen to stone.

Judge Henry approached him, saying, "Edmund, what is this I hear about your peculiar behaviour tonight? Do not try any of your tricks on me; what is the matter with you?"

Edmund did not reply, but continued to stare at the far corner of the room, as if there were something that entranced him.

The Father saw that the boy was really almost beside himself with some strange emotion, whether fright or illness he could not tell, but evidently under some strange spell he could not overcome; so, putting his arm around the child, he drew him to a sofa nearby and said to him very gently: "What is the trouble, my son? Tell Father what it is," and with a wave of his hand he ordered everyone to leave the room. Then, holding him close to his side, after a few soothing words, prevailed upon him to speak.

"Father," he said, "I have seen mother!" and then he sobbed bitterly. "I am afraid you will not believe me, Father, but she came to me and spoke to me."

"Are you sure you were not asleep, son?"

"No, Father, I was writing my Latin exercise when my hand stopped and I felt that there was someone in the room. I could neither write nor move. I looked around and saw no one, but in the corner behind the piano I saw something like a white handkerchief lying on the floor, and as I looked at it it seemed to move and to grow larger. I watched it as it grew larger and larger, until it was the size of a grown person. Then it moved from behind the piano and advanced toward me. I tried to run, but could not move. As it came near I saw that it was a woman. Her hair was black and her eyes were looking right at me and I recognized my mother. She came up to me and leaning over me, put her arms around me and said, "Try to be a good boy, my son, and meet me in heaven; it won't be long." Then she disappeared.

From that evening Edmund was a changed boy. After a few days he told his Father that he wished to join a church. "My mother asked me to be a good boy and try to meet her in heaven, and I intend to keep my promise to her," he said. He was received into church membership and was a zealous and consistent Christian and church worker. His school reports were perfect and the village boys became his friends.

On an afternoon in August he promised to go with his brothers and some of the village boys in swimming. The others started, but his sister asked Edmund to run down to the village drygoods store and get something for her that she needed immediately. He did so, and then ran to the river to join his party. He was overheated, but without waiting to cool off, threw off his clothes and jumped into the water. He was immediately seized with cramps and before rescue was possible was drowned.

GREENWOOD

IN February 1759, Act of the General Assembly established the town of Fairfax, later renamed Culpeper, on "a high and pleasant situation in the County of Culpeper, where the courthouse now stands," and set apart thirty acres of Robert Coleman's land to be laid off into lots and streets by these trustees: Thomas Slaughter, William Green, William Williams, Philip Clayton and Nat. Pendleton.

Before the Revolution William Green, a Captain in the Navy, lost at sea on the brig Defiance, and a son of Colonel John Green, married Lucy Clayton Williams, daughter of William Williams and Lucy Clayton.

Lucy Clayton's home was named Catalpa after a tree her father brought from Essex, the first of the species in Culpeper County.

"Greenwood" was built by William Williams as a wedding present for his daughter. The old house is to be found on a hill amid a grove of trees, about a mile from town.

The kitchen, ice and smoke houses alone remain of the group of buildings, beehives of industry always in evidence not far from the houses of Colonial and pre-Revolutionary days.

Of special interest at Greenwood more than a generation ago, was the house occupied by the overseer and his wife, Edwards by name. After their death and the changing occupations of plantation life necessitated altered conditions, Mr. Green put a colored family to live in the dwelling. Subsequent events lead us to believe Mrs. Edwards resented this desecration of her former home. Very soon the negro tenant came to Mr. Green and told him it was impossible to live in the house as Mrs. Edwards threw stones at them! Investigation proved the truth of this remarkable story. Showers of stones, some of considerable size, would at times fall from the ceiling! Again they appeared to come out of the walls zigzagging across the room, or entered by way of the windows! Some stones were found to be wet, while again others were hot! Tales of these

Greenwood, Culpeper County, Virginia

curious happenings spread over the county, and every day and all day long the family at Greenwood was harassed by a stream of visitors arriving in buggies, dearborns or on horseback, curious to see the remarkable demonstrations. Clearly something had to be done; so a group of determined and resourceful men of the Caucasian race, declaring it to be their opinion the negroes were responsible, laid plans to strike terror into the hearts of every colored person on the premises! Each resolute crusader armed himself with a pistol, and lining up every member of the suspected race, declared in loud and menacing tones their determination to shoot any and all negroes who so much as stirred throughout a perscribed period of time.

They had not long to wait. The pistols were scarcely leveled before a shower of stones tumbled from the ceiling around and upon the investigators and their weapons! Mrs. H. St. George Tucker, who was Miss Mary Williams of Culpeper, tells me it was found necessary to tear down the house in order to rid the premises of this remarkable phenomenon.

FABRIC OF A VISION

NEAR Culpeper, Virginia, there stood many years ago a large brick building, flanked on either side by immense chimneys, with dormer windows in the high-pitched roof. Long the home of the Grimes family, today the inscriptions on a few tombstones in a little burying-ground not far off, alone bears witness to this fact. A simple marble slab, guarded by five tall cedars, is inscribed to the memory of Alice Grimes.

In later years the house was occupied by the Daingerfield family, afterwards moving to Lexington, Kentucky, where one member, Elizabeth Daingerfield, is the leading woman breeder of thoroughbred horses in America, and has at present under her care Man o'War, Morwich, and other famous horses.

Miss Daingerfield tells the story of the reappearing of Alice Grimes, her sisters and other members of the household amply substantiating the facts. The ghost girl did not come to frighten, but rather to seek the companionship of the young women living where once her home had been. The latter never ran away nor were they conscious of anything strange in the appearance.

"Elizabeth," her nephew said, as they sat by the fire awaiting tea, "when did you first see a ghost?"

"It was in Virginia, more than twenty-five years ago, but I never pass a clump of cedars without thinking of her. She was very real and very vivid and I was never in the least afraid of her. Even today I should like to see her again. Jule saw her first in the parlor. Heneberger was visiting us at the time. I recollect Jule was a very practical unemotional girl. She walked the entire length of the parlor, thinking the girl sitting at the piano was Mary Heneberger, and said: "Sing 'When I Remember.'" The ghost turned a lovely face to her, with a sort of reminiscent, questioning smile. The choice of the song was strange, for the last verse goes—

> 'When I remember something promised me
> But which I never had nor can have now,
> In that the promiser we no more see
> In country which accords with earthly vow.'

"It was in early Spring, quite early in the evening, about six, and there was nothing alarming even when she saw her no more, and knew her for a ghost."

Henderson Daingerfield Norman saw the ghost many times. Once she was walking around the yard in front of the house with a young man from the village. Just ahead of them the ghost girl appeared. Henderson pointed out the apparition to her companion and dared him to follow and speak to her. The young man walked faster and then ran, the ghost always keeping a little before him. Once he called over his shoulder, "That's no ghost. It's Elizabeth."

"Then catch her."

He did try, but finally lost sight of the girl among the five cedars surrounding her grave.

In the late afternoon one day Mrs. Daingerfield, Elizabeth's mother, saw Alice Grimes as she came into the drawing-room. The girl, her back turned, was sitting at the window looking out into the yard towards the little group of cedars. Mrs. Daingerfield went up to her and spoke. Alice turned. There was the same wistful smile, the same gentleness, the same regret—and then as with the others who saw her, she was no more.

"There were a number of times," Elizabeth said, "when a number of us saw her at the same time. This was apt to be when we were happiest, planning a party. We rarely saw her at night. Never suddenly or in unsuspected corners. Often when alone I have wished she would come and stand near me. There is no explanation other than we saw her. Often when we were sitting together, often when alone, she was there. She was gentle, she was beautiful, always smiling just before she went away.

"Once I remember going out of my room into the long hall upstairs and this figure being just in front of me in the hall light, I called, thinking it a friend staying with me: 'Mary, wait, our ghost may join me,' and followed one step behind down the long stairs into the lighted hall below, where the figure turned and a far more lovely face than Mary's laughed into mine and faded.

"Again when a young doctor, a most matter-of-fact soul, walked with me one brilliant moonlight night, laughed at my stories of my ghost, and when I said 'She is right in front of us now,' looked scornfully a moment and then said, 'Nonsense, that is Henderson,' and reaching out to touch her, his hand went through—there was no substance.

"Alice Grimes was very real and grew to be rather an omen of good times. One evening Jule followed her into the parlor, we all seeing the figure lead the way and sit down by the piano. One of us strolling up threw an arm around her shoulder—but only the vision was there.

"After the house burned we never saw Alice Grimes again."

SALUBRIA

B UILT in 1742 by the Rev. John Thompson for his home, Salubria stands in Culpeper County near Stevensburg, a large commodious dwelling of brick and one of the first pretentious
houses on what was the western frontier of Virginia. Rev. John
Thompson was born near Belfast, Ireland. His ancestral home
Mockomon Abby, County Antrim, was given to the Thompson
family at the Reformation. The clergyman was a Master of Arts
of the University of Edinburgh and accounted "an accomplished
gentleman and a very handsome man."

Of Presbyterian inheritance, in 1739 "Parson Thompson" returned to England for ordination in the Anglican Communion. A
special service was held in the Chapel Royal of St. James. "We
have the original certificate signed by Nicholas, Bishop of St.
Davids," writes the clergyman's great great granddaughter.

Rev. Mr. Thompson married Butler Brayne, daughter of Richard Brayne, and widow of Sir Alexander Spotswood. They moved
to Salubria after her home "Germanna," built in 1724 on the banks
of the Rapid Anne, was burned. Her son Robert Spotswood, an
officer under Washington in 1755, was killed by the Indians. His
body they never found, but the moccasin he wore was sent to his
mother and for many years preserved as a family relic.

Mr. Dandridge Spotswood writes: "Lady Spotswood's second
son was Captain Robert Spotswood, who commanded a Company
under Colonel George Washington in the French and Indian Wars.
Robert was a particularly promising young man. While a student
at William and Mary he married one of the daughters of Colonel
Prentiss of Williamsburg. In the same letter to his mother he told
of his wedding, of the death of his wife three days later, and of the
burial from Bruton Church. The late Murray Forbes of Falmouth
owned this letter."

Mr. Spotswood adds: "So long as Robert Spotswood's moccasin
remained at 'Salubria' fate dealt kindly with the house. After its
loss none of the family connection have held the old mansion any

Lady Spotswood

Salubria, Culpeper County, Virginia

length of time. One can at times hear distinctly the tread of the moccasin over the floor of the upper hall, and in the room Lady Spotswood occupied."

Rev. Mr. Thompson's will was probated November 16, 1772. He and the former Lady Spotswood were buried at "Salubria," but all trace of the little cemetery has vanished.

Mrs. Jennie Thornley Grayson, wife of Mr. John Cooke Grayson, who lived for a time at "Salubria," writes that one night she stood combing her hair before the mirror in the room in which Lady Spotswood is said to have died. Turning toward the door in order to call the maid, something, she never knew what, made her look again in the glass. "A white mist seemed to have enveloped my form. I could not move nor utter a sound. As I looked intently the mist slowly took the form of a face peering over my shoulder and reflected in the glass before me. I felt oppressed and unable to move. A shriek rent the air and I was discovered in a faint."

"One night at supper the sugar bowl needed replenishing. Two of the Grayson boys were told to get the sugar from the barrel upstairs. Taking the lamp they journeyed up the steps. Crossing the dark hall guided by the dim light of the little lamp they carried, one boy leaned over the barrel while his brother John held the lamp. As he arose from his stooping position to put the cover on the barrel, both boys saw very faintly a figure dressed in white with black hair falling over her shoulders, her arm outstretched, as she floated noiselessly down the hall! One look was sufficient! Uttering loud screams, head over heels they, lamp and sugar bowl tumbled down the stairs! The colored servant exclaimed, 'Dose boys done seen de Spirit!'"

Admiral Cary T. Grayson writes me:

"I was born at 'Salubria,' and when a boy was told a Mrs. Hansborough hung herself in a bedroom on the second floor."

AVENEL

A VENEL stands in Fauquier County, near Little Georgetown, at the foot of Bull Run Mountains, in a grove of splendid old trees, and overlooks Thorough Fare Gap Trail.

A comfortable house was built on this property by William Beverley, of "Blandfield," Essex—for a summer home. Avenel is owned by members of the family leaving the Tidewater section many years ago, to build a new home in the then far distant region at the foot of the Blue Ridge Mountains.

Mr. Brad. Beverley, son of Mr. William Beverley, related that a lady dressed in white had frequently been seen by a number of persons. "My brothers and sisters have seen her. Guests have from time to time met her walking in the garden or coming towards them through the woods. Members of the family have seen her coming down the road or standing by the gate as though in the expectation someone would enter. The servants tell of passing her near the house."

"I have only seen her twice myself—once when a little boy she pushed by me on the road in the twilight and entered the gate in front of me. Once at 10 o'clock at night when returning from Warrenton on horseback with my uncle. We rode towards the gate and saw a lady come through it and walk towards us. My horse trembled and sank down on his knees, but uncle, seeing it was the ghost that he had so wanted to meet, leaned down and caught at her as she passed near him and disappeared. He held nothing in his hand nor did he touch any solid substance.

"A boy once put his arms around the white figure, but she melted away in his embrace! Thereafter on many occasions we waited for this lady in white, or the 'grey lady,' as she is now known to the whole countryside, but we never saw her afterwards.

"Twice in the last ten years she has been seen—once by passing hunters, whom she almost frightened to death, and once by one of the tenants on the farm, who walked up to her and put out his hand. She disappeared and was never identified."

Avenel

FAIRFIELD

ABOUT twenty miles from Warrenton in Upper Fauquier County, James Markham Marshall, brother of the Chief Justice and son of Colonel Thomas and Mary Keith Marshall, built his home in 1833 and called it "Fairfield." Upon an eminence commanding a splendid view of the distant Blue Ridge Mountains and almost within sound of Firery Run plunging from its source in those great hills, the old brick home may still be found. Two stories in height, with a steep roof, and the usual large rooms on either side of the great hall. From the walk you step upon one large stone, then into the door. A long lane broken by several gates wanders hither and thither from the highway to the mansion, behind which in the spring, petals from an ancient apple orchard drift upon the graves and old stones lying in the tall grass.

After the Civil War the property was sold to the Yates family. In course of time Miss Mary Ambler and her mother were living not far away at "The Dell," and Miss Yates planning to have a masquerade party, Miss Ambler suggested the attendance of all her kin residing in the neighborhood in order to make the ball a success. During a pause in the dancing Miss Ambler looked to where a group of her cousins and aunts were standing watching the gay scene and said to her cousin close by: "May, who is that lady in the old fashioned costume and mob cap standing with the family?" May declared she saw no such figure. "Oh, yes, she has a black dress with a very full skirt; blue eyes, fair skin, and a mob cap. I wonder who she can be?"

Later, removing masks and arranging their hair in an upstairs room, Miss Ambler exclaimed: "There she goes, May, down the corridor!" May saw no one.

The next day Mrs. Yates calling with a basket of fruit for her mother, Miss Ambler asked concerning the lady wearing a mob cap. Mrs. Yates had seen no guest answering the description.

The following week Miss Ambler went to the old Marshall home, "Leeds," five miles distant. Seating herself in the parlor, the walls of which were lined with portraits, one presently attracted her attention. "Why, there," she exclaimed, "is the lady wearing

Mary Keith, Mrs. Thomas Marshall

a mob cap I saw at the ball." It was Mary Keith Marshall, mother of James Markham Marshall, builder of "Fairfield."

Mr. E. Marshall Newton, "Hume," Fauquier County, writes me: "It was in the hall on the stairway that Miss Ambler was seated when she saw the old lady. I was not present at the time, but Miss Yates, afterwards my wife, told me of the incident which was very remarkable indeed."

The Gaol, Warrenton, Virginia

THE OLD GAOL

ONE of the landmarks in Warrenton, Virginia, and said by many to be haunted, is the old stone gaol. Situated in close proximity to the rear of the court house, it still serves in the same capacity for which it was constructed, and in its appearance bears witness to the passing of the years. It is an oblong two story building surrounded by a yard to the rear, inclosed in a high stone wall. The resident gaoler lives in a brick dwelling a few feet in front of the gaol, and separated from it by an open air passage surmounted by stone walls.

Judging by appearances, this institution of the law was built about the middle or latter part of the eighteenth century, and is one of the very few old buildings left within the business section of Warrenton, so many of the others having been removed to make room for larger and more imposing structures.

An interesting story connected with this gaol concerns an old gentleman by the name of McG. who owned and lived on a farm in upper Fauquier County. He conceived the idea that some distant relatives were endeavoring to take unfair advantage of him by seizing his property. With this in mind, and with the aid of several gallons of kerosene, he determined to prevent their intention by setting fire to the house; his desire being to destroy himself at the same time. He was rescued however, and having given a full account of what had been planned, he was put under arrest for attempted suicide and arson, and brought to the Warrenton gaol for confinement and observation. The shock and excitement incident to the affair was too much for one of his age and infirm condition, and pneumonia developing it was decided to remove the old gentleman to a residence nearby that he have more comfort and suitable nursing. Before this could be arranged he passed away.

Some months later a woman arrested for a misdemeanor was placed in the same cell which had been occupied by McG. and where he had died. On coming to trial, the presiding judge asked if anyone had visited her since her arrest, to which she answered, "No, sir! not anyone I am acquainted with . . . but a little old man with a long white beard comes to my cell every night. He won't speak to me, and every time he's been there he's tried to take away the bed clothes." Judge Edward S. Turner asked her to give a description of him, whereupon she told exactly the appearance of McG.

Mrs. McDonnell writes me:

"This experience occurred in 1924 or '25, and my authority for it is a lawyer, Major Robert A. McIntyre, who was present in court at the time the woman made the above statement. He was unable to remember her name, however. He had also been engaged to represent McG. at the time of his apprehension and visited the old gentleman many times before his death."

GRACE CHURCH

GRACE CHURCH is situated on the old Fredericksburg-Winchester road—half way between Fredericksburg and Warrenton. The old "Rogues road" runs back of it. About an acre of ground cleared out of the wilderness surrounds the church and a well is near the road on the left of the church where the traveller may be sure of cool water for himself and beast.

The church, a square frame building, has an outside vestibule and four large windows, with wooden shutters on each side—a country "burying ground" on the right-hand side of the grounds and at the back of the church is nearly filled with graves old and new.

For over two hundred years this road, once an Indian trail, has been travelled by all sorts and conditions of men. In the past century, the ladies in their carriages going to the mountains for the summer, or to the springs; travellers on horseback, men hauling to Warrenton and Winchester the produce of Tidewater, fish wagons, oyster wagons in season, and all summer long, watermelons and cantaloupes, packed in huge covered wagons. "Mountain Arks" my grandfather called them. No wonder, considering the convenience of water and wood aplenty, and a cleared spot in front of the church, that it was customary to camp there at night from the time the trail was blazed to the time the church was built and up to the present.

Having been born in Tidewater and being accustomed to drive over to my mother's farm near Warrenton, where we always spent the summers, every June, returning in September, twice a year we stopped, camped and fed horses, had a lunch, rested and drove on, to reach "Fenton" about twilight, having started from home about dawn. Often, when we met other travellers there would be conversation and many times I would hear some of them remark that that old church was haunted and that unless there was a big party, it was a spooky business to stay there at night.

Even now the loneliness of the place and the sighing of the wind in the pine trees makes it an inexpressibly desolate spot. The huge

Grace Church

pine forest toward the west shades the sun soon after noon and a shaded early twilight comes on before 4 o'clock.

When I was about seventeen years old my Father sent me with his overseer, old Mr. Kirkpatrick, to Fredericksburg, to bring back a load of melons. We went in the big covered wagon, stuffed with straw and as we were travelling light made the trip down in a day. The next morning we purchased the melons, loaded carefully, and started the forty-mile drive home. The road was a rough unimproved country road and as it was middle August, the heat was intense, so we made poor time, reaching Grace Church at dusk. We had travelled toward a dreadful thunderstorm, the lightning flashing and thunder growling, and wind rising, as we made the last mile. Mr. "Kirk" knew my mother's fear of storms which I had inherited, so he said we would feed and stake the horses and ourselves camp under the wagon. All of which we finally accomplished before the rain came. It soon became apparent that we could not sleep under the wagon as a regular downpour of rain sent the water running under our blankets and straw bed. We decided to try and gain entrance to the church and to our consternation every window and door was sufficiently barred to keep out any and all who came.

About 11 P. M. we succeeded in making a comparatively dry place to sleep in the porch-vestibule; at any rate it kept off the rain. It seems to me I had been asleep about a minute when the horses began to be restless and snort and try to shy away from their stakes. We had not quieted them before a furious noise began inside the church as if some one or many were throwing over the benches, or dropping them on the floor with loud bangs. At first we thought it was wind roaring or perhaps thunder. But the noises became so loud that Mr. "Kirk" gave me the lantern and helped me to climb up and look in to see who or what was inside. However, as long as we remained at the windows there was absolute silence and as soon as we would get down and start to rest the tumult would begin again. We stood the strain about two hours. In fact, we informed the ghosts or whatever it was, in no uncertain terms, that "we would be damned if we moved before the storm was over," and sat down on the porch and stuck it out, noises and all, until the storm passed and a pale moon came out. Then old "Kirk" said, "Let's get from this awful place, Will," and we started harnessing the horses and were busy about it when a Mr. Beach, of Stafford County, drove up in a big wagon loaded with melons. Said he had missed the worst of the storm as it had not passed in his direction, and he had decided to camp the rest of the night at Grace Church if he found any other travellers there, but said he, "I wouldn't camp here alone for a thousand dollars. This old place is haunted and haunted bad! I know dozens of people who have heard noises in this church, like throwing the benches around and moaning, and two or three of my friends have heard a woman shrieking, and once there seemed to be a fight in the church that lasted fully ten minutes, followed by complete silence." We then acknowledge we had heard the noises and had been dreadfully frightened, so were harnessing up then and were moving on home. Mr. Beach said, "I'm going too, you bet, nothing doing with me camping here alone." So in a few minutes we were all on our road.

Looking back at the experience it seems even a more unhappy occasion than at first, for several times since I have been practicing medicine I have met and conversed with people whose stories duplicated my own experience, and while travellers still stop in the day there are never any who are bold enough to spend a night in that remote spot.

W. J. CHEWNING, M. D.

NOTE:—April, 1930. I invited Dr. Chewning, as an interesting experiment to see what would happen, to spend another night at Grace Church with a load of melons.

He says: "Not for a king's ransom!"

GREEN VIEW

"GREEN VIEW," standing in lower Fauquier County, near White Sulphur Springs, and not far from Warrenton, is a huge rambling frame house, built about 140 years ago. It is in the shape of an L, with a center chimney, and can be found near the headwaters of the Rappahannock River. It is part of an original grant to Hancock Lee. A wing was added one hundred years ago. The drawing-room is graced by a beautifully carved panel over the mantel, rolling aside, a spring being touched, and revealing a closet of two shelves.

This property was given to Mary Jeffries Chewning by her father, who bought it from William Henry Fitzhugh. Mrs. Chewning and her husband, Dr. George Chewning, occupied Green View as a summer home for ten years. When their son William was about fourteen years old, he, his sister Agnes, his mother, and a friend, Mrs. Maria Daniel, were spending August at this place, and they all four tell the following story:

William was in bed and asleep in the room next to his mother's The door was open into a hall where a small lantern was burning. He awakened suddenly, sat up in bed, and saw distinctly an old man with a long beard, fully dressed, but without a hat, standing at the foot of the bed, his hands resting on the footboard, and he was looking down at him. The boy thought his grandfather had come while he was asleep, but looking intently at the figure, realized

he had never seen the old man before. Jumping out of bed and rushing into his mother's room he told her. The commotion aroused Mrs. Daniel and Agnes. Although an hour was spent searching the house from garret to cellar, no trace of the midnight visitor could be found.

Two days later, quite unexpectedly, the Grandfather, Mr. Enoch Jeffries, came for a visit. His explanation was "something impressed him they wanted to see him." He was told of the old man seen by William, standing at the foot of his bed. The boy was asked to describe the figure as accurately as possible, whereupon his Grandfather exclaimed, "My God! That was old man Fitzhugh I bought this place from, and he died before you were born!"

Green View

THE HAUNTED KITCHEN

WARRENTON, the County Seat of Fauquier, had its origin in the selection of a Court House site in the vicinity of Alexander Cumminghame's "Red Store." June 17, 1760 the Sheriff gave notice that at the August Court the Court would agree with an "undertaker" to build a Court House of brick, 36 feet long by 20 feet wide.

A tavern had been opened by Andrew Edwards, to whom a license was granted July, 1759. A few houses sprang up. The name of the settlement was Fauquier Court House.

Early in its history Warrenton appears to have been chosen as a school location, and significantly, its name is derived from that given to the first Academy established there. In 1779 Hezekiah Balch, a graduate of Princeton, organized a classical school in Fauquier, finally incorporated November 28, 1780 as the Warren Academy, named in honor of the hero of Bunker Hill. From the Academy the town apparently took its name.

Mrs. Kitty Belt McDonnell enriches the book "Virginia Ghosts" with several interesting contributions. The Haunted Old Kitchen is a part of her home, and on Culpeper Street, Warrenton.

On the property owned by Mrs. John H. Belt in the town of Warrenton is a very old, detached kitchen with large brick chimney and spacious fireplace, such as was used in Colonial days for cooking.

For some years Mrs. Belt used this kitchen in summer, but the negro population always said the old building was haunted and talked a great deal among themselves about it. A colored girl employed by Mrs. Belt who slept in the second story, claimed she often heard queer noises but was never frightened by them, as she said she was well acquainted with the spirits and was used to them.

One night this girl (whose name was Eva Gibson) worked later than usual preparing bread for breakfast the next morning, when she heard a soft, swishing sound behind her which appeared to come from the direction of a small stairway leading to the room

Haunted Kitchen, Warrenton, Virginia

in which she slept. Taking little notice of the noise, except to pause and look about her, she continued making the bread as before. In a few moments the same noise occurred again, louder this time. As she turned from the table near which she had been standing, she saw clearly the figure of an aged woman ascending the stairs, carrying a bundle in her arms about the size and shape of a young baby. On reaching the turn in the stairs, the old woman paused a moment and looked directly at her before going up the rest of the way. Eva was frightened this time, but managed to recover sufficiently to reach the house and tell Mrs. Belt what had happened. She described the old woman minutely. She was a small negro, wore spectacles, large white apron, and a "white 'kerchief" tied about her head. The bundle in her arms was wrapped in a plaid shawl or piece of plaid blanket. Eva was a little afraid to sleep over the kitchen that night, but as the old woman never appeared again she soon forgot about the experience.

In the autumn of 1930 Mrs. Belt had some repair work done on chimney and fireplace in the old building by a negro named Charles Marshall. "He came to this vicinity from Fredericksburg a few months after the close of the Civil War. While working one day replacing some bricks in the fireplace, he mentioned to me that he used to know a woman who worked for many years as cook in that same old kitchen, and he remembered well seeing her stooping over the fire basting a ham or turkey roasting there, and he showed me how it was done. I asked him to tell me the woman's name and what she looked like. The name had vanished, but his description of her tallied exactly with the old woman Eva had seen.

'And,' said Charles, 'she was a real good woman too . . . did what was right and 'tended her church regular. One of her kin died, I 'member, and lef' a weeny young baby. She 'dopted that baby, took good keer of it and raised her to a grown gal'!

"I had said nothing to him about the ghost or anyone having seen it until he volunteered the above information."

AFTER MANY DAYS

GEORGE KEITH, 10th and last hereditary Earl Mareschal of Scotland that bore the name, born in 1685 and died May 25, 1778, was the eldest son of William Keith. He was descended from Robert Keith, Mareschal of the Scottish Army under Bruce. His youngest brother James, born in 1696, wounded at the battle of Shiriffmuir, and later Frederick the Great's greatest field marshal, was killed at the battle of Hochkirchen, October 14, 1758, after an eventful military career. His cousin James Keith was the son of a bishop of the Episcopal Church. The bishop was a professor in Mareschal College, Aberdeen, and also uncle and guardian of the Earl and his brothers. James Keith was born at Peterhead, Scotland, and educated with his cousins, who later took part in the rebellion of 1715, fled to the continent, from where through James they continued to foment dissension.

In course of time the secret correspondence was discovered, James fled to France, and after a sojourn in Spain came to Virginia. He was educated for the church, but like most of the youth of his day was tainted with infidelity. He had in Scotland a very close friend and fellow student, one William Frazier. Their confidential discussions led them to disbelieve in the truth of the Bible, and in a state of future reward and punishment. "Though they had Moses and the Prophets, yet they thought if one should arise from the dead they would believe." They therefore made to each other the solemn pledge that he that died first would return to the other and impart the truth or falsity of the Bible. The contract having been written and sealed in their own blood, the young men went to opposite extremities of the earth—Frazier to India, Keith later returned to England from Virginia, for Orders. His first church was St. John's, Richmond, in Henrico Parish, prior to 1730. This charge he resigned October 2, 1733.

The first minister known to have officiated at the Dumfries Church was Mr. Keith, and while minister of Hamilton Parish he continued to preach at Dumfries until that church was transferred to the new parish of Dettingen in 1745. Mr. Keith's services were then retained at Hamilton where he officiated until his death, in 1751, terminated an interesting and eventful life.

This Scotch clergyman was buried beneath the altar of "Old Elk Run Church," about fifteen miles below Fauquier Court House, in that day a substantial brick building near a small stream from which it took its name. It is said the Reverend James Keith's doubts were never wholly removed. He married Mary Isham Randolph and became the grandfather of Chief Justice John Marshall, his daughter having married Colonel Thomas Marshall of Oakhill, Fauquier County. It is of interest to note that Chief Justice Marshall always wore a ring with an amethyst setting, upon which was the motto *Ventas Vincit,* the same engraved on a silver coin brought by James Keith from Scotland.

Years passed. Nothing had been heard from William Frazier. In 1750 there lived at the rectory a white servant, a Mrs. McLeod, who attended to the dairy and milked the cow. One evening while engaged in her duties a stranger in military garb appeared before her and said he was the spirit of William Frazier who had just died in India, and who in life had been the friend of James Keith. He told of the compact and ordered her to tell her master the Christian religion was true, that he must prepare for death as he would die within one year. The woman, alarmed and afraid of her master, failed to deliver the message. The following evening the soldier again appeared, and threatening her exacted a promise she would give Keith the message.

When the clergyman heard the story and description of the man he was convinced of the reality of the apparition, exclaiming "That was my friend Frazier!" He immediately began to set his affairs in order. He died six months later.

It is stated inquiries were instituted and in course of time it was ascertained William Frazier had died in India a few days prior to his appearance in America.

"This tradition is supported by the evidence of all the older members of the family"—(Wm. M. Paxton, "The Marshall Family") —and is corroborated by the fact that the McLeod family of Baltimore have a record of it in their possession. In 1868 two descendants of Mrs. McLeod went to Kentucky to confer with Markham P. and Colonel Charles A. Marshall concerning a Scottish inheritance. They represented that Mrs. McLeod's Bible was still an heirloom, and reference to the apparition had been written in it by Mrs. McLeod. This confirmation of the old family legend was a matter of much interest to the Marshalls.

Rev. James Keith had a sister to whom he was very devoted, and who died in Scotland when a child. He brought to Virginia her nurse, who apparently possessed clairvoyant powers. In the year 1751 a malignant fever was a scourge in Fauquier County, and as Mr. Keith rode off daily to visit the sick, Janet would say, "He is all right for I see the child with him." Finally the clergyman himself was stricken, and when Mrs. Keith and Janet would enter his room the old nurse spoke of seeing the little spirit pass out.

Mr. Keith's daughter married Colonel Thomas Marshall. One of her sons was Colonel James Markham Marshall. His granddaughter Miss Mary Ambler tells me her grandmother related these facts concerning her grandfather.

KINLOCH

THOMAS TURNER of King George County, Virginia, chose a site on a hill among trees and commanding a fine view of the mountains for the home he built in 1816 in Fauquier County. This he named Kinloch.

The house is stone, and originally had two frame wings covered with vines. A fire long years ago brought about many changes. In the olden days there was an inconspicuous opening to the attic in the roof where it is now suggested soldiers may have found refuge and safety during the war.

Not far from the house a stone wall surrounds those who have fallen on age-long sleep, and the stone walk remains, leading a century ago to a tiny school house attended by Robert E. Lee, and the Turner children, Thomas Turner being the guardian of the future leader of the Confederacy. The slave quarters—some were close by, others at a distance—cannot be found, and it is to be regretted a famous pigeon house we would gladly see, fell down only a few years ago. The Mt. Vernon silver was hidden in the pigeon house during the Civil War. It was sent to Kinloch by the Washingtons in a very large wooden box, the wagon drawn by oxen and the box covered with fodder. On receiving it, Thomas Turner told his many slaves he was unwilling to have the responsibility of the silver, and insisted it should be shipped back to Mt. Vernon at once. After careful thought, Mr. Turner decided to secrete this much valued silver in the pigeon house, then sheltering a great many birds. In the dead of night he removed the valuables and carefully repacked the box with rocks, fastening it securely. This was shipped back to Mt. Vernon next day. The silver remained in this hiding place throughout the war. There were over a hundred slaves at Kinloch. The house servants had cabins near by, later reduced to ashes. The field hands lived about a mile away.

Uncle Tom Brown lived close to the kitchen. He had a noted oven and for many years baked bread for the family. Tom was a favorite slave and the Turners were devoted to him. His death was the tragedy giving to Kinloch its ghost.

Kinloch, Fauquier County, Virginia

One night Uncle Tom Brown went to the village and engaged in a dreadful brawl! Towards morning the old mammy in the cabin heard the terrible noise as of a mortal choking to death. The sound came nearer and nearer. The old slave, dreadfully frightened, cowered in her bed. Presently there was the sound of someone crawling up the steps, opening the door and falling by her side. When they got a light, Uncle Tom was found on the floor dead! His throat had been cut.

Mrs. Carleton Rutledge, who was Miss Anne Turner, writes me that afterwards Tom's ghost was seen by the different members of the family, also by visitors, and from time to time the slaves saw him.. They each and all described the ghost as walking with a long butcher knife in one hand, and always the horrible noise of catching of breath, through a cut throat. Mrs. Rutledge does not know that the noise has been heard, or the ghost seen, since the Quarters were burned.

Leeds Church, Fauquier County, Virginia

LEEDS CHURCH

CHIEF JUSTICE JOHN MARSHALL built his home, "Oak Hill," in Fauquier County. On "Leeds Manor," a large tract of land given to his son, was built, after the English fashion, a Chapel; and here the family worshiped. This church was burned during the Civil War. The smoke of conflict having at length cleared away and peaceful pursuits resumed, the present sanctuary arose upon the ashes of the old, and stands amid the graves of the children of men. To this churchyard was brought from Siberia the body of Dr. James Markham Ambler of the Jeannette polar expedition; and here unknown soldiers bivouac. In accordance with the request of one dying soldier, his cartridge belt was nailed to a tree at the head of his grave.

Beneath the trees in peaceful seclusion stands this church, fashioned of white stucco, the windows guarded throughout the week by green shutters.

During the Christmas holidays of 1888 James J. Marshall returned to his home, "Evergreen," from the University of Virginia. One night after 11:00 o'clock he was returning on horseback from a visit at Clermont, the home of Mr. Stribling. While still at quite a distance from the church, strains of organ music could be heard.

Wondering who could possibly be practicing at such a late hour, he rode nearer, and passing a bend in the road, saw even through the closed shutters that lights were burning within. As he sat on his horse listening, the hymn "Nearer My God to Thee"—in the well remembered voice of his cousin Sally who had been a member of the Choir—floated out upon the night air! Astonished and puzzled, Mr. Marshall tied his horse to the fence and started to investigate. The door was locked. Thinking someone had suddenly turned out the light, in as much as when close to the window no light was visible, he waited a while for someone to appear from within, but at length rode home. Next morning early Mr. Marshall went to the home of the Sexton, a white man, and inquired if anyone had taken the church key the day before. No one had! The mysterious music heard beneath the stars that December night was never explained.

LEETON FOREST

HON. CHARLES LEE, Attorney-General of the United States under Presidents Washington and Adams, spent his last few years at "Leeton Forest." He was born in 1758 at "Leesylvania" near Dumfries.

Located about two miles from Warrenton, Virginia, on what is known as Sunset Hill Road, is the site of the home of Attorney-General Charles Lee and called "Leeton Forest." Charles Lee was the father of Mrs. Charles Pollock who inherited the place upon her father's death. Several years ago the old house was burned, nothing remaining but a high stone foundation and four stone chimneys, as the main portion was built of wide clap-boarding.

"Ever since I can remember," writes Mrs. Kitty McDonnell, "I have always heard Leeton Forest was haunted and none of the negroes living in the vicinity would stay there after sundown. Love nor money could ever induce them to do so, and many refused to work in the house even during the day. Mrs. Pollock left the old home to an unmarried daughter who lived there many years. After her death the place was rented repeatedly to desirable tenants, but none of them ever remained long, and many had tales to tell of the queer happenings which took place. The last occupants who rented it were a Mr. and Mrs. Dillingham from Philadelphia. I knew them quite well, and made frequent visits to Leeton Forest during their sojourn there, though I must admit I wasn't particularly interested in spending a night in the old house; in fact, I don't believe I could have been persuaded to do so. However Mrs. Dillingham often told me of the experiences she had while living there, none of which ever frightened her in the least, or any members of her family. If anything, they were greatly interested in the manifestations.

"Their first experience that there was anything out of the ordinary about the place, was about the door to one of the bedrooms in the second story. Because this room was unoccupied and but partly furnished, the door was kept closed, but every night it would open and would be found open in the morning. After trying every possible means, such as new locks and latches, they finally resorted to padlock and chain fastened to the woodwork with heavy staples, but even this did no good, for in the morning the door would be open and the padlock unfastened. At last they gave up trying to cope with the situation and allowed the door to do as it pleased. In this same room which adjoined that of Mr. and Mrs. Dillingham would be heard distinctly the sound of someone rocking in a heavy chair. This occurred every morning at seven or thereabouts. After a while the rocking would cease, then would be heard footsteps walking lightly across the bare floor, and water being poured into a basin, followed by the sound such as is made when washing the hands and face. Upon repeated investigation the room was always vacant and nothing disturbed. Sometimes voices talking in low tones would be heard, but this did not occur as frequently as the rocking of the chair and washing of hands.

"Mrs. Dillingham also told me that in the mornings when her children were at school and she knew most positively there was no one in the house but herself, she would hear talking in fairly loud tones which seemed to come from the back of the house where pantry and kitchen were located. She was never able to distinguish just what was being said, and on going to that part of the house the voices would cease and no one was to be seen.

"Mr. and Mrs. Dillingham lived at Leeton Forest longer than any of its former tenants and after they moved to Baltimore, Maryland, in the settlement of the estate, the old place was sold to Mr. F. He had lived there but a short while when one night the house caught fire and was destroyed but for foundation and chimneys. The morning after the fire a colored carpenter living in the neighborhood visited the remains of the old house, and to also extend sympathy to Mr. F., as it was generally known that he carried no insurance on the place. In walking around and looking over the ruins, both of them noticed a stone on the inside wall of the foundation near a chimney, which appeared to have no mortar to hold it in place. Mr. F. succeeded in removing this stone, and behind it was a recess which contained a good sized metal box similar to the kind used nowadays for keeping money. The carpenter tells me he never saw what the box contained, as Mr. F. made tracks for the barn and locked himself within, where he remained most of that day. Shortly afterwards Mr. F. commenced arrangements for building a new home upon the old foundations, and when completed proved to be of much larger proportions than the old house. To this day it is not known just how much the metal box contained but the evidence is that it helped considerably in building the new home.

"I saw Mrs. Dillingham less than a year ago in Baltimore and we quite naturally turned the conversation to Leeton Forest. She is sure the phenomena there were caused by that hidden box, and some spirit guarding it perhaps, was endeavoring in a remote way to communicate its whereabouts. As far as I know there has been no unusual occurrence since the box came to light and the new home was completed."

LONGWOOD

"LONGWOOD," near Catlett, Virginia, is a lovely place in Lower Fauquier County. It is a long two-story frame house, lower wings on either end, standing on a hill in the center of a huge lawn dotted with many trees, sloping down to Cedar Run. This property is spoken of as "an original grant to the Hooe family." The identity of one of the ghosts reported to the writer of this sketch to be seen at Longwood is said to be Kate Hooe, who died many years ago. She steps into the parlor in the evening, sits in a low rocking-chair by the fire, with a book in her hand, reading intently, until someone entering, she disappears!

One afternoon, in the late Fall, the mistress of the house being very tired, lay down on a long sofa by the window in this room to rest before supper. She fell asleep. The maid, desiring to ask her a question concerning the evening meal, went into the parlor about dusk and found what she took to be her mistress sitting in the rocker near the fire with her face in her hands, apparently in deep grief. Inasmuch as she did not look up at the sound of the opening of the door, the maid went out, shutting the door after her.

Mrs. Hooe said the closing of the door awakened her, and seeing how late it was, found the maid and said, "Carrie, why did you let me sleep so long? I should have been up long ago."

The reply was: "Miss Sue, I did go in but when I saw you sitting there by the fire so sad like I hated to speak to you."

Mrs. Hooe said, "I was asleep on the sofa by the window, not sitting by the fire."

Carrie exclaimed, "Well, then, Miss Sue, I've seen Miss Kate's ghost, for she was sitting just as I told you, in great grief, by the fire."

"Did you see her sweetheart come, too?" asked Mrs. Hooe. "No," said the maid, "just Miss Kate."

A week later Mrs. Hooe went upstairs to bed. Her husband was already in the room reading. A room supposed to be haunted was at the end of the corridor. As she walked along a man came out of the room, went down the hall to a small room, entered and shut the door. Thinking it was her husband, Mrs. Hooe called to

Longwood

him. He answered from the bedroom. She went in and said "I met a man coming down the hall. He went into the little room."

They took a lamp and looked everywhere, but found no trace of him and nothing had been disturbed. Then Mrs. Hooe recalled having heard that from the date of Miss Kate's death her Confederate soldier sweetheart had been seen every now and then going down the hall and into the "haunted" room to look for her.

One more interesting ghost visits Longwood, and the room he enters is the "haunted room." Miss Sallie Jerriette Meetze tells us his story.

When I was a child Mr. Rhys (Rice) Hooe, who married a Miss Daingerfield—I think of Alexandria—told the following ghost story to his daughter Catherine, and to me:

When a young man, Mr. Hooe and some friends went to "Longwood," the home of his cousin, Mr. Howison Hooe, to a party. A big thunderstorm came up and many of the guests had to spend the night. The house was very crowded and it was announced someone had to sleep in the "haunted chamber." They drew straws to settle the matter and Mr. Hooe was obliged to occupy the room. Fearing some of the others would try to get in after he was asleep and scare him, he locked the door and put the key under the pillow. About half-past two in the morning, Mr. Hooe related, he was awakened by the sound of the door opening, and a man came in dressed in a Confederate uniform and wearing cavalry boots. He walked over to the window, sat down and began pulling off his boots. Mr. Hooe, believing one of his friends had dressed up after this fashion, sprang from the bed and grasped the coat collar. His hand clutched only the air! The man had vanished. Mr. Hooe said he was so weak he could hardly walk back to the bed, get the key and unlock the door. This he somehow managed to do before collapsing upon the hall floor. The noise of his fall aroused one of the guests. He was helped up, given a drink of whiskey, and the rest of the night was passed three in a bed, but not in the "Haunted chamber!"

Note: This weakness of which Mr. Hooe spoke, and his subsequent fall, were not due to *fear,* but to the fact that he had touched the ghost. This is a condition well known to students of psychic phenomena. Mortals have been known to faint, unaware they had walked into an apparition!

Loretta

LORETTA

ABOUT four miles from Warrenton, on the Bethel Road in Fauquier County, can be seen "Loretta," an old dwelling, overshadowed by unhappy memories of experiences in the hearts of those still living, time is powerless to erase, and believed to be haunted by the spirit of a woman whose children suffered from the tyranny and injustice of a stepmother.

"Edmonium" was built in 1741 by Richard H. Foote, with his first wife's money. Later in its history the name was changed to "Loretta" by a school girl, in honor of a nun to whom she was attached.

A brick building of three stories, the chief interest centers in its attic. A large room with but one door opening into the hall. The roof, about twenty-five feet above the ground, and impossible to approach from the outside, is pierced by four dormer windows. The house has the unique history of having been built upon an old burying-ground. While excavating for the cellar quantities of Indian weapons, bones and other relics were unearthed, silent reminders of a people long extinct and of a warfare ended.

Are the distressing and disturbing noises, described by those once making their home at "Loretta," the spirit of the unhappy mother, as many of her descendants believe, and do the Indians return from the happy hunting-grounds to revisit their ancient burial-mound desecrated by the "pale faces" nearly two hundred years ago?

Mrs. Thomas Smith, whose mother was born at Loretta, says, "Every night they could hear sounds of digging, digging, beneath the house. Sounds as of heavy barrels rolling down the stairway and terrific crashes against the doors—the occupants fearing the blows would surely break the door to pieces, but investigation proved everything in normal condition."

Mr. Marshall Jeffries owned the property at one time and Mrs. Jeffries writes me interesting historical notes.

"We did upon many occasions hear many strange noises while

living there. Again and again at night it would sound as though every dish in the house had crashed together in the dining-room. Upon going downstairs everything was found in perfect order!

"At other times one would believe a large party was in progress."

Violin music was heard not alone by Mrs. Jeffries, but by her guests.

"These phenomena always happened after the house had been closed and locked for the night, usually about midnight."

"One night I was waiting for dinner to be placed on the table," writes Mrs. Jeffries, "when an old clock that had not run in years struck twice. The servant said, 'There will be two deaths in your family in less than a year.'"

"There were two deaths—my mother's and that of a child. The clock never made another sound as far as I ever heard."

Mrs. Jeffries speaks of a lady in white being met on the stairs several times by others—she herself never saw her.

A letter from Mrs. Fanny Blackwell, a great-granddaughter of Mr. Richard Foote, tells of "the woman seen roaming about." This restless spirit, Mrs. Blackwell, with other members of the family, believe to be that of Richard Foote's first wife.

The most unusual phenomena occurred in the attic, where a heavy piece of mahogany furniture would be pulled across the only door, making it impossible to enter. "The combined efforts of several men were required before the wardrobe or bureau would push back sufficiently to enable a man to enter."

Are these efforts on the part of the unhappy spirit to make its identity known?

A SOLDIER'S VISION

SIX weeks before his death which occurred in October, 1915, Captain Robert E. Lee and his wife moved into a new house built by them a short mile out of the village of Upperville, Virginia. They named the place "Nordley." A three-story house of stone, it stood in a small wood, many trees around about.

Mrs. R. Walton Fleming tells me she made a visit at Nordley in August, and Captain Lee's mind was then much occupied with the events of the Great War. In his opinion we would eventually take part.

Some months after Captain Lee's death Mrs. Lee told Mrs. Fleming that they were seated on their porch one evening the last week of his life. As bed time drew near she fancied he was dozing, when looking into the distance Captain Lee exclaimed: "Look at all those tents! The soldiers have encamped in our grove!" Getting up to go into the house, he said: "Juliet, leave the front door open tonight, some of these poor fellows may want to come in."

A MYSTERY

"BEFO' de wah" there lived in upper Fauquier County, Virginia, "Old Doctor W." Of all his many attributes, but one, that of jealousy, assists in the delineation of this hazy outline of a drama, very vivid and very real when Dr. W. played the leading part, and upon which tragedy the curtain fell and the light went out many years ago.

Old Dr. W. was the husband of a young and beautiful wife, the former Miss Nannie S. The wedding of December and May has been called to our attention in other places than upper Fauquier County, Virginia, and we have remarked the name May is ever that of a woman!

To his wife, in the words of the bard of Avon, Dr. W. was "a little more than kin, and less than kind." Parties were more frequent and young men more numerous in those days than in this degenerate age; and when a picnic, dance, or other form of merrymaking was heralded, where the youth of the neighborhood was sure to foregather, word comes to us, Dr. W. locked his wife in her room! An estimable Virginian is responsible for the remark, "Fortunately he did not live long."

Sunny May did not pine for December frost, and presently a cousin, a Mr. S., came courting, and found favor in the eyes of the young and charming widow. It is recorded that upon the evening of the day Mr. S. ascertained he was to be taken for better or for worse, he lingered late in the company of his lady love, and a terrific thunderstorm breaking (as the tantalizing revealer of so much and yet so little, remarked, "making it impossible for him to go home, or so he thought"), his hostess ordered the maid to prepare the guest-chamber for the happy Mr. S. He retired about half after eleven and, undressing, set the lamp by the bed to be put out after he was "tucked in."

Fancy his horror, as he got in one side of the bed, to see old Dr. W. get in the other side! Mr. S. did not remain to argue. He scrambled out, and amid the sound of the crashing thunder and flashing lightning, assembled a few garments as hurriedly as possible and got out of the house into the pouring rain.

The story finally got out, too, and Mr. S. constantly admitted its truth.

All's well that ends well. On the appointed day the wedding bells rang and the bridegroom taking the precaution to take the bride to his own rooftree, they lived happily ever after.

Roland

ROLAND

IN Fauquier County in the heart of the Bull Run Mountains, such silence as only profound isolation can give surrounds Roland. One end of a large wing of great age touches the side of High Point Mountain and a marvelous stream old as the everlasting hills, fed by springs far out of sight, splashes down the steep incline

Who can unfold for us the history of that pioneer woman rejoicing in this great stream, and placing the first crock of milk in its cool depths? Before 1850 Roland was built by J. Bradshaw Beverley for his daughter Rebecca when she married Thomas Henderson.

After the second battle of Manassas, Mr. Thomas Henderson, desirous of rendering assistance, inquired of General Corse what he could do. The General pointed out a young man, also from Alexandria, and for six weeks this desperately wounded soldier, William Gardner, was nursed at Roland. The doctor came at night to visit him from Middleburg, twelve miles away.

Many years later Mr. Gardner told the writer of this sketch that "Mrs. Henderson hid Confederate soldiers in her house."

Mrs. Sarah Chichester Page, a niece of Mrs. Henderson, writes me that fifty years ago she and three of her cousins were spending the night at Roland. The hour was late. "We were talking over tales of the Civil War. Some one said: 'Did you know there is a place in this house big enough to hide a man in and keep him hidden for several days? I've heard time and again Aunt Becky had soldiers hidden here, and the Yankees never found them once.'

" 'Let's look for the manhole,' said Jane.

"I replied: 'There are six more rooms as big as this, and all those great rooms downstairs. Nevertheless we started by opening the door of our big clothes closet, and one of the girls stooping down found her finger caught in a crack in the floor! To our horror and utter amazement, the whole floor lifted, and we saw a great space beneath, quite large enough for a man to sit in, or lie at ease! As we four stood silent and awestruck, suddenly just out of the air close at hand a bugle blew clear and sweet, and it sounded *Taps!* Four of us heard it, and none ever forgot the wonderful experience. I knew there was no man within miles of Roland that night.

Snow Hill, near Warrenton, Virginia

SNOW HILL

A GREAT many of the older generation living in and near New Baltimore, Fauquier County, Virginia, claim they have encountered the ghost of Kirk, the supposed pirate, who resided between his periodical voyages at "Snow Hill' farm.

Two gentlemen, Mr. Aleck Smith and Mr. George Gray, planned a visit there fifty or more years ago, when both of them who died some years ago were adventuresome youths. They knew about the crock of Spanish coins which had been ploughed up on the farm and were determined to make a search for the rest of the treasure.

Without telling anyone of their plan they drove over to Snow Hill one misty night in early spring, fortified with shovels, picks, crowbar, and lantern. At this time the old place was unoccupied, so they felt fairly secure in that no one would be likely to intrude upon them, particularly on such a night. After reaching the entrance on the main highway, they drove some distance into the grounds before halting to light the lantern. The night was becoming mistier, but not a current of air seemed to be stirring. Suddenly they heard some one running behind them and breathing heavily. They looked back but could see nothing. The footsteps on the rocky driveway could be heard distinctly however, and when nearly up to them there was a gust of icy wind, and their lantern was extinguished. Not suspecting anything supernormal they pushed on up the steep hill leading to the house, but owing to the thick mist could see but a short distance in front of them, when again they heard the running footsteps, this time ahead of them. The horse they were driving then stopped dead in its tracks and refused to go on. The footsteps grew fainter, finally the sound of them faded off in the direction of the house, which by this time could be faintly discerned in the gloom. At last they drew up to the gate leading to the lawn, but the instant they halted the icy wind was again felt and as they looked toward the house, every window was brilliantly lighted. Neither of them had had time to alight from their vehicle, and although they had heard many reports of queer lights being seen at Snow Hill their first thought was that someone was ahead of them this time in the hunt for the treasure, which caused these adventurers much alarm. Just as they were deciding whether or not to investigate the lighted windows, the door opened suddenly and there silhouetted against a luminous background, stood the figure of a very tall man. . . . They had no recollection of the costume he wore, and it is hardly probable that they could remember under the circumstances. However they did recall quite vividly that he was heavily built with very broad shoulders, and the outline of a beard was plainly distinguishable.

Our two adventurers were thoroughly scared by this time, and their horse must have realized too the uncanniness of the place, for it reared sharply and turning tore down the driveway pell mell. The two young men were so frightened by what they had seen they could make no attempt to gather up the reins or stop the horse in its mad run for home. There is little doubt that Kirk's ghost is what they saw, and it seemed determined to prevent any possibility of the treasure being unearthed. Since this encounter many courageous persons have tried to locate the prize, but all to no avail. Anyone visiting there today will find excavations in the cellar, while others are scattered about the old house and outbuildings.

VIRGINIUS DABNEY

JUST after the Civil War Mr. Virginius Dabney, author of "Don Miff," was staying at an old place in Loudoun County, Virginia. He was visiting a kinsman and reading law. He slept in a house in the yard which consisted of two rooms. A passage ran parallel with the rooms and there was a door at each end of the passage. In the room adjoining Mr. Dabney's, a friend had been sleeping but he was now away. The first night nothing happened. The next night while absorbed in Blackstone he was startled just as the clock struck, by hearing the south door of the passage noisily open, heavy footsteps stalk its length and then out of the north door! He supposed some belated servant was taking a short cut home, and thought no more about it, taking no notice of the occurrence for several nights.

At last coming to the conclusion the noise was a nuisance, he barred both doors with a primitive and very heavy wooden beam which rested on wooden sockets. "The intruder shall go all the way around tonight," he thought; but lo! at midnight the door opened noisily as usual and the footsteps hurrying over the bare planks might have been those of a giant in seven-leagued boots! The north door banged to as Mr. Dabney jumped out of bed. The moon shone brightly, and no moving form appeared on the sweep of greensward.

The next night he sat up, and just as the wild footsteps came down the passage rushed out, lamp in hand! The footsteps were still sounding and there was a slam as of a door going to, although the door was barred.

One special night the scurrying was so tremendous that Mr. Dabney opened the north door and peered out. It had been snowing since nine o'clock—not a footprint! After a week or two the friend returned who had been sleeping in the house. Just at midnight the south door opened and loud footsteps sounded! Quick

as a flash both men jumped out of bed and into the passage. In a twinkling they had unbarred the door and were out in the yard—to find nothing!

Mr. Dabney said, "Have you heard it before?"

"Many, many times."

"Spoken to it?"

"No."

They decided to speak to their host. He told them candidly that he had heard it often; frequently the footsteps sounded even within his own distant chamber. "How do you account for it?" asked Mr. Dabney.

"When this house was built, twenty-five years ago," the host affirmed, "the carpenter and my father's overseer had a personal difficulty, which resulted in the shooting of the carpenter by the overseer one night at twelve o'clock. In his death agony and fright the carpenter entered the south door of the house which he had first finished, ran along the passage and out of the north door where he fell."

IVON

REDUCED to ashes in 1926, but a short time after they had closed its door for the last time, whose abiding place, and that of their ancestors it had been for 175 years, "Ivon," home of the Chichesters, is only a memory. But a beautiful pool fashioned by nature amid her rocks and trees, fed by mountain springs, flows on as when in 1750 Thomson Mason decided to build "Ivon" within the sound of its waters. In Loudoun County, Virginia, three and a half miles from Leesburg, at the foot of the Cotoctin Mountains, this property was a part of the "Raspberry Plantation" granted to Sir William Thomson. He left it to his granddaughter, Ann Thomson, who married George Mason 1st. In due time it was bequeathed to their second son, Thomson Mason, brother of George Mason of Gunston Hall, and descended finally to George Mason Chichester, his grandson. Captain Arthur Mason Chichester and Mary Beverley of "Avenel" lived at "Ivon" with their family when the "bear" paid frequent visits to those living beneath this ancient roof-tree.

The oldest portion of the house was of stone construction—low of ceiling, a walnut stairway; lovely deep window seats made possible by the massive walls, and quaint high mantels are day dreams that still abide. In 1854 a frame addition was built rambling beneath the trees, and upon it the hand of Time draped a wealth of vine.

Miss Maria Williams of Kentucky was housekeeper at Ivon for six years, and to her Mrs. Chichester and the whole family were much attached. Mrs. Sarah Chichester Page writes me:

"I slept in that room for fifteen years and never saw the bear but once, or heard him there again, but it is perfectly true that Miss Williams told my mother the bear came to her nearly every night, rising on its haunches and pawing at the bed, so after one particularly trying experience she declared she would give up the situation rather than live through another night of it! After my experience mother forbade our ever speaking of the bear again for fear Miss Williams would leave."

Again Mrs. Page writes: "I had been away all winter, and when I got home late in the spring, mother said, 'Your sister is in your

Ivon, Loudoun County, Virginia

The Pool, Ivon, Loudoun County, Virginia

room with her babies; would you as soon go into your grand-mother's old room for a while?' 'Quite as soon,' I assented, 'for I'm sure it's cooler.' Sleeping profoundly for some hours, I awakened before dawn to remember the window toward the East was open, and decided to go and pull down the shade. While crossing the floor, I heard padding beside me, and concluding of course the noise was made by my father's dog, Tawney, I said: 'What are you doing upstairs, old fellow?' Immediately I recalled the door was closed, and with an old iron lock no dog could possibly open. I went back to bed rather rapidly, but the "dog" kept even pace behind me. A bit disturbed, I was conscious that the animal stood close beside the bed and that he was twice as big as Tawny, the bull terrior. No electric lights in those days, so I just *cowered* and after a while he just *wasn't there!*

"In the bright summer morning the incident seemed rather absurd, yet at breakfast it was still so real to me I couldn't help remarking: 'I had rather a large bear in my room last night,' and was dumfounded to get a vicious kick under the table from my mother—gentlest of women! I said no more. After breakfast she exclaimed: 'How *could* you mention that bear before Maria Williams! I gave her that room but she insists a bear came nearly every night, stood on his hind legs beside the bed and fairly pushed her out the other side! She refused to stay in the room, so I moved her out just before you came home.'

"But evidently the bear had a fancy for me and kept in touch. The week following I went over to visit my cousins, the Turners at Palmerstone. One night in the cool open sun parlor I related my experience to Randolph Turner. Early in the story we both heard distinctly what we thought was a large dog get up from the floor and come towards us. As I finished the tale the animal gave himself a big, heavy leathery-sounding shake. No one could have failed to hear it. Randolph instantly struck a match—to find no animal in the room! He declared there was no dog on the place!"

LESSLAND

LONG before the Civil War Hon. Jeremiah Morton owned three farms in Virginia—"Moreland," "Stillmore," and the smallest he called "Lessland." The latter is to be found about a mile from Raccoon Ford and quite near Culpeper. Lessland is today the home of his great-granddaughter Mrs. Stearns Halsey, and her two children, Carol and Glassel.

Facing the north, the Blue Ridge Mountains a line of haze in the distance, Lessland stands on a hill bordered by that stream once quaintly called the Rapid Anne. Superb white columns bearing capitals of Ionic design adorn a porch evidently once beloved by many mortals who, from some other state of activity, now and then revisit their former rendezvous and can be seen by those with clairvoyant power. A beautiful molding finishes the low pitched roof, harmonizing with the Ionic atmosphere embellishing this spacious and comfortable mansion. A trellis was placed to one side years ago by old Mrs. Jeremiah Halsey who was particularly fond of the arbor and careful of the vines trailing over it. Frequently if wanted she could be found twining the tendrils or removing faded flowers or dead leaves. A relative, Mrs. Margaret Halsey Weir of Fredericksburg, has several interesting facts to furnish of mysterious happenings on the banks of the Rapid Anne.

Last summer it seems there occurred a terrific storm. The wind snapped off a huge tree right by the porch and demolished the trellis beloved in years long gone, by old Mrs. Halsey. Hearing next morning of the damage occasioned by the storm during the night, Mrs. Halsey's young son Glassel went out before breakfast to view the scene. He came in immediately and told his mother there was a little old lady with big skirts on leaning over the railing and looking at the broken trellis. His mother was at first inclined to treat the matter lightly, but in view of other mysterious happenings, and the fact the boy was noted for the accuracy of his statements, she finally came to the conclusion he had really seen his grandmother contemplating the wreck of her trellis.

In late September Mrs. Halsey and Mrs. Weir were driving home from Culpeper. Entering the gate and approaching the house, Mrs.

Lessland, Orange County, Virginia

Weir exclaimed: "Look, Fanny, you have company!" "What do you mean?" replied her cousin. "Why, don't you see the old gentleman sitting in a big leather chair on the porch? I do believe he has side-whiskers! I thought they had gone out of style." Mrs. Halsey could see no one. "On the left side of the porch," persisted Mrs. Weir, "don't you see him, wearing a linen suit?" Arriving a minute later at the door, no old man and no chair were to be seen! Mrs. Weir at once insisted upon searching the house for such a chair as she had described. Mrs. Halsey then admitted, "We have a chair of that description; my husband's grandfather used to sit in it on the porch when he came for visits, and I must say you have described him accurately, but he is dead."

One evening Glassel and his teacher were upstairs doing arithmetic. Hearing a great clamor and chattering on the porch the teacher stepped to the window in order to call down and request the group to be less noisy. Glancing down she was astonished to find no one to be seen, nor had anyone been there!

One afternoon Mrs. Halsey and Mrs. Weir were standing at an upstairs window and saw a friend, Mr. Norris, arriving in a car. When half way from the front gate he turned and drove away. In a few days Mr. Norris called, and the ladies naturally asked to know the reason for his hasty retreat. Their caller replied, "As I drew near I saw so much company on the porch, and not having taken time to dress before coming, I thought it wiser to go back and come another time." He was astonished when told that he alone saw the company on the porch, the mysterious group being invisible to those standing looking out of the window.

Newington, Orange County, Virginia

NEWINGTON

ONE can still find traces of the first Court House a few hundred yards from an interesting old homestead called "Newington," Mountain Run, Orange County, Virginia, standing twelve miles southeast of the present County Seat. William Taliaferro was born at "Snow Creek," Spotsylvania County, August 9, 1726. His wife was Mary Battaile, the wedding taking place October 4, 1751; but it was on the property of his second wife, Elizabeth, daughter of Francis and Elizabeth Taliaferro of "Epsom," Spotsylvania County, whom he married August 5, 1758, he built "Newington" "up on a hill, half a mile from the highway." This property was an extensive grant to John and Lawrence Taliaferro in 1728. Here William Taliaferro died April 21, 1798.

As is so frequently the case, a part of this ancient rooftree antedates 1758, and its origin fades from us into the mists of those far off days nearly two hundred years ago! One fine old walnut tree lingers, its branches sweeping across the dormer windows, and the green nuts dropping one by one in October's frosty air. It comes to me that the "greate" room is beautifully wainscotted in walnut. At one side a built-in desk adds a note of interest, and opposite, we find one of those tiny cupboards beloved of our pioneer ancestors. Mr. W. B. McGroarty, of that ancient lineage, tells us that features of "Newington" are its hall and stairway; and about one hundred yards distant is the ancient burial ground. About this will be woven in part the thread of my little mystery.

After the death of William Taliaferro, his widow married Captain Benjamin Hume, and not until she reached the ripe old age of ninety, in 1830, did her journey end in that shady spot, quite near her old home. For seventy years prior to 1910 this property was owned by Mr. Lawrence Sanford, from whom it was bought by Mrs. J. P. Walters, now living in Orange, and who writes me of her interesting and remarkable experience one night in the early fall of 1914. The graveyard, she tells me, is in the garden and shaded by many beautiful trees. Several streams or springs, water the property, but the effacing hand of Time has removed one by one that group of detached buildings the complement of all Colonial homes,—such as the little office to which the Master so frequently turned; and the smoke house bountifully provisioned in summer against winter's needs. Mrs. Walters writes: "There was a very unsightly space overgrown by bushes in the garden back of the graveyard. Mr. Walters told an old man who had worked on the place fifteen years, to clean off this rank growth, and plow the land. The man replied: 'It can't be done.' He said he had done this every year, and had 'several times tried to plow, and every time the swingle-trees would snap off as fast as I put them on. Then we tried iron swingle-trees and the mules dropped in graves every few steps, so we left it alone!' "

One day Mrs. Walters ordered some plowing done in the garden and while this work was in progress the horse sank into a cavity. Upon investigation, this was found to be a grave containing a skeleton! That night at about eleven o'clock she was awakened by a loud noise apparently in the yard. Careful investigation revealing nothing out of the ordinary, Mrs. Walters once more retired to bed. Very soon this noise was heard twice in quick succession, and presently the figure of a woman appeared at the foot of her bed! This apparition spoke, calling Mrs. Walters by name, and giving her own name as Ethel Cavanaugh. She asked her not to be afraid; that the grave disturbed in the garden was hers; "Newington" had been her home long before it was that of the Sanford family, that she made periodic visits to her old home, and had died in the room above the spiral stairway.

Mrs. Walters writes: "You want to know why I mention one special room that Ethel died in. She told me what room she died in, and where she was buried. I said: 'I have never seen your grave in the enclosed graveyard.' She smiled and said: 'No, only the Sanford family are buried in the enclosed lot. I was buried in the garden. You see I lived here years and years before the Sanfords ever owned this place, and I died in the room upstairs over the room you now use as a dining room.'" Mrs. Walters was occupying a room on the first floor. Her description of the ghost is interesting: "Ethel Cavanaugh was tall and slender, perhaps five feet ten inches, weighing 140 pounds. A round figure, not flat like the figures of today. The only color about her was her jet black hair, and large deep blue eyes. She had a high forehead, and thin lips. Her pallor was the only thing about her that looked like a ghost. The dress is not very clear in my mind, except that it was thin and lacy and fit her figure, and it must have been long as I did not see her feet."

Mrs. Walters said she later asked the County Clerk if there were any Cavanaugh names mentioned in the Court records; and he said back a number of years ago he found those of the name living in that neighborhood.

The room above the spiral stairway may have been Ethel's before 1758 when William Taliaferro found both Elizabeth and her broad acres lovely, and to be desired! Or again, she may have been some relative seeking shelter from life's storms beside Elizabeth's fireside, such, a familiar picture incidental to woman's long struggle to economic independence.

THE McCHESNEY GHOST

D R. JOHN McCHESNEY, an intelligent physician, lived on his farm, about a mile north of the village of Newport, Augusta County, and the same distance west of the main road leading from Staunton to Lexington, by way of Middlebrook and Brownsburg. His wife was a sister of Thomas Steele, who lived on the main road, a mile from Dr. McChesney. Mrs. Mary Steele, widow of Captain William Steele and mother of Thomas and Mrs. McChesney, lived in Rockbridge, two miles west of Midway. William Steele, a son of Thomas, is now (1889) one of the few surviving witnesses of the occurrences to be related, and to him we are indebted for all our detailed statements. He was a child at the time, six years of age, but distinctly remembers what he saw and heard, and, we may add, his veracity is unquestionable. His testimony before any tribunal in Augusta County would be implicitly believed.

In 1825 Dr. McChesney's family consisted of his wife, four young children, and sundry negro servants, one of the latter a girl named Maria, probably eight years of age.

One evening in January or February, while the white family were at supper, Maria came in from the kitchen much frightened, apparently, and saying that an old woman with her head tied up had chased her. Little or no attention, however, was given to the incident, but Maria continued for some days to complain of being frightened when by herself and other circumstances connected with the girl attracted the attention of the family. Soon after this, volleys of stones began to descend upon the roof of the dwelling-house, and continued to fall at intervals, in daytime and also at night. The stones averaged the size of a man's fist and some of them were too large to be thrown by a person of ordinary strength.

Occasionally some of the stones were hot and scorched the dry grass on which they fell. Reports of the stone throwing circulated through the county and hundreds of people from miles around came to witness the spectacle. On some days the yard was full of people, on all sides of the house, eagerly watching to see where the stones came from; but all retired without making any discovery. The descent of stones did not occur every day and visitors on offdays generally went away incredulous about the whole matter.

During the whole time Maria complained of being chased and frightened. As Maria seemed to be the center of the disturbance, Dr. McChesney concluded to send her away, and ordered her to go to the residence of his brother-in-law, Mr. Thomas Steele. While she was on the way across the hills Mrs. Steele and her children (including her son William), a young negro woman, and her children were under a tree in the yard. Mrs. Steele was knitting and the negro woman was engaged in washing. Mr. Steele was not at home.

Suddenly a loud noise was heard in the house as if it were full of frightened and stamping horses. The negro woman ran first to the house and called to Mrs. Steele to come. In the center of the large room all the movable furniture was piled up promiscuously,— bed, bureau, chairs, andirons, etc. While the spectators were look- ing and wondering, stones began to fall on the house, and then Maria was seen approaching. She stated, as usual, that she had been chased by an old woman, and her evident terror was distress- ing to behold. Maria was sent home, but the fall of stones con- tinued at Mr. Steele's. The missiles entered the house, how and from whence no one could discover, and broke the glass in the cupboard doors and many of the plates and dishes. The furniture was severely pitted and some articles still preserved show the marks to this day.

There was no cessation of the occurrences at Dr. McChesney's. One day in the Spring, the weather still cool, the family were sit- ting around the fire. The persons present were Dr. and Mrs. McChesney, Mrs. Mary Steele, Mr. and Mrs. Thomas Steele, their son William and others. The doors were closed and the window- sash were down, when a stone, seeming to come from a corner of the room near the ceiling, struck Mrs. Thomas Steele on the head. She was the only person struck at the time. A lock of her hair was severed as if by scissors and her scalp was cut to the bone, causing bleeding. Mr. Steele became enraged and denounced the invisible agent for "taking its spite on a woman" and not on him. He then took his seat in the front door, and immediately was pelted with clods of sod and earth, coming from the inside of the house. He sat there until the missils were piled around him and then at the earnest solicitation of his mother, who cried that "the thing" would kill him, left the spot and was not pursued.

Wishing to remove the McChesney and Steele children out of the way, they were sent to their grandmother's, near Midway, but Maria was sent also. Soon the disturbances began at Mrs. Steele's—stones flew about, furniture in the kitchen moved of its own accord, etc. One day a large kitchen bench pranced over the floor like a horse. The children present were at first amused, and young John M. Steele (afterwards Dr. Steele) proposed to bridle the steed and ride him. They did so, but became so much alarmed at the antics of the bench that young Steele fainted.

During this time, Mrs. Steele's farm servants found that food and tools taken by them to the fields disappeared and turned up at the house. While at Mrs. Steele's, Maria complained of being beaten. Mrs. Steele took her between her knees, drew her skirts about her, and with a stick struck around as if to beat off an invisible foe. Maria continued to cry out that she had been beaten and pricked with pins. The "slaps," says William Steele, were distinctly heard, but no one could see the vindictive enemy. At last the victim fell upon the floor, exhausted and apparently dead, but soon revived. She continued to be punished, as described, for many weeks.

Worn out with these troubles, Dr. McChesney, as a last resort, sold Maria, and she was taken South. As soon as she left, the disturbances ceased and they never followed her in her new home.

From the Annals of Augusta County, Virginia from 1726 to 1871
by
JOSEPH A. WADDELL
Member of the Virginia Historical Society

The descendants of these McChesneys and Steeles still live in Staunton, Virginia, people of character and of substance. William B. McChesney, head of the house in Staunton, was one of the student guard-of-honor over the remains of Robert E Lee, he having been a pupil at Washington and Lee University at the time of the General's death.

Selma, Staunton, Virginia

SELMA

SELMA was built in Staunton, Virginia, in 1856 by Colonel H. L. Opie of the Confederate Army. On the outskirts of the town, the house was placed on an eminence in the midst of a large well-wooded estate, and was approached by a long shady avenue. Spanning a little stream, a rustic bridge added a picturesque touch to the park. The large mansion of white stucco is typical of many southern homes. Tall pillars lend dignity to the front façade, and large green shutters give a touch of color. Before entering, one pictures the plan to be a generous hall with two spacious rooms on either side. During the past seventy-five years several families have called Selma home; each inheriting a thread of mystery, a presence intangible yet not to be denied.

During the Civil War the Opie family was in residence and had as visitors a lady and her son. The latter was in the Confederate Army and one day was chased by a Yankee into the house, through the hall, and killed by the dining room mantel, where his blood still stains the floor.

In 1872 the property was owned by the Williams of South Carolina. Miss Serena Williams told Mrs. H. Arthur Lamb, an English lady who later occupied Selma, that the ghost of a soldier was constantly seen by members of her family, and by the servants. On the night of their arrival in the new home, a visitor arose from the tea table to go upstairs. Returning she asked: "Who was the gentleman entering the room as I went out?" The surprising response was: "Why, no one came in!" She insisted that a soldier in uniform had passed her as she went out. Later he frequently was seen by the Lamb family. He passed them on the stairs or entered the dining room. Again they would find him standing quietly by the blood-stained hearth as if he were a member of the family circle! A new servant once asked if she should lay a place at table for the gentleman. Asked "What gentleman?" she replied: "Why, the soldier gentleman!"

Mrs. Harry Green, daughter of Mrs. Arthur Lamb, states she

was a very small child when they lived at Selma, but recalls being terribly afraid to go near the room which had been occupied by the mother of the soldier, for she knew that in that room he had often appeared.

Fifteen years ago the place was bought by Colonel William Beard of Tallahassee, Florida. They had great difficulty in getting servants "on account of the ghost." Members of the family distinctly heard steps of a ghostly patrol, night after night, passing and repassing across the rustic bridge on the grounds; but desiring to sell, they were reluctant to talk about the ghost of the Confederate soldier haunting Selma.

CARTER HALL

F ROM an old family Bible we learn that Nathaniel Burwell was
born at Carter's Grove, near Williamsburg, April 15, 1750.
He was the seventh child of Carter Burwell and Lucy Grymes,
who were married at Brandon, Middlesex, January 16, 1738.

Col. Burwell was a man of great wealth and of commanding
position in the community. He journeyed from Williamsburg to
ClarkeCounty, and there built his splendid mansion, choosing a
site commanding superb views of the Blue Ridge Mountains and
close to a great spring flowing in the cool shade of immense forest
trees. This new home he named Carter Hall. It was built after
the Revolution, before 1790, and stands today, a massive three-story
stone structure some sixty feet in length, and bearing on either end
long wings adding grace and symmetry to the whole.

Nathaniel Burwell married Susanna Grymes at Brandon, November 28, 1772, and to her he was devotedly attached. She died
at Carter's Grove, July 24, 1788, age thirty-seven, and her death left
him so crushed and lonely he felt unable to bear his misfortune
without a companion in misery who could understand his great
loss and render the sympathy he felt he must have. After reflecting
for a few months a happy inspiration was vouchsafed. Col. Burwell
prepared for a journey.

Mounting into his immense coach swung upon strong leather
thongs, the great wheels designed to withstand deep ruts and heavy
mud, the driver and footman high on the box guiding the sturdy
horses along rough and well-nigh impassable roads, they wended
their way to "Rosewell."

Arriving at his neighbor's hospitable mansion, and doubtless
seated before a cheerful fire, with a cheering glass close at hand,
Col. John Page listened sympathetically to the widower's tale of
woe. The story comes to us that Col. Burwell asked Col. Page to
send for his half-sister, Mrs. George Baylor, that he might marry
her. We do not find that Col. Page found this type of courtship
hasty or unusual. The widow, we learn, was young and beautiful.
Possibly this fact occurred to the Master of Carter Hall even in the
hour of his deepest bereavement, and as he jolted over the rough
roads in his great coach.

Carter Hall

She came and promptly rejected the disconsolate widower's proposal!

"Lucy," he said, "your brother John and I arranged it all before you came."

That seemed to settle the matter. After the ceremony the bridegroom said, "Now, Lucy, you can weep for your dear George, and I can weep for my beloved Sucky."

Nathaniel Burwell died in 1814 at Carter Hall. More than a hundred years of summer suns and winter storms, Gilead's unfailing balm, have visited Carter Hall since its Master, Nathaniel Burwell, shed his last tear for his beloved "Sucky." "There is no name with whatever accent of passionate love repeated whose echo is not faint at last."

Mr. J. Townsend Burwell, present owner of Carter Hall, in his very courteous answer to a stranger's letter of inquiry, entertains an unbelieving spirit, but admits "several times I have heard the arrival of a vehicle at the front door and have later discovered that nothing was really there!"

Yet it is to be believed the spirits of Nathaniel Burwell and Susan Grymes keep company in another sphere, and possibly have appeared before the eyes of astonished mortals.

Mrs. Lily Jolliffe Tappling relates that her aunt, Mrs. Lucy Burwell Jolliffe, and her two sons were visiting at Carter Hall. One night sitting before the fire in the dining-room, they heard the sound of a carriage being driven to the front door. Taking a candle, Mrs. Jolliffe followed by her sons, opened the door and all three saw a big old-fashioned coach with heavy wheels, two large horses, and coachman and footman high upon the box. They could see someone was in the carriage. The footman jumped down, opened the door, letting down the steps. No one descended! Before their astonished gaze he put up the steps, closed the door, and jumping to his seat beside the coachman, the crack of the whip was plainly heard as the great lumbering vehicle disappeared into the night. Mrs. Jolliffe's description coincided with what was known of the great coaches belonging to the day of the Master of Carter Hall.

Abraham's Delight

ABRAHAM'S DELIGHT

ABRAHAM'S DELIGHT is the quaint name of an old mansion, one mile from Winchester, Virginia, with an interesting history. It has the honor of having been one of the first stone houses built in the valley of the Shenandoah, and the fine spring on this property supplies the entire town of Winchester with water.

The homestead and a flourmill were built in 1754, by Isaac Hollinsworth, one of the chimneys bearing that date. He was a Quaker whose grandfather Thomas, came to America from England with William Penn in 1682 and settled in New Castle County, Delaware.

Abraham Hollinsworth, Isaac's father, married in 1737, Anna Robinson, and bought 582 acres near Winchester, upon which his son built a home, still owned by his daughter. A steep flight of steps lead to a small porch, from which the house is entered through a massive door. On the wall of the wide hall may be seen the horn used in an earlier age to summon help when herds of buffalo still roamed through that part of the country.

Mary Hollinsworth stated that when her grandfather Abraham died his funeral was attended by every white man in Frederick County, ten in number!

The Ghost of Abraham's Delight is a very tall man, well over six feet, and dressed in a costume of a bygone century. This apparition has been seen throughout the years by a number of people; the phenomenon of its appearing a matter of community interest.

The ghost walks up the front steps and on to the porch, passing through the closed and often locked front door. In about ten minutes the figure emerges once more through the closed door, and upon reaching the grounds, walks a short distance, then vanishes! So familiar is this apparition, that workmen, seeing the ghost enter the house, would lean on their shovels and watch for its reappearing. They were never disappointed.

Miss Hollinsworth had varied and interesting experiences in this old mansion with visitants from another sphere of existence. When in her younger days she sat down at the piano and sang hymns, a woman's voice joined in; and late in the night, from her bed she would hear in the parlor below, laughter and music, as though a party of young people were making merry. This did not annoy, being as familiar to her as the call of the whippoorwills outside the window.

After the Civil War the acres of Abraham's Delight had been denuded of timber; the soil was untilled, the live stock long since appropriated by the Union soldiers. The old house and poverty alone remained to the intrepid Mary Hollinsworth. It is reported that she disappeared and was lost to that part of the country for years. Brave in spirit and caring only to recoup the depleted fortunes of the home of her Fathers, this intrepid pioneer in the emancipation of women "went west," and doning man's attire, sought and found remunerative employment.

We are told that in order doubtless to enliven the monotony of existence, Mary unfortunately became engaged to be married! The fateful day drawing near, Mary once more disappeared, but this time with considerable savings, the result of industry and thrift.

Suitably clad, Winchester knew her once more. A mystery unsolved by the recorder of this chronicle is how the intrepid Mary was traced; but a lawsuit resulted and her savings vanished, either to the bride-elect or to the lawyers.

BELLE GROVE

BELLE GROVE stands some fifteen miles from Winchester, Virginia. This imposing mansion of native sandstone is 135 feet long and said to have been designed by Thomas Jefferson for his friend Isaac Hite, Jr., grandson of Joist Hite, ·the pioneer. After six long years the building was completed in 1783, standing on a tract of the original estate of "Long Meadows," owned by his grandfather. Each pillar on the impressive portico is one large forest tree. The keystones and cornerstones, it is said, were brought from England and hauled over the Blue Ridge Mountains from Alexandria with ox-teams, a distance of seventy-five miles. The slave quarters have disappeared, but at a becoming distance can be found the big stone smokehouse, approached by a path of flagstones, and a picturesque old icehouse stands beneath the trees. Four of the massive gray-white chimneys tower fifty feet into the air, while the nuts covering a magnificent old English walnut tree are today ripening in the warm September sun.

Major Isaac Hite was Aide-de-Camp to the Revolutionary General, John Peter Muhlenburg, later a preacher of note in the Episcopal Church. The major was a charter member of Phi Beta Kappa Fraternity in 1777 at William and Mary College.

His house finished, he went to Montpelier in Madison County, where he was married to Nellie Conway Madison, sister of President Madison. The groom kissed the little daughter of the officiating clergyman and was told by the mother she should be his second wife. Twenty years later they were married!

President and Mrs. Madison spent one week of their honeymoon at Belle Grove and it is said that in 1814 he and Dolly, of more heroic mould, sought refuge beneath its hospitable roof.

Before the Civil War one Benjamin Coolie occupied this property and had for a cook a young negro woman. This girl had been heard to declare that if a mistress ever entered that house she would not live long. In course of time Coolie married, and one morning all hands in the harvest fields, or otherwise occupied at a distance, Mrs. Coolie going into the basement to give some directions to the

Belle Grove

cook, was struck on the head with an ax. She fell upon the hearth of the huge stone fireplace, and the body dragged out of the door along the flag walk and thrown into the smokehouse. Some one chancing to pass saw the negro. She was arrested, tried and convicted. Some legal technicality claiming the attention of the court, the woman was remanded to jail. While in jail the Federal forces arrived; the negro prisoners were released and the woman disappeared. Ever since the ghost of Mrs. Coolie has walked.

Mortally wounded, the Confederate General Ramseur was nursed by a Federal officer, Col. Henry A. du Pont, a classmate at West Point, as General Sheridan slept in the adjoining room.

Stonewall Jackson also made the dwelling his headquarters and after the battle of Cedar Creek it was a hospital.

More than fifty years ago an Englishman named Rose occupied this estate. Miss Lucy Jones, of Winchester, visited the Rose family frequently, she was Miss Rose's intimate friend. Miss Jones states that the different members of the Rose family saw the ghost frequently—a white figure standing by the stone fireplace in the basement; gliding along the flag path to the smokehouse; again in the hallway of her former home, or looking from the windows at the big walnut tree.

Byrd House, Winchester

THE BYRD HOUSE

WHERE the Shawnee Indians selected a spot with a fine spring for their village, two hundred years ago, one Joseph Wood founded some believe to be the second oldest city in the State of Virginia and called it Winchester. Memories of Washington as a surveyor in the employ of Lord Fairfax still linger; the building he later used as headquarters, and solid stone houses built by Hessian soldiers, are reminiscent of Revolutionary battles,—while those now living can bear witness to the fact the town changed hands twenty-seven times during the Civil War!

There stands on north Washington Street a house, the rear portion of which is very old. One authority speaks of it as "The house of Judge Robert White, one of the earliest built brick houses in the town." Erected by Judge White, or by a prior owner, the front portion was added prior to the Civil War, about seventy-five years ago, by Nathaniel B. Mead. In 1873 the property was acquired by George H. Byrd, and is known as "the Byrd house." He deeded it to his brother, Col. William Byrd, who in 1865 moved to Winchester and practiced law. The house does not today belong to the Byrd family. The writer is informed by the aunt of Governor Byrd that long before their taking possession, the house had the reputation of being haunted by the spirit of a little child, who apparently appeared frequently and made itself very much at home. This lady writes, "Upon one occasion she appeared in a room full of people!" The child, it is said, was from time to time seen standing beside a high-backed oak chair with her hands resting upon the arm of the chair.

Mrs. Margaret Worthington, brought up in Winchester, daughter of Rev. Nelson P. Dame, for many years rector of the Episcopal Church in that town, tells me the little child seen so often standing beside the tall oak chair died of diphtheria sitting in that chair, before the Byrd family bought it, among other articles, with the house.

Mrs. Worthington was frequently at the Byrd home, and told

of a "sweet faced woman often seen wandering about." One evening the family related they locked up the house and went to make a call. Returning they were astonished and alarmed to see the entire third story brilliantly lighted and figures moving to and fro. Thinking the house was on fire and firemen within, they rushed in only to find all dark and silent as they had left it. This phenomenon occurred several times and was witnessed by a number of people.

The writer is unable to obtain further details of these very interesting and evidently very frequent manifestations nor the names of those so fortunate as to see them. Neither can she ascertain whether or not the members of the Byrd household ever met the specter described as "a tall and shrouded figure of a man, possessed of piercing and glowing eyes, full of sorrow and of anguish," frequenting the garden walks and unexpectedly emerging from some shadow.

A wonderful "hand-writing on the wall" was the little spirit appearing again and again, bearing a message from the unseen world, hoping some understanding heart would be present to interpret and to understand.

Possibly the shrouded figure was some Monk drawn to the inmates by religious affiliation, or possibly some earth-bound spirit, imprisoned in awful loneliness, seeking a friendly word of greeting and sympathy.

Let us hope that some day the shrubbery will once more blossom in the sunlight on north Washington Street; the old Monk and the little child walk hand in hand in that "light that never was on sea or land," but shines reflected in some human face.

THE FORK IN THE ROAD

L ATE in the eighteenth century a large mansion of Georgian architecture was erected high on a hill in Winchester, Virginia, by Dr. Daniel Conrad. Terraces separated the residence from the road of that day and many fine trees gave a touch of cool green and afforded privacy in summer-time.

Dr. Conrad was a man of conspicuous attainment in the medical profession at a period when experienced physicians were few in the Valley of Virginia. His advantages had been many. His father possessing a comfortable fortune enabled the son to study at the University of Edinburgh, where he graduated with honors, afterward returning to practice medicine in his native state. Natural talent soon gave Dr. Conrad a standing in his profession, and his love for humanity endeared him to all with whom he came in contact.

Throughout the summer of 1806 a low fever prevailed in that part of Virginia. The calls upon the Doctor's time and strength had been incessant. The distances to be traversed were often great, and the rough country roads of that early day were in places well-nigh impassable in times of heavy rain. All summer both the physician and his faithful horse had started out early and frequently returned to home and stable long after dark.

One night in September at a late hour he was on his way to the bedside of Miss Charlotte Norris. Her home was on the banks of the Shenandoah River at a distance of some fifteen miles. Dr. Conrad had seen her two days before, and believing the crisis imminent prepared to remain at the Norris home for some time. As he drew near "Ash Hollow" a depression among the thickly wooded hills, and 125 years ago far from any human habitation, a lovely silver vista stretched ahead of him, but quite nearby the road forked. By the light of the moon the dial of his big watch could easily be read as he drew it from his pocket. Finding the hour to be half after one, later than he had expected, the doctor decided he must hurry. *And at that moment he saw her!* His patient was on horseback riding rapidly; looking at him as she beckoned to him with her hand to follow her up the turn in the road. But what was the mat-

Home of Dr. Daniel Conrad, Winchester, Virginia

ter with his horse? Instead of responding to the spur with a forward plunge, the animal turned tail and galloped at full speed toward home! Finally controlling the horse and after a little arriving once more at the parting of the ways, Dr. Conrad called loudly, but only the wind in the pines answered.

Believing Miss Norris to have eluded her attendants and saddled her horse in order to ride to meet him, greatly disturbed in mind, the Doctor pressed his horse into a gallop, and at length beneath the overarching trees in the lane reached the door of the house. The old butler John soon answered his loud knocks, and to his hasty question, "Your Mistress, where is she?"—rolling his eyes, John whispered, "Oh, Marse Doctor, she's daid! She done die jes' a while ago."

"At what time did she die?"

The old negro turned and pointing to the tall clock said in a solemn tone: "I done stopped de hans 'zactly at half past one."

The following day as Dr. Conrad rode home through the haze of the late September twilight his eyes resting on the distant mountains, he pondered the problem of Life and Death; of the Vision in

"Ash Hollow," and of the mystery furnished by the dial of his watch and the face of the silent clock standing in the hall. Doubtless physically exhausted from overwork, three weeks later he too turned at the fork in the road, and

"Fled along a pathway fleet
Worn smooth by many, many feet"

———

"By medicine life may be prolonged—
Yet death will seize the doctor too."

Elmwood, Winchester

ELMWOOD

THE interesting happenings occurring in the old dwelling called "Elmwood," once standing near Winchester, Virginia, are recounted by Mrs. Custis James, of Williamsburg, the former Miss Mary Walker, and by her sister, Miss Frances A. Walker, who were living at Elmwood when it met the fate of so many old houses. Its smoke-stained walls stand silent witnesses to a great truth, "What time brings, time will take away."

Elmwood had no pretentions to beauty. A square brick house with the usual center hall and large rooms on either side. Its lack of grace and charm was, however, overshadowed by a setting of beautiful trees, and from the porch a lovely view greeted the eye where here and there a vista had been cut affording a glimpse of distant blue hills and far-reaching green fields.

As were many other Virginia dwellings of any considerable size, Elmwood was at one time the headquarters of General Sheridan; at another, was occupied by General Custer of the Confederacy. This was the home of General and Mrs. John G. Walker and family for more than forty years. General Walker commanded the 3rd Cavalry, the "Brave Rifles," in the old Army and was a General in the Army of the Confederacy.

Built by Alexander Tidball about 1840, owned by the Ward family, and lived in by the Walkers, Elmwood was the scene of two tragedies. A spy was hanged in the yard during the Civil War, and before the advent of the Walker family there had been a murder committed in the cellar under the dining-room. The phenomena, the frequent aftermath of such tragedies, were not absent from Elmwood. In the dining-room strange sounds were heard as of barrels being rolled out of the storeroom; loud knockings on the back door startled the family from time to time; sounds as of dancing in the kitchen when the room was empty; in the dining-room could be heard the crashing of dishes.

Miss Frances A. Walker writes: "I was writing on the dining-room table with door open into the drawing-room when I heard a crash and looked up to see a large blue vase that was on the mantelpiece in there sail by the door and everything slapped off the side of the mantel. The crash was a Japanese teacup and saucer that was broken on the hearth. The vase landed in a big armchair on the other side of the room and I picked it up and restored it to the mantel. The windows were all down and the door shut and there was no one on that floor. It was about 1 o'clock in the day. A heavy candlestick was also knocked off and I found the candle that was in it a few minutes before stuck behind a photograph on the piano!" Miss Walker remarks, "This was queer."

"My sister, Mrs. James, saw an alarm clock suddenly knocked off the mantel in a bedroom. It flew across the room and landed on its feet by the bureau. It went on ticking. This was at night, but the firelight was shining in the room. We were used to strange sounds and occurrences about the haunted house, but in as much as we were never harmed, we paid no particlar attention to these extraordinary happenings, which seemed to have no significance that we could read or comprehend. Nothing ever appeared."

Those Spirits demonstrating after this manner possessed only the power of telekinesis; raps or the movement of objects without contact. This is inferior to the power of materialization. By means of raps they could probably have been able to answer questions; have made their identity known, and to have delivered their message. At Elmwood these Spirits drew attention to their presence by the only means possible to them. With the aid of paper and pencil, the slow repetition of the alphabet, noting each letter as it is followed by a distinct rap, valuable information unknown to the questioning mortal has often been received, and, after investigation, found to be true. By this method many mysteries are solved; many secrets unraveled; many tragedies understood.

THE MIDNIGHT VISITOR

THE land on which Forest Lodge stands, some miles from Winchester, Virginia, was patented to one Lewis Stephens before the Revolution. He and subsequently his son John ran one of the most important taverns on the Valley turnpike, where a change of horses was made. This property was bought about 1869 by Lady Fitzgerald, wife of Viscount Fitzgerald, seeking health for the latter among Virginia's mountains. They moved into the old Inn on New Year's Day 1871 and that night the building burnt, destroying all Lady Fitzgerald's property, and a young maid she brought out from Ireland was burned to death. The large brick house now standing was then erected, and ready for occupancy in 1872.

In 1890 this estate was bought by an Englishman by the name of Doe. The house stands alone at the foot of the mountains about fifty feet above the valley and some distance from the nearest dwelling. It is of brick, a commodious and comfortable dwelling, in the style of a typical Irish country house.

Mr. Haines writes: "My mother's niece Miss Marie Swift graduated at Hannah More School, in Maryland, and later became a governess to Annie Doe, the daughter of Colonel and Mrs. Doe, remaining with the family a number of years. One evening Miss Swift sat reading in the living room, all the other members of the household having retired early. At last to her dismay the clock struck the hour of midnight! She quickly put out the lamp, and groping her way into the hall tiptoed up the stairs. Turning on the landing towards her room, a hand caught her skirt, holding it firmly for an instant! Tearing herself loose she fled into the room in almost a fainting condition. The next morning at breakfast someone sitting near said others had had similar experiences.

Some time later a large house party being entertained, Miss Swift suggested taking a smaller room in another wing of the house, and invited "for company" little Annie Doe, as a roommate. All went well for a short time. Late one night Miss Swift was awakened out of a sound sleep hearing Annie's shrill shrieks of terror! Sitting up in bed beside the frightened child she *saw distinctly* a woman standing at the foot of their bed who stared fixedly at them, and then faded—vanished! Had not Annie also seen this vision my cousin could have persuaded herself she had simply been dreaming, but when both beheld the visitant it was absolute proof they *had* seen a ghost!"

It is just possible this apparition was that of the Irish maid who perished when the Inn was burnt. Hauntings can frequently be traced to a tragedy.

The psychic element in the above sketch—the data of importance—is authentic.

Presented by Mr. William S. D. Haines

My cousin, Marie Swift, died three years ago. At that time she was teaching in St. Timothy's Seminary, Baltimore. Before telling you these ghost stories, I first wrote to my cousin's sister, Mrs. Paul H. Swift of Chicago, who corroborates what I here relate.   WILLIAM S. D. HAINES.

WAVERLEY

NOVEMBER 12, 1735, Alexander Ross, a Scotchman, patented 2,373 acres. He was a prominent Quaker, and established a settlement and erected a meeting-house north of the present town of Winchester. By will, dated October 24, 1748, he left to his widow Catherine, the portion of this patent adjacent to the house "and the house in which we now dwell." The property was called Ross' Spring. This portion passed through several hands named in the deed of Taliaferro Stribling when he sold, March 4, 1826, 578 acres and the house for $15,000, to George Fayette Washington, a great-nephew of George Washington, acting as executor for a descendant of Alexander Ross. Called for more than one hundred years after the magnificent spring becoming the stream of Clearbrook as it flows through the land, the Washingtons changed the name to Waverley.

Standing five miles from Winchester, this old mansion did not altogether escape the ravages of the Civil War. George Fayette Washington's mother was a Miss Frances Bassett, and a portrait of her sister in Philadelphia today, wears a blue ribbon painted across the forehead to hide the scar of a Yankee bullet fired at the beautiful portrait as it hung on the wall of the drawing-room at Waverley seventy years ago.

Major Burwell Byrd Washington inherited the property at his Father's death, in 1867, and it was during his lifetime and that of his widow that the ghostly appearances about to be recorded occurred.

Miss Lily Jolliffe, living within walking distance, went over one afternoon to spend the night. Mrs. Washington and her daughter had their room in the old wing, while Miss Jolliffe was in the guest chamber over the parlor. Mrs. Tappling, formerly Miss Jolliffe, relates that she bolted her door and went to sleep. In the middle of the night she was awakened by the sound of steps on the stair. Believing Mrs. Washington to be ill, Miss Jolliffe called out, "Wait Birdie, I'll let you in," and sat up in bed. Before she could arise the door opened and the gray figure of a man entered. He walked

Waverley

over to the window and stood as though watching the branches of the great sycamores swaying in the October wind. The moon was very bright, the air clear and cold. Presently the figure turned and walking to the foot of the bed looked for some moments down at her. Then turning, he walked out of the room. Miss Jolliffe heard distinctly the door being bolted. The day following she went home and told her father of the terrifying experience.

"Well," he said, "I'll tell you what I know about that room. One night Byrd Washington and myself with two other men were playing cards. We had four candles lighted. In the middle of the game the door opened; a man entered and blew out 'the candles! I can tell you we four left the cards and ran!"

A few days later Miss Jolliffe mentioned to Mrs. Dabney Harrison, of Winchester, that she had been to Waverley.

"Did you see anything?" Mrs. Harrison asked. "Many times I have seen the ghost in that room. One night my little dog was asleep on the foot of my bed. I was awakened by it springing up close to me and trembling all over. Opening my eyes I saw the ghost standing at the foot of the bed."

Ten years later Miss Jolliffe had married and was in Vermont seated on her veranda one afternoon with some friends to whom she was relating her experiences with the ghost at Waverley. Just then the postman brought a letter from her mother. Excusing herself she opened the envelope. It began:

"My dear Lily. Do you recall an experience you had with a ghost one night some years ago at Mrs. Washington's? Nannie Dandridge has just been there and had the same experience, in broad daylight, in the room you occupied."

Mr. Dabney C. Harrison, of Winchester, who lived at Waverley for nineteen years relates the following interesting occurrence:

"I can tell you one peculiar thing that happened. My grandfather was, all his life, an unusually healthy man, never sick. One evening the family was gathered in the dining-room. The old Grandfather clock in the hall had never run in the memory of man. Suddenly it commenced to strike, and struck seventy-nine times. Grandfather was nearly seventy-nine years old. We all talked about it. He was perfectly well. In a few months he died."

A MOTHER'S LOVE

ABOUT the middle of the last century there lived in Appomattox County, Virginia, Dr. and Mrs. Joel W. Flood, who, when he was but a few weeks old, at the death of his mother, adopted their grandson, afterwards Major Joel W. Flood of the Confederacy, and grandfather of Governor Harry F. Byrd of Virginia.

The grandmother placed the little crib in the very center of her large, old-fashioned bedroom, procured an efficient white nurse for him, who slept in the dressing-room that opened into her chamber, and the frail little mite throve lustily and grew into a magnificent baby. He was really a beautiful child and naturally a source of unending comfort and pleasure to his grandmother.

The doctor had a large practice and was often out late at night. On such occasions his wife would not sit up for him, but lighting the swinging lamp on the front porch, leaving the hall light burning, and placing a tray of biscuits and milk on his study-table, would betake herself to slumber.

One night after having been asleep some time, Mrs. Flood wakened with a feeling someone was in the room. Supposing it to be the doctor, she peeped out from between the curtains of her big four-poster bedstead and saw, not the doctor, as she had expected, but the form of a young woman bending over the crib and weeping as though her heart would break. The old lady, astonished and too terrified to speak, fell back on her pillow and covering her head continued to tremble and shiver until her husband came, when she clung to him and told him what she had seen.

The doctor, a practical, unromantic matter-of-fact Presbyterian elder, insisted she had been dreaming, asked what she had eaten for supper, and declared there were no such things as ghosts. His wife was highly indignant at such indifference to her fearful experience, and long after her husband fell asleep remained awake listening to the creaking of the shutters as the wind soughed through the bare branches of the trees, and dreading a return of her ghostly visitor.

At breakfast next morning the doctor made light of his wife's experience to the other members of the family, but could not shake her belief that she had seen the mother of the baby.

A week or so after this the phantom appeared just as before, and again the grandmother was terrified, but the Spirit did not seem inclined to approach the big bed and its trembling occupant, but confined its attentions to the baby sound asleep in the crib.

The grandmother, in spite of her fear, was a woman of great dignity and common sense. Thoroughly convinced God had permitted the young mother to visit her baby, and ashamed of her own cowardice, she determined if the ghost reappeared to speak to it. Always devoted to her son's wife, she felt no harm would befall her. Informing the family of her resolution, she calmly awaited another appearance of her daughter-in-law.

Before a great while the Spirit reappeared, and although unable to keep from trembling with fear, Mrs. Flood raised her head and said, "Daughter!" The ghost looked at her. "Don't be so grieved, my dear, I promise you I will be a good, kind mother to your child." The mother looked at her and smiling sweetly, bent over the baby for a moment, then disappeared. She was never seen again.

The grandmother lived to be an old woman, and to her dying day was firm in the belief that she had seen and spoken to the baby's mother; and the baby, who grew to middle age and past, would mention the occurrence with the greatest reverence and faith in its veracity.

A STORY OF LONG AGO

ON a winding country road in romantic Old Virginia there stood, many years ago, in Appomattox County, a rambling, picturesque old mansion that had been the birthplace and home of four generations of the same family. At the time of the occurrence about to be related the owner was Speaker of the Confederate Congress, and later, for many years represented his State at Washington. The house made no pretensions to architectural beauty, but the various additions made by its successive masters, its irregular front, its old-fashioned diamond-paned casement windows, made bright with boxes of pretty flowers, its many vine-covered porches, some of them very small and in unexpected places, together with its large beautifully shaded lawn, its lovely flower-bordered garden beds and grape arbors, its pretty walks about the grounds and its charming little summer houses placed here and there, made up a picture that was wonderfully attractive and would have satisfied an artist's ideal of Home. Indeed, no more restful, peaceful and comfortable-looking place ever gladdened the eyes of a weary wanderer longing for the scenes and haunts of his childhood days.

The house had originally been painted a dark brown, and it had always been allowed to remain so, and this, together with its steep roof and overhanging eaves, might have given it a sombre look, but all that was offset by its bright windows and pretty porches and grounds, while at night there was always a perfect blaze of light and merriment. It was a hospitable old house. No matter how many guests were gathered there it never seemed to be be crowded and seldom was the week end that did not find a company of "merry gentlemen" and beautiful women seated around its festive board enjoying the cordial hospitality of its master and mistress.

This house, however, like many other old houses, had its mystery, its reputed ghost. The neighborhood knew of it and the servants whispered of it, but no one dared to speak of it to the host, who bitterly resented any suggestion of the kind, although he was said to have seen it. Some few persons professed to be afraid to venture there, but the house was so pleasant and the family so bright and happy, that they could not bring themselves to stay away and the story had almost died out when on a cold, snowy morning in a Christmas week, a sister of the Chatelaine, a young girl of nineteen, whose beautiful voice had been cultivated by several years of study in Europe, and who had never before been in Virginia, and had come to spend Christmas with her, went into the parlor to practice.

The front hall was panelled to the ceiling in dark wood and the stairs, which ran from the far end around to the front, were finished in the same dark wood, consequently this part of the house was very dark, being lighted only by the two side lights of stained glass at the sides of the front door. The door was usually kept closed, so that the front hall got the ill will of servants and children, who imagined it haunted and pretended to have sometimes seen the ghost of an old lady there who smiled at them pleasantly and looked like "Miss Annie" an old aunt of the Master, whom everyone had liked, but who, being a ghost, was to be feared and dreaded. This suspicion, however, was so severely frowned upon by the heads of the house that the subject was rarely mentioned.

When the dinnerbell rang on this particular day the young girl who had been singing looked around the table and said, "Why sister, where is the old lady who came into the parlor while I was singing? I hope I did not offend her. She seemed to be enjoying my song, so I kept on until I finished it, and when I turned to greet her she had left the room. Please apologize to her for me."

The hostess replied, "Why, Elinor, no one has come here today. It has been snowing hard all day and no one could go out or come in during this weather. The snow is fourteen inches deep."

"Well, sister, I am sorry to differ from you, but a strange old lady certainly came to the parlor door this morning while I was singing. She did not enter the room but stood in the doorway with one hand on the doorknob and the other cupped at her ear as if she were deaf, and she had a pleasant smile on her face as if she enjoyed the music. She wore no wraps but seemed as if she belonged to the house."

"How was she dressed?" asked someone. "She wore a black silk dress, with a scarf of some silky material. Her hair was gray and pompadoured; she wore silver-rimmed glasses, and at her side was a silver chain from which hung a bunch of keys."

The people gasped, for she had accurately described the old aunt of the host who was said to haunt the house, and who had lived there and acted as housekeeper for years. She had been very fond of music and had had the habit of standing in the parlor door for a few minutes at a time listening with one hand to her ear to the musician.

The host excused himself and left the table immediately, and the lady of the house said, "Elinor, for God's sake never mention this circumstance again. You saw my husband's aunt, to whom he was devoted, and he cannot bear any mention of her as a ghost. The servants and children have been pretending that they saw her, but we thought it was only a superstitious fancy, but as you had never seen or heard of her nor had ever been here before, I am forced to believe that you really saw her."

VISITORS FROM THE BEYOND

ON a very warm midsummer afternoon, a few years ago, I returned home from my office later than usual and found the hall and drawing-room brilliantly lighted and company present. It was an old fashioned, very high-pitched house, with a wide hall and long staircase on which was a landing and a door that gave entrance to the rear portion of the house, in the passage of which was a south window that was usually kept open because of the breeze from it that cooled the entire upper hall.

Feeling too hot and tired to enter the drawing-room, I started upstairs to my bedroom, and on crossing the landing, midway, I saw a large black dog lying on the steps beyond it and just opposite the rear door that led to the south window. He was apparently asleep, and as a refreshing breeze was blowing in I thought he had selected this place for his afternoon nap because of its cool shadiness, especially as the second floor hall was but dimly lighted, so I was not much surprised when he refused to move or even to open his eyes and notice me when I spoke to him. I again asked him kindly to move and again he refused to notice me. The third time, however, I spoke quite peremptorily, ordering him to get up and let me pass. Then a strange thing happened that startled me very much. Without rising, or moving his head or limbs and continuing to lie on his side with his eyes closed, he glided up the steps and along the hall until he reached the far end and then, without a door being opened, disappeared.

The next night the same thing happened. The dog was lying in exactly the same spot and disappeared when I stamped my foot at him. I did not take my meals in that house and at breakfast time I was always in too great a hurry to meet the family, so they heard nothing about my ghostly visitor. The third night was cool and the dog did not appear; later in the evening the doorbell rang. I was expecting a friend and went down the steps a little way to greet her, and when I got to the place where the dog had lain I felt something jerk my arm violently and I jumped away as if I had been shot. I looked up and down and all around, but not one living thing was in sight except my friend, who was coming up the steps on the other side of the platform. Nothing happened when she came to my room, but when she left, when she got to the place on the stairs where the dog had lain, she fell headlong and struck her head very hard on the oiled floor. She suffered with violent headaches for three months and died from the effects of that fall. I never saw any more of the dog, but shortly afterwards a friend spent an evening with me and we played checkers in my room. The night was warm and I became very thirsty and excused myself to get some water from the cooler in the hall just outside my door. We had been rather jolly and our play had not been very skillful, and as I reached the door I looked back and said, "Now, don't move the men, for I mean to beat you when I get back." Just then I opened the door and started back with a loud cry, for in the very doorway stood the full-length, black, shadowy form of a man. My friend ran to me and as she came the figure moved back into the dark part of the hall and disappeared just as the dog had done, without moving its head or limbs.

I told my friend I was too nervous to play any longer and that I had to pack my things, for nothing could induce me to spend another night in that house. I had a beautiful room with a pleasant family and hated to move, but I was thoroughly frightened. The next day I stayed away from the office and told my landlady I was going to move out and related the circumstances that had occurred to cause my departure. She replied that she and her children had often seen those apparitions and they were not afraid of them, for they recognized the man as being her husband and the dog as his pet dog, who had had a habit of sleeping on the stairs in that very spot in warm weather. She said they never attempted to hurt or frighten anyone, but seemed to wish to be with them and frequent their old home. Her husband, she said, often passed through her boudoir when she was alone there. She asked me if I had ever seen a young lady, and when I said "No," she replied that it was her daughter who often appeared to them, and added that if I were to remain she would appear to me. I moved that day and not very long afterward the old lady passed away and the daughters rented the house and lived elsewhere. I have heard nothing of them for a long time, but I shall always have pleasant recollections of their mother's kindness to me and of her beautiful character. She believed these apparitions to be the spirits of those who had been members of her family who wished to be about her sometimes, and who can prove that they were not, nor blame them if they still loved her and missed her sweet face and loving nature.

ELLERSLIE

IN Brunswick County, Virginia, some miles from the present town of Lawrenceville, may be found today a house representative of the time in which it was built and of the locality in which it stands.

"Ellerslie," built before the Revolution, far from the rooftree of friend or neighbor, standing upon a lonely eminence, remains an interesting reminder of leisurely pursuits and tranquil pleasures; days of plenty and years of prosperity. Shut in in winter by roads well-nigh impassable, and separated by many miles at all seasons from the towns of that period, it stands, a large two-story and basement mansion of frame construction, its depth but that of one large room. The great columns guarding the front door and extending to the roof and the graceful overhanging elms lend dignity and charm. The magnificent box bushes transplanted to the Bishop's garden in the shadow of the walls of the Cathedral of Sts. Peter and Paul, Washington, belong to Ellerslie.

In the rear, among the roots of century-old trees, bubbles forth, as of old, the splendid spring beside which the slaves once churned the butter and placed the pans of milk and jars of cream in water flowing cool beneath the long, low springhouse.

In the kitchen, built not too far from the dwelling, in order that from its great fireplace the contents of the tureens and dishes might be placed smoking hot upon the dinnertable, still may be seen the great iron pot hanging and the spit on which the big roast was turned and returned by some patient little darkie.

Almost out of sight stands the old smokehouse, once filled to the roof with hams and bacon against the coming winter, and here and there, and all around, the little cabins tell their own story and we picture dark forms seated at the doorsteps in the evening, and we listen if perchance some echo from the beautiful tune, "Swing Low, Sweet Chariot," may drift to us upon the summer air. The songs of the darkies are hushed, but now as then the music of Meherrin River sings at the foot of the hill. The stream furnished fine fish for breakfast and all manner of game was plentiful in the surrounding woods.

The property was built and owned by the Hartwell family, and I am told "Old Miss," the mother of the last of the name to dwell beneath the roof of "Ellerslie," was frequently to be seen, dressed in stiff silk with tight bodice and full skirt, coming down the front steps.

The place was bought by Mr. David Dunlop; his niece, Mrs. Elizabeth C. Pearre, writes me of a visit she made with her little girl to "Ellerslie" some twenty years ago. The bedrooms were very large. She with her friend, Mrs. J., slept together, while the children occupied another bed. The night previous there had been much moving of objects in the kitchen. Pots and pans removed from their hooks and placed on the table or in the sink or elsewhere. "Old Miss" was reported again to be walking.

Mrs. Pearre writes, "During the night one of the children was taken slightly ill and Mrs. J. and I both got up to make the child comfortable. We were talking to each other after the children had dropped off to sleep, standing at a little distance from the bed, not close enough to touch it, when we both exclaimed in one breath, 'What is that?' Having simply laid the two fresh sheets on the bed what we saw, and saw plainly, was the sheets being quickly and deftly tucked in all around the big bed by unseen hands! We looked on in silence. When the work was finished the bed looked smoothly and neatly made. Not frightened, only mystified, our sleep the rest of the night was sound and undisturbed."

Did "Old Miss" enter the room and rebuke as best she could the careless ways and habits of mothers of today whose care of children did not meet with her approval?

GREEN HILL

IN Buckingham County, about fifty miles from Lynchburg on a high grassy hill overlooking the very wide and deep river a quarter of a mile below, the woods in the dim distance, and surrounded by locusts, "Green Hill" stood for 170 years, and was once the home of Col. John Cabell.

Within, amid weeds and briars, may be found the sunken tomb of Colonel Cabell.

Built in 1762 of heart pine, two stories, with a cellar and dormer windows in the shingled attic; two sturdy chimneys stood at either end. Approached by steep flights of steps, the roofs of the high porches were supported by tall white pillars.

Beyond the garden two splendid springs still flow ceaselessly beneath ancient spring houses, and the office in the yard survives the desolating hand of Time.

John Cabell, born in 1742, was the third son of Dr. William Cabell and Elizabeth Burks. He married Paulina, daughter of Col. Samuel Jordan, May 20, 1762, at 8 P. M. His second wife was Elizabeth Brierton Jones, the wedding taking place July 19, 1787. Colonel Cabell was a man of importance and of influence. In 1774 he was sheriff of Buckingham County and delegate to the Convention at Williamsburg. Represented the county in the General Assembly of Virginia in 1777, etc., etc. His brother William, under date of April 14, 1769, writes in his diary: "Swap'd my blazed-face mare with John Cabell for his grey horse." "Nov. 30, 1769, paid Mr. Pattison of Williamsburg fifteen shillings for repairing John Cabell's watch."

Colonel Cabell is said to have been a man of a fiery temper and strong will. Those who followed him seemed to regard his memory with a good deal of awe and to feel that on small provocation he returned to overlook in Spirit where he had ruled in the flesh.

Like many of his time, Colonel Cabell had his superstitions, and he also had Spirits to overlook his welfare. In his early days it seems he was not a religious man. One night, probably after the death of his second wife in 1802, he was lying in the big parlor before a huge log fire. Suddenly the great hall upon which the parlor opened was filled with an unearthly wind. Turning to see what was causing this Colonel Cabell saw, standing by a large table upon which rested the family Bible, three female figures. The pages of the Bible were turning rapidly, from beginning to end, although no hand touched it. Colonel Cabell felt this was a call to him to study the Holy Book, which from this time he did, and became a devout believer.

Long after his death in 1815 one night the family and some friends were trying "table rappings." After calling for several Spirits, someone asked for Col. John Cabell. Again and again the mortal demanded the return of Colonel Cabell. No response at length caused him to exclaim, "Oh, he was a hot tempered, contrary man when living and he is the same man when dead." At this moment the large mahogany-table with heavy marble top rose up bodily high into the air, flinging the candles to the floor and crashing down again, scattered those formerly gathered around it never to gather again!

The hall doors at Green Hill were not only locked but barred with heavy wooden timbers held in place by iron hooks. One evening while the family and a visitor were in the sitting-room laughing and talking, from no visible cause, the heavy bar across the front door was flung aside and the door burst open! An immediate search revealed no normal explanation. Someone remarked: "Something must have displeased Colonel John!" Constant rappings were heard in different parts of the house. Everyone felt the Colonel continued to hold sway over his family and earthly possessions long after he had gone to the Spirit world.

The vicissitudes of war removed Green Hill from the possession of the descendants of Colonel Cabell, the property passing into other hands. The purchaser evidently had reason to know that the ghost of Colonel Cabell continued his interest in his old home, for it is said he became so terrified he refused to sleep alone in a room, declaring Colonel Cabell came and pulled the clothes off the bed!

IVANHOE

IN Campbell County, Virginia, near the James, the mountains a lovely ridge of blue along the sky line, stands a large but unpretentious old dwelling full of psychic romance and charm.

In December 1819 Sir Walter Scott published his novel "Ivanhoe" and sent an autographed copy to his kinsman Colonel Edward Ball Withers in Campbell County, Virginia. I am indebted to his granddaughter Mrs. Cora L. Mosby and to Miss Anne Rodé, the present owner, for the following events in the history of their old place. Miss Rodé's father purchased it sixty-four years ago, and repairs since made, suggest the house to have been built about 1780.

The ghost in lavender, whose dust doubtless rests in an ivy covered grave in the old burying ground, is believed to have been the wife of the original owner. This old property, once comprising several thousand acres, has from time to time furnished generous farms for branches of the family tree; charming log houses erected in the shade of old sycamores and locusts, and bearing such happy names as "Crystal Spring" and "Hickory Hollow." Mrs. Mosby tells me of a pedlar murdered in one of the upper rooms in the long ago. The family was never disturbed, but guests occupying the room heard alarming noises, had the bedclothes removed in the night, or found them on the floor upon entering to retire! Two young men saw a pillow fly across the room! All Miss Rodé knows about the pedlar is the bloodstain on the floor. She always occupied that room. All means to remove the stain were unavailing. Shortly after staining the floor, the spot would reappear! Marks remain where evidently an attempt had once been made to burn it out! During her father's lifetime frequently could be heard between nine and ten at night the sound as of a heavy weight or body falling; he would investigate but could never discover the cause. A guest once asked if the noise did not prove annoying. "By no means," Mr. Rodé replied, "I would not give my ghost for one thousand dollars!" Some nights could be heard apparently near the house the sound as of the heavy strokes of an ax chopping a tree; and very noticeable was the well known labored breathing incidental to the exertion of chopping. No servant could be induced to leave, or approach the house after dark.

Miss Rodé has had but one experience with the ghost on the stairway. Late one night she recalled having left a borrowed book on a bench in the yard. After securing the volume, as she reached the steps a woman she imagined to be her sister appeared on the stairway. Putting out her hand to take her arm, Miss Rodé was amazed and frightened to have her hand go clean through the figure! In the moonlight, the dress appeared to be white, or some light color, and the figure very lifelike.

Mrs. Mosby tells me of a lovely ghost dressed in lavender frequently seen coming down or going up the stairway; at night sometimes; again during the day. She was slender, had dark hair, and wore on her breast a bunch of violets. As she passed, the scent of the flowers was strong and delightful! Until quite recently, Miss Mary Rodé, whose hearing is imperfect, had never heard of the Lavender Lady of those far off days when the Mosby family lived at Ivanhoe. Upon being told, Miss Mary seemed quite startled and exclaimed: "Why, do you know, upon several occasions in the hall after shutting the front door, I have noticed the scent of violets. So unmistakable has been the perfume that I have said to myself, 'What nonsense, there can be no violets at this season.'"

One summer afternoon, all doors and windows wide open while the family were from home, some people drove up seeking direction, having missed their way. Seeing a lady dressed in lavender seated on the porch, a man approached, hat in hand. His astonishment may be imagined when the figure in lavender suddenly vanished from sight!

TELEKENESIS IN LYNCHBURG

M R. WILLIAM NELSON WELLFORD of Roanoke, Va., writes me that about 1840 his grandfather Colonel James Maurice Langhorne built and owned the house at the corner of Jackson and Eleventh Streets, Lynchburg, "and the ghosts were at work as far back as I can remember."

Mrs. John Wallace of Fredericksburg, sister of Mr. William Nelson Wellford, writes that when her grandfather William Nelson Wellford lived in the house it was "dreadfully haunted." The remarkable phenomena were so numerous and of such frequency she can by no means recollect them all. Her mother told her she often had seen the servants drop on their knees exclaimnig "Oh, God!" then stand up and say "A ghost brushed by me!" Her mother and oldest sister told her that on numerous occasions after the servants were through in the kitchen in the afternoon, everything left in order, closed and locked up; from upstairs it would sound as if many servants were busily preparing for a great banquet—hurried footsteps to and fro; the opening and shutting of doors, rattling of china and silver, etc., etc. Investigation would reveal pantry doors open, kitchen range door open, pots and pans strewed all about; everything in confusion!

One day when Mrs. Wallace was a child her mother herself prepared a guest room for an old uncle arriving from New York. Just before train time she went in to put water in the pitcher. To her horror the bed had been unsheeted, and all the linen and bedclothes had been tossed into the middle of the room in a bundle; all bric-a-brac, pictures, etc., were piled on the floor; the room in a state of utmost confusion! Her mother had often seen the keys in the little old leather key basket kept on the side table, jump up and down as if some one was shaking the basket violently.

Mrs. Wallace herself has seen "the walls shake up and down, and felt it too!" Such remarkable and unbelievable tales were told of happenings in the old house that two of her mother's nephews, Norwell and Wister Langhorne, said they would go there alone some day and see for themselves if there be any truth in the tales.

What with unseen hands touching them, walls shaking, keys dropping, doors slamming, they not only believed but had had enough and left!

Mr. Wellford writes: "I will tell you some of the antics. An old sewing machine would run just any time it got ready. A cradle would rock in the same way. The doors to the kitchen stove would open just any old time, and it was useless to lock a door because it would open as soon as your back was turned.

"Just below this house a few blocks, there was a row of shanties for negroes, owned by Colonel Leftwich and known as Leftwich row. Just in front of this row there was a small stream. Every night a white mule would graze, and on account of no one being able to capture the mule the negroes became frightened, moved away, and it was finally necessary to tear down the shanties."

When Mr. Wellford moved, the house was so haunted no one would either rent or buy. It was finally sold for a boys' school. The demonstrations gradually subsided. The house has been repaired and is now a dwelling once more.

Center Hill, Petersburg, Virginia

THE SPIRIT AT THE WINDOW

THE Marquis de Chastellux in his Memoirs says: "Mrs. Robert Bolling's house, or rather houses, for she has two on the same line resembling each other which she proposes to join together, are situated on the summit of a considerable slope which rises from the level of the town of Petersburg, Virginia."

The large mansion "Center Hill" was built prior to the Revolution by Robert Bolling, whose grandfather bearing the same name emigrated from England. Robert Bolling 3rd served in the Revolution as Captain of Volunteer Cavalry, and married November 4, 1781, Mary, daughter of Robert Bolling of Chellow.

The massive old brick mansion facing the square as you approach is embellished by a splendid flight of steps leading to an immense porch, an architectural design of dignity and charm. Until quite recently an office with rooms above, and built near the old burying ground, stood just to the rear. A little passage connected the two buildings.

Forty-five years ago Mrs. Campbell Pryor who was Anne Bannister, a direct descendant of the builder of "Center Hill," lived there for ten years. To her I am indebted for an account of the remarkable happenings of which she had personal knowledge.

Every evening anyone passing by about twilight could see "a beautifully dressed lady" seated at the second story window over the front door. One morning at the breakfast table, Bannister Pryor, aged six, asked: "Mother, where is the pretty lady who came and sat on my bed last night. She held my hand and talked to me. I do not see her?" The child then described the Spirit seen by so many seated at the window. Her identity was never discovered.

Mrs. Pryor speaks of a little melodeon standing in one corner of the library. "Many, many times familiar airs have been heard played by invisible hands, as no mortal was in the room."

For some time Mr. Pryor sought to occupy as a bed chamber a small room on the first floor near the office. The attempt was abandoned! No matter how securely tucked in were the bed clothes, soon after the lights were turned out invisible hands jerked the coverings off the bed and threw them onto the middle of the floor!

For ten years on the 24th day of January at half past seven in the evening a demonstration occurred of interest to the entire neighborhood. Friends gathered in the drawing room to await the never failing phenomenon. On that day of the year the clock pointing to the half hour, the door leading into the office was heard to open. Then a noise such as of a regiment of soldiers marching! The clank as of sabres suggested the occupation of those tramping along the passage; up the stair and into a room over the office. After about twenty minutes the sound was again heard descending the steps, crossing the hall, then finally the slamming of a door and all was quiet.

A CONTINENTAL CHAPLAIN

THE Reverend John Braidfoot, second rector of Trinity Church, Portsmouth, Virginia, was a Scotchman who came to this country at the solicitation of his friend, Reverend Charles Smith, first rector of the parish. He was ordained in London in 1772 at the same time as John Peter Muhlenburg, and in charge from 1773, he remained faithful to his parish during the Revolution, serving as Chaplain in the Continental Army.

At the formation of the State of Virginia the Legislature confiscated all glebes where the vestries were unable to purchase them. The glebe formerly belonging to Trinity is now a part of the Port Norfolk section of Portsmouth.

The Reverend John Braidfoot married Blondine Mosely and had one son, William. A great-granddaughter of the Rev. John Braidfoot and also another relative state that after the Revolution, the Anglican Communion being disestablished and many churches closed, throughout this period her great-grandfather continued to live in the rectory at the glebe, visiting his scattered flock in order to keep in touch with them. In this way he passed much time making parochial calls.

Driving home one evening, his horse stopped suddenly, and Mr. Braidfoot perceived an "apparition" standing in the road. Astonished, but not unduly alarmed, he awaited in silence some further demonstration from this Spirit from another sphere. The Rev. Mr. Braidfoot's great-granddaughter informs me her grandmother stated the apparition spoke to her grandfather, telling him that upon the following 6th of February he would die at home. This prophesy was imparted to his wife. Upon three or four occasions, in the same manner—while driving along some country road —the phantom appeared and repeated the same dire prophesy.

As the fateful day approached Mrs. Braidfoot, hoping to divert her husband's mind, made plans for a large dinner party to be held on that particular day. While this dinner was in progress, the clergyman excused himself and went up to his room. He did not reappear, and later was found dead. There were no signs of violence.

Rev. John Braidfoot

Rev. Mr. Braidfoot was buried at the glebe. There seems some discrepancy as to the year of his death. A "marker" bearing his name was placed in Trinity Churchyard by the Daughters of the American Revolution. The records of Trinity Parish give the date 1784.

SOLDIER'S JOY

"GREEN HILL," Buckingham County, Virginia, once the home of Colonel John Cabell, and to which after death he returned again and again to oversee his former possessions, is no more; but journeying into Nelson County we may find the home of his brother Colonel Samuel Jordan Cabell, a gallant soldier throughout the Revolution. This dwelling bears, even unto our day, the inspiring name of "Soldier's Joy." Built by Colonel William Cabell of "Union Hill" for his son, records inform us that Samuel Cabell and his wife left "Union Hill" and went to live in their new home in 1785.

After the passing of 145 years "Soldier's Joy," a two-story frame building, still stands surrounded by many locusts and other forest trees; but the two long low wings, adding a note alike of charm and of comfort, have disappeared; and the famous paneling carved in France for the large lofty ball room, alien hands in our day have sold to embellish the walls of "Mirador," the former home of Lady Astor.

Miss Caroline Cabell writes me: "Remodeled, the house bears faint resemblance to the old 'Soldier's Joy' we knew and loved." Over the old graveyard in springtime the scent of locust blossoms still perfumes the air; and here, 113 years ago, the Revolutionary officer ended life's warfare.

Miss Cabell writes me: "The ghost at 'Soldier's Joy,' while invisible, is distinctly audible, and has been heard in the dead of night by many."

One stormy night, not long after Samuel Cabell moved into his house, there was a loud knocking at the front door, and a servant ushered in a repulsive looking pedlar, who demanded lodging for the night. Colonel Cabell—the soul of hospitality—at first declined to take the man in owing to his forbidding countenance; but the pedlar was loudly insistent, almost threatening; the rain was descending in torrents, and neighbors far distant, so Colonel Cabell finally gave a reluctant consent and told the servant to give the stranger supper, and to take him for the night to a room in the far wing. About one o'clock in the night Colonel Cabell awoke suddenly. The storm had subsided and by the pale gleams of a watery moon he saw the evil-faced pedlar standing over him holding in his hand a long sharp knife! Ere the weapon accomplished its purpose, a blow delivered with terrific force landed, sending the pedlar reeling backward! His head striking the sharp edge of a heavy old wardrobe, the man fell to the floor like a log and the blood from a deep cut streamed upon the pine floor! Colonel Cabell called for lights and the servants. The pedlar was dead! "The stain has never left the floor," says Miss Cabell. "I myself have seen it, but I have never heard the thud. In my youth I was too much afraid of hearing it to be willing to spend a night at 'Soldier's Joy.' I have talked with those who have heard it, and who say 'the sound is inexplicable.'"

Since that night more than a century ago, when Colonel Cabell's presence of mind saved his life, at about that same hour of the night there has often been heard near the ancient stain the dull heavy thud as of a body falling!

Oakridge, Nottoway County, Virginia

THE VOICE

"**O**AKRIDGE," Nottoway County, Virginia, was built about 1800 by Richard Smith. The plantation of four thousand acres necessitated among other buildings the master's office, kitchen not too far off, and at some little distance quarters for the slaves. This old dwelling may still be found four miles from a small village grouped about Nottoway Court House. Mrs. George W. Cabell, "Englewood," Shipman, Va., writes: "My grandfather, Captain Warner Wortham Guy, was born at 'Song Credit,' Caroline County, Virginia, in 1797. He married his first wife, Hannah Scott, January 3, 1822. She died in 1840. In 1842 he moved to 'Oakridge,' and here married Mary Peyton Smith. His first remarkable experience occurred about 1853, and the second in 1859—grandfather died in 1863. My father told me he was at home and in the hall when grandfather was told to 'take the ten o'clock train'! The vision in lavender, descendants believe to have been their grandmother."

The following was told by Colonel William Scott Guy: "My father was much worried—he was certain he had paid a large sum to a wholesale place from which he had been getting supplies. After several months it was discovered he had not been credited with this payment, and, if the receipt could not be produced the money must again be paid. Diligent search had been made in every possible place, but without success. One morning father had again looked everywhere, and was resting on the sofa believing the receipt lost. In a few moments he raised up and asked his wife who was sewing nearby, 'Who was that touched me?' She told him no one had been in the room. Whereupon he explained that some one touched him and said, in an urgent way, 'Look in the bank book!' Mrs. Guy assured him he had been dreaming. He lay down again, and in a few moments jumped up declaring he had again had this experience! He then decided to go to the office and look in his bank book. To his surprise and delight, there in the book was the missing receipt.

"Several years after this he was once more in trouble! If he could raise a considerable sum in cash he could make a very desirable investment. He had been trying for a week or two to dispose of some stocks without sacrifice, but finally decided he must either borrow the money or give up the investment, neither of which he wanted to do. As it happened, he was again lying on the same sofa one afternoon when he felt someone touch him and say, 'Take the ten o'clock train'! Turning, he thought he saw a woman in lavender near the door. He sat up, rubbed his eyes and no one was there! Going into the hall, he told the family, sitting there talking. They were sure it was a dream, having forgotten the episode of the lost receipt. He lay down once more, but in a few minutes returned to say that someone had again touched him and said as before: 'Take the ten o'clock train'! By this time someone recalled the lost receipt and then all fell to urging father to take the ten o'clock train, which did not go until the next day. Next morning in good time for the train, he ordered his horse, and rode to Nottoway where arrangements were made to care for his horse several days. The train was then boarded without knowing how long the journey would be. While sitting beside a friend, a man approached and spoke to father's friend. An introduction followed; in a very few minutes this man said he wished to buy some South Side Railway stock. My father owned such stock, and found the stranger was willing to pay cash and to purchase for the price father was anxious to obtain. Needless to say he got off at the next station, and caught the first train for home!"

BACON'S CASTLE

A SUBSTANTIAL and picturesque old brick dwelling pronounced to be "the only surviving Jacobean house in Virginia," stands in Surry County, and brings to us from the far-off Colonial period a picture of stormy experiences and uncertain tomorrows. The massive hand-wrought beams, low ceilings, deep window seats, curiously fashioned fireplaces, wide floorboards and narrow stairway speak to us of far-off things, a time of simple living and of frugal habits. The day of the tallow dip, when bedtime closely followed the setting of the sun. Those who in bitter winter weather sought such comfort as the burning logs furnished in 1650 when Arthur Allen built this home, faced many hardships besides winter's cold and many days of anxious uncertainty, the depths of which we can dimly imagine, but never completely fathom. Indians were never very far off and disease and death an ever-present menace.

Owned in 1667 by Arthur Allen, Jr., a Speaker of the House of Burgesses, and a warm friend of Sir William Berkeley, the homestead was seized by Nathaniel Bacon, whose troops made of it a stronghold for nearly four months. Ever since that time it has been known as Bacon's Castle.

Mr. and Mrs. Charles W. Warren are the fortunate owners of Bacon's Castle today. Mrs. Warren has very kindly furnished some interesting data concerning happenings within the old Castle.

"A Baptist minister we all liked, and who was a frequent visitor, asked one night that he might sit up for a while after we went up and do some reading. The next morning he said:

" 'Mrs. Charles, I had an experience last night. Sitting here reading my book with great interest, I heard footsteps coming downstairs. Thinking you had sent the maid for something, I did not look up even when the door opened and the steps came by me, but when a chair on the other side of the fireplace began to rock, I did look, and possibly said something! The chair stopped and there was no other noise.' "

One morning at breakfast a guest asked, "Mrs. Warren, is there

Bacon's Castle

someone ill in the room over mine?" When told there was no one sick or well in the room, he said, "I was awakened by such sounds of distress I thought of going up and offering to help if possible, but decided to wait. After a while all was quiet and I went to sleep."

In that room is a very interesting loveletter scratched on a pane of glass.

Mrs. Warren tells of her personal experiences.

"Many nights I've lain awake listening to footsteps on the stairs, never stopping, just step, step. I've gone to my door and looked out, thinking surely I would see someone.

" 'The Castle light' has been one of mystery for so long and seen by so many. Often after a stay from home the servants have asked me to look in this room or that one. 'The light stayed in there a long time last night,' they would say. I never found any disturbance. So many times we have watched it going from field to field, around the barns and stable, but the nearest it ever came was a night when we were sitting on the porch. A beautiful ball of lovely colors suddenly appeared, stayed a minute, then left as quickly as it came."

"One night I was awakened feeling there was someone looking at me. I opened my eyes and sure enough I saw a sweet white face, large black eyes, black hair neatly parted, and a white scarf around the head. I called the maid who answered from her bed; then I called 'Charlie!' There seemed a long breath or deep sigh, and she was gone. Another time she appeared. I was not asleep, but felt this same presence. Sure enough, there she was! The same sweet white face. I said nothing. We just looked into each other's eyes. The same breath of air, and she was gone!"

One morning the maid as usual called under the window for the key. Soon she came, asking if I had been in the sitting-room. I was the last to come up the night before and had left the room in order. This is what I found, a large nickel round burner-lamp had been taken off the table and was leaning against the pedestal. Not a drop of oil anywhere. The globe smashed in many pieces and scattered about the floor. A large Webster dictionary opened and placed carefully on the sofa; the stand moved to another part of the room. To move these articles required some force."

THE PASSING OF A SOUL

THE following remarkable phenomenon is related by Miss Anne Seymour Ames. It happened to Miss Ames' Father and aunt—Alfred and Elizabeth. Her Father, Alfred Ames, was born on the old family plantation "Ames' Ridge" in Accomac County, on the Eastern Shore of Virginia. The Ames house, a large double brick house, constructed with the usual wide hall and four square rooms, was a typical Southern home, designed both for comfort, as it was understood in that day, and for a generous hospitality for which that region has for generations been noted.

Of a family of staunch Protestant Episcopal inheritance, young Alfred Ames was sent to Dickinson College, Pennsylvania, where he embraced Methodism and became a minister of power and high standing in that branch of the Christian Church. At one time Rev. Mr. Ames was pastor of the old McKendree Southern Methodist Church, one of the largest congregations of that denomination at the Capital. Miss Anne Seymour Ames' Aunt Elizabeth—her Father's sister—married the Rev. Charles Hall. Dr. Hall was many years ago rector of the Episcopal Church of the Epiphany, Washington, D. C., and was quite a noted preacher. Later he was called to be the rector of Holy Trinity, Brooklyn Heights.

Alfred Ames was nine years old when he and his brother Edward, two years older, were both sick of malarial fever so prevalent in that part of Virginia. The boys were in separate beds in a great big old-fashioned nursery. They were nursed by members of the family and by the servants, trained nurses being unknown at that time and in that locality. Neither of the children were thought to be very ill; Miss Ames' Father was considered the more seriously affected of the two.

It so happened the two boys were alone in the nursery in their beds, the family and servants for the time being out of the room. Suddenly this boy of nine who knew nothing of death, his mother having died some time before, suddenly became aware that his brother's soul was passing—that he was dying!. The game most played by these three children was battledore and shuttle-cock, and to the child nine years old what he saw was most like one of the white feathers of a shuttle-cock.

Alfred Ames never told this experience, but the episode was indelibly imprinted on his mind and memory. His brother had died very suddenly and entirely unexpectedly. In after years he wrote of the event in his diary, but his diary was his sole and secret confidant.

Rev. Mr. Ames and his sister Elizabeth died within six days of each other. About two or three years before their deaths, both being in perfect health, with no apprehension of death for either, Elizabeth, who was at the time of her brother's sudden death a child of about five, said to Rev. Mr. Ames one day: "Brother Alfred, I want to tell you something I have never told a soul. *I saw the soul of our brother leave his body!* I opened the nursery door and crept in, and I saw his soul—like a white feather—freed and floating upward." Mr. Ames answered, "Sister, I too saw the same thing happen. I have never spoken of it to a soul, but here it is recorded in my diary," and he showed her the place.

These are the testimonials of a man and a woman of unimpeachable veracity and integrity, of standing in the Church and in the community.

It is interesting to recall that the philosopher, William James, writing of the aura, says that if he could describe what is indiscribable, from the very nature of the case, he would liken the phenomenon to the resemblance of a white feather in form and motion.

A GREAT MYSTERY

THE Rye Cove Virginia Consolidated School stood on a high plateau in the rolling hills between the mountains. A frame two-story building of seven rooms. Of its complement of 250 pupils, over two hundred were in attendance on the morning of the third of May, 1929.

Sweeping into the Nolichuckey Valley the tornado struck about half a mile down the valley from the school, overturned several buildings before ripping the two-story frame school asunder and strewing the wreckage over a distance of several hundred yards. Some of the children were blown one hundred feet from the building, while others were buried in the debris. Twelve children and one teacher were dead; fifty-two children and some teachers taken to the hospital. Floyd Noblin, principal of the school, said, "I saw the storm coming up the valley and ran into the building. The schoolhouse collapsed just after I entered, and I knew nothing more until I had been pulled from the wreckage."

The tornado literally lifted the building from its foundations, leaving the floors. The upper story disintegrated as the wind tore it asunder, pieces of the wreckage being blown in some instances more than four hundred yards away.

One of the corps of eight teachers, Miss Effie Flanary, a seventh-grade teacher, of whom the division superintendent speaks as "a mature woman and very reliable," writes me as follows:

"About 10 o'clock in the morning I was teaching a review class in the sixth grade mathematics and was solving a problem on the board for their observation. Suddenly something like a nicely finished mahogany table appeared at my right side, and a flash of something like lightning came down the wall and across the table and split it in two along an irregular line. I can't say if it were a voice or thought which came to me in these words, 'Rye Cove is not a safe place to be.'

"I turned from the board to my desk, laid my book on the desk and thought I would go to Prof. Noblin and ask him to dismiss the school. I looked about the room to find some pupil to send to him, and then I decided I would go myself as I believed I could tell him better than anyone whom I might send. Before I took one step towards the door the thought all left me as suddenly as it came! I never thought of the incident until that afternoon after I had been brought home, probably about 4 p. m. The tragedy occurred about 1:30 or 1:45.

"About a month before the building was destroyed I dreamed of teaching in a new and entirely different building, and all about were evidences of a newly constructed building.

"Again I dreamed of going back to begin school in a new and strange building, but with a number of my regular students, but they seemed strange and different."

Lying in a baggage car, being taken to the hospital at Bristol, someone said to a child of eight, "Sonny, are you tired of waiting?" The reply was, "Mister, after what I've seen today, I'm glad to be alive. I could wait the rest of the night."

A FARMER'S DREAM

IN 1909 there was a lonely cabin situated in the woods of Wythe County, Virginia, in the vicinity of Wytheville. This cabin was owned and occupied by two brothers, elderly men, of retiring habits, and walking into the town only when it was necessary in order to make such small purchases as their needs required.

As fancy generally attributes wealth to those who shun society and bury themselves in the solitude of the woods, so these men, T. C. Stuart and W. J. Stuart, although poor, were generally spoken of as possessing hidden treasure.

Two or three miles from the home of these peaceful and harmless old men lived a farmer, their nearest neighbor. On the night of April 17, 1909, he dreamed he saw three men going up the road towards the cabin. He saw them plainly—two negroes and one white man. One man limped as he walked.

In his dream the farmer followed them and saw them pause under a crooked tree at the turn of the road. They seemed to be plotting murder and robbery. They went on. In his dream the farmer did not see them enter the cabin, but he seemed to go ahead, and saw the two old men murdered on the floor. One lay near the hearth, with one hand stretched out towards a hole in the floor near the fireplace. In the hole was a tin box. The other brother lay in a corner of the hut with his head crushed. Papers were scattered about. The farmer awakened and told his wife of his dream. He asked if she had seen the two brothers pass by recently. She had not seen them for three days. Her husband said he felt sure there must be something wrong, and though he tried to again go to sleep, he could not do so.

He arose at daylight, called the sheriff, telling him every detail of his dream. The sheriff and others accompanied the farmer to the lonely cabin. As they passed the old tree at the turn of the road they found an empty tin box and papers scattered around. The box was such as the farmer had seen in his dream.

They continued to the house and found the cabin had been set on fire and was still burning and within the partially consumed bodies of two human beings. These were identified as those of the brothers. The smaller of the two skeletons was lying near the fireplace, and a physician who examined the skull discovered leaden pellets embedded in the bone which he identified as shot. The remains of the other man were found in a corner of the room with the head missing, as though severed from the body.

The community was aroused and active measures taken to apprehend the guilty parties. The farmer's description of the two negroes —one lame—and a white man seen in his dream was so clear that two months later the three men were arrested and sentenced.

Later the Court of Appeals reversed the decision of the lower court, on the ground of insufficient evidence, and the men were released. To date this was the only record of a dream being admitted as evidence in a trial for murder. Supreme Court of Appeals of Virginia January 12, 1911.

THE RETURN OF THE PRODIGAL

ONE Spring the vestry of the Episcopal Church at Berkeley Springs, West Virginia, engaged a clergyman, Mr. Arnold by name. Mrs. Arnold was a native of New Orleans and a relative of Lady Astor.

Miss Belle Cross, the well-known and gifted psychic, lived then at Berkeley Springs and had a summer cottage at Blue Ridge Summit.

In the late Fall the vestry of the church decided to retrench by closing the church doors for the winter. Miss Cross, endued with a Christian spirit, offered Rev. and Mrs. Arnold shelter in her mountain cottage. This offer they gladly accepted. Later Miss Cross joined them.

The first week passed comfortably. One night the rector was called to Washington for the week-end. Mrs. Arnold, after sitting by the fire reading "Fifty Years in a Maryland Kitchen," went into her bedroom adjoining, leaving the door open for the extra heat. Miss Cross put aside her knitting and went to her room upstairs.

As Miss Cross entered her room she perceived an overpowering smell of stale liquor, the atmosphere close as though unaired after a carousal. She seemed obsessed by a great sense of fear, something never before experienced by her in the cottage.

Suddenly she saw a large man of blonde type, hair brushed back from his forehead, and handsomely dressed. Miss Cross said mentally, "What does this mean?" He heard, for he pointed down the stairs to Mrs. Arnold's bedroom and said, "I belong to her." With that he vanished.

The next morning Miss Cross said to Mrs. Arnold, "Did you have anyone who drank among your connections?" As Miss Cross said this the man appeared again, standing between herself and

Mrs. Arnold. She could describe him accurately and again felt a sense of terror.

As Miss Cross spoke Mrs. Arnold's face blanched, alarming Miss Cross to such an extent she said, "I will not tell you any more."

Mrs. Arnold replied, "Go on, you have described my first husband, of whom I have not spoken for thirty years, and who died of wine and women. I know nothing of spirit return, but I believe it possible and would like a word from him."

Miss Cross then picked up a pencil. The pencil was violently controlled, digging deeply, and writing in wild haste, "What one word could I say but *forgive! forgive! forgive!*

A few minutes later the pencil moved slowly and wrote in a fine delicate hand:

"My dear child, God is love. Love can bring no evil to its object. What you thought evil was but given you to strengthen you spiritually. I am with you often. I love you still."

Mrs. Arnold said, "That is my mother's writing and I will give you evidence of it for your work."

Mrs. Arnold's husband appeared to her a week later and asked to be forgiven. At first she refused, but forgave him, asking him to help her.

Very shortly Mr. Arnold obtained supply work leading to a comfortable country parish where they now live.

A STORY OF CIVIL WAR DAYS

DURING the years of the Civil War there lived in the little village of Bath, Virginia—now Berkeley Springs, West Virginia—the family of Capt. Johnson Orrick, of a well-known Virginia family. Capt. Orrick was in the Confederate Army camped near Winchester. His wife and three little children lived in a cottage having two long porches upper and lower, across the entire side length of the house. At the extreme end of the house and opening upon the lower porch was a sleeping room for "Millie," the one maid who had remained in Mrs. Orrick's service. This room had no door opening into the house, and it was Mrs. Orrick's custom to lock the maid's door from the outside, and take the key, in order to get to Millie if need arose late in the night. Millie was a very tall and slender mulatto, quiet, of much dignity, and little given to conversation.

One night about 9 o'clock Mrs. Orrick had seen Millie to her room and locked the door as usual. She then entered the cottage, closed and locked the doors, and ascended to her own room where the three little children were sleeping. This room had two small windows and a door opening onto the *upper* porch. There was no entrance to this porch, save through this bedroom, and all doors into the room were locked.

Mrs. Orrick had but a dim candlelight in order not to disturb the children. The moonlight was very bright, and chancing to glance towards the windows looking upon this upper porch Mrs. Orrick was surprised to see Millie walking up and down the porch. She had on her blue checked dress and her little brown shawl was pinned around her shoulders. Going to the window Mrs. Orrick spoke to her gently, but received no response. She then stood and

watched her for several minutes. The woman stopped from time to time and gazed steadily far away toward the low mountain range walling in the little town. As this was in 1863 all ears and eyes were tuned for sights or sounds suggesting a coming attack of the enemy. Thinking Millie might be hearing some distant sound,

Mrs. Orrick quietly opened the door onto the porch to question the girl. Lo, Millie, in plain view a moment before, had vanished!

There was no place for Millie to go! Only through Mrs. Orrick's room could entrance to the gallery be gained. She closed the door and hurried downstairs. Passing along the lower porch she reached Millie's room. Unlocking the door, the girl was found fast asleep and completely undressed. All questions next day failed to throw any light upon the strange occurrence.

But two days later, as Mrs. Orrick was on her way to meet her husband, who had obtained a twenty-four-hour furlough and permission to meet her beyond the lines, a messenger hailed her carriage and took her to a house where her husband lay dying, the victim of a "bush-whacker's" bullet. Capt. Orrick smiled in recognition and was gone.

A few months later Mrs. Orrick again saw Millie, this time about midnight, walking to and fro in the yard. At the time the girl was sound asleep in the room adjoining that of Mrs. Orrick, due to the illness of one of the children. Less than forty-eight hours later Mrs. Orrick's father was stricken with paralysis and passed away.

Some years later Mrs. Orrick removed to Baltimore. Millie was either dead or lost down in Virginia; the family never knew. Mrs. Orrick, lying on her bed, awake and with a light burning, saw Millie walk through her room, wearing the familiar blue checked dress. The next night Mrs. Orrick's mother was stricken with apoplexy and never rallied.

Similar instances are related by other members of the family of seeing Millie when she was known to be miles away; but only just prior to death or grave illness. It was the custom, whenever possible, to bring Millie to do the "laying out" for all the kith and kin of "her folks." She never accepted her freedom. The travelling of the astral is a well-known phenomenon.

PRIEST'S FIELD

From the Shepherdstown, West Virginia, *Register* of Thursday, November 8, 1922; and extracts from a letter written to Mrs. C. G. Doll, April 11, 1839, by the Missionary, Rev. Prince Demetrius Augustine Gallitzin, son of Prince Demetri Alexeiewitch Gallizin and Countess Amalia Von Schmettau. Born at the Hague, December 22, 1770; died at Loretto, Cambria County, Pennsylvania, May 6, 1841.

A VERY interesting service was held last Thursday, All Soul's Day, at the "Priest's Field," near Middleway, Jefferson County, when Right Reverend Dennis J. O'Connell, Bishop of the Catholic Diocese of Richmond, Virginia, celebrated three masses for the repose of souls connected with a strange event in our local history.

The tale of "Wizard Clip" has often been told, but it is such a well-authenticated ghost story that it is always interesting. There are records, as well as traditions and oral facts, that have been handed down describing this remarkable occurrence, and Rev. Alfred E. Smith, editor-in-chief of the *Baltimore Catholic Review* and secretary to the late Cardinal Gibbons, says that this is "the truest ghost story ever told."

In the year 1790 a man by the name of Adam Livingstone came from the village of Lancaster, Pennsylvania, and settled on a tract of seventy acres of land that he had purchased near the village in Jefferson County, Virginia, now known as Middleway. All went well for four years. Sometime in 1794 a stranger appeared in the night at Livingstone's home and asked for accommodations. He was taken in, as he appeared to be ill, and was cared for by the Livingstones. As several weeks passed he grew worse and, realizing that his end was approaching, he told his host he was a Catholic and begged that a priest be sent for. Livingstone, who was a. Protestant, had neither the time nor the inclination to send away

for a priest, and he told the unknown guest that he knew of none in the neighborhood, and if he did would not care to have one come to his home. The stranger died unshriven.

Immediately things began to happen at Livingstone's home. Indeed, before the stranger was buried there were strange occurrences. The corpse was "laid out," and one of the neighbors, Jacob Foster, agreed to sit up, as the custom was, through the night. When night came Livingstone and Foster lit candles in the room where the body lay. The candles flickered and went out. Others were lighted and they, too, mysteriously were extinguished. Some half candles were brought, but the result was the same. Foster excused himself and went home early. Livingstone had a bad night of it. He was not superstitious, but he just couldn't stay in the room with the dead man. As he lay sleepless in another room he heard the sound of a horse galloping around and around the house. He jumped up and investigated, but could see nothing, though the moon was shining almost as bright as day. Livingstone was glad when daylight came. The same day the stranger was buried, but he was interred in unconsecrated ground.

A week after Livingstone's barn was burned from some unknown cause. A number of his cattle sickened and died; the fowl of the place dropped dead. In the house there were strange manifestations by day and night. The chinaware would fall from the shelves and smash to pieces on the floor. The furniture would bang about the rooms in which there was no living person.

The strangest manifestation of all was the sound of invisible scissors and the clipping of cloth. Blankets and sheets and clothing were clipped by the invisible shears, and though the sound could be heard, nothing was to be seen until the holes appeared in the garment or the sheet or whatever was attacked. This attracted attention from far and near. Many Shepherdstown persons visited the place, and though some of them went there skeptical, most of them came away believing. One good woman had a valuable shawl ruined by the invisible scissors and a well-known man wearing a swallow-tail coat had the coattails snipped into shreds. He was treated especially badly, perhaps, because he had ridiculed the idea that such things could happen. Visitors from Winchester, Martinsburg, Charles Town and other places had similar experiences. Usually the cuts in the clothing were in half-moon shape.

Livingstone and his family, naturally, were greatly worried by these weird happenings. The manifestations occurred at irregular intervals by day and by night. An old writer states that Livingstone "lost much rest." One night he had a dream in which he envisioned himself toiling with much difficulty up a steep mountain. Reaching the top he saw a man in clerical robes, and a voice said, "This is the man who can help you." The next day Livingstone rode to Winchester and interviewed Rev. Alexander Belmaine, the Episcopal rector. The rector gave him but little encouragement, and Livingstone was not satisfied that he was the right man. He returned home and the strange occurrences continued. Three months of being harassed in so strange a way had humbled Livingstone, and when someone suggested that he put his case before a Catholic priest he agreed to do so. He consulted with Richard McSherry, a Roman Catholic who lived near Leetown, who informed him that Rev. Denis Cahill, a Catholic priest, was to say mass in Shepherdstown the following Sunday. In company with Mr. McSherry and a Mr. Minghini, also of that neighborhood, Livingstone came to Shepherdstown Sunday morning and attended the service in the little Catholic Church which was then standing on what is now known as "Chapel Lot" at the west edge of town. When Father Cahill appeared and began the sermon, Livingstone was greatly agitated. "This is the very man I saw in my dream," he gasped; "his is the voice that said he would relieve me."

After the service Livingstone told the priest his story and related the dream. At his insistent urging, Father Cahill went to his home with him and there he learned sufficient to verify the strange tales that had been told. He sprinkled the house with holy water, and though the manifestations were modified, the clippings continued. A few days later Father Cahill said mass for the repose of the soul of the stranger, and the uncanny annoyances ceased forever. Livingstone soon afterward went back to Pennsylvania to live, but before he died he deeded thirty-four acres of his farm to the trustees to hold for the benefit of the Catholic Church for all time. It is said that he and his family became devout Catholics.

This strange story has found its way into most histories that treat of our local affairs. Fifty or sixty years ago there were persons who had gotten the story from those who had actually witnessed the manifestations. Rev. Demetrius A. de Gallitzin, the prince-priest who became famous as a missionary and explorer, was interested in the affair and came here to investigate it. He spent three months in Middleway and vicinity investigating the story and securing proofs. Though he did not believe it at first, in his memoirs written in 1797 he declares that after having examined and cross-examined witnesses in a way that no court could surpass and after having investigated every word of his witnesses' testimony, he was forced to the conclusion that such things had happened. In the same year letters written by Mrs. Anastasia McSherry gave similar testimony.

The village where these events occurred was originally called Smithfield, after William Smith, who in 1729 had been granted a considerable tract of land by Governor Gooch of Virginia. After the spook had made it famous it was called the Wizard Clip, and to this day it is better known as Clip than it is by its latter-day official name, Middleway.

"Priest's Field" lies a half-mile or so west of the main turnpike leading into Middleway. It is a sterile piece of ground, though pleasantly located. The upland is hardly susceptible of cultivation, as the soil is shallow and the shattered limestone rock is very close to the surface. The foundation of an ancient house may be seen, but no vestige of the building itself is left. The leafless trunks of some old pear-trees are still standing, habitations of woodpeckers and owls. The Opequon creek flows through the lower part of the property, where there is a bit of pleasant meadow overshadowed by tall sycamores. A spring of water that emerges from the hill side is at present dry, though usually it is a clear running stream.

The deed conveying the thirty-four acres known as Priest's Field to trustees for the Catholic Church was executed by Livingstone February 21, 1802.

The house in which the supernatural visitor did his weird work disappeared many years ago, though its site is still pointed out. The grave of the stranger who caused so much trouble is unknown.

The following, from a letter written April 11, 1839, to Mrs. C. G. Doll by Rev. Prince Demetrius Augustine Gallitzin from Loretto, Cambria County, Pennsylvania:

"My view to coming to Virginia in September, 1797, and remaining three months, was to investigate the extraordinary facts at Livingstone's of which I heard so much and which I would not prevail upon myself to believe, but I was soon convicted to a full belief of them. I spent several days penning down the whole account. The first beginning of this business was a destruction of property, by clipping, burning, and removing, all done by invisible hands. Showers of stones were thrown. For a considerable length of time Livingstone was persecuted and his property destroyed by the agency of evil spirits. The clothes belonging to him and to his family were cut to pieces by invisible hands; fire bursted repeatedly from out their beds at broad daylight; articles of furniture displaced. Strange and frightful apparitions and strange noises terrified them very often at night. Chunks of fire rolled over the floor without any apparent cause. Some of the clothing bore the impress of a hand burnt on the cloth, or an I. H. S. made in the same manner. Once before their eyes a burning hand was impressed upon some clothing. Fourteen persons were converted in one winter by these things.

Adam Livingstone was of Dutch descent, a Lutheran in religion, an honest and industrious farmer. He was kind and hospitable.

It was a poor and sick Irish traveller he welcomed beneath his roof.

The Rev. Dennis Cahill, during his first visit, sprinkled the house with holy water. On his going away, having one foot over the doorsill and the other inside, yet, suddenly, a sum of money which had disappeared from out of Livingstone's chest was by invisible hands laid on the doorsill between the priest's feet.

An old Presbyterian lady from Martinsburg, to satisfy her curiosity, went to Livingstone's. Before entering she took off her new black silk cap, wrapped it up in a new silk handkerchief—when she opened it, she found her cap cut into narrow ribands.

Mr. Livingstone and a portion of his family became members of the Catholic Church. Mrs. Livingstone was never sincerely converted. They had scarcely made their profession of faith before a bright light awoke Mr. Livingstone one night and a clear sweet voice told him to arise, call his family together and pray. The voice led them in prayer. No sooner were the Livingstone family relieved from the torments of the devil than they were visited by a consoling voice which remained with them for seventeen years.

Mr. Livingstone moved from Virginia to Bedford County, Pennsylvania, about twenty miles from Loretto, where he died in the spring of 1820. I had mass at his house repeatedly. He continued to the last very attentive to his duties."

Index

245

Bloodstains, 24, 185, 215, 224
Blow, Mr. and Mrs. George Preston, 94-5
Blue Ridge Mountains, 142-3, 176, 187, 191
Bocock, Thomas Stanley, 205
Bolling, Mrs. Robert, 219
Booth, George Wythe, 72
Booth, Thomas, 72
Bower, Jennie, 75
Bowling Green, 55
Boys and youths, and ghosts, 16, 33, 53, 65, 142, 176
Braidfoot, Rev. John, 221-2
Brandon, Middlesex County, 187
Bransford, Alice Carter, 112
Brayne, Butler, 140
Brayne, Richard, 140
Bremo. *See* Recess-Bremo
Brent, Giles, 34
Brides, greeted by a ghost, 53
British soldiers (Redcoats), 86, 94
Brockenbrough, Mrs. B. B., 69
Brooke, John, 62
Brooke, Robert, 13
Brooke, Sarah Taliaferro, 62-3
Brooke's Bank, Essex County, 63
Brooks, Mary, 125
Brother relationship, 229-30
Browne, Junius Brutus, Jr., 79
Brunswick County, 211-12
Brunswick Parish, 43
Bruton Church, Williamsburg, 92, 140
Buchan, Helen, 15
Buchan, John, 15
Buckingham County, 213-14
Bull Run Mountains, 142, 169
Bunker Hill, *See* Warren, Dr. Joseph
Burks, Elizabeth, 213
Burwell, Col. Carter, 187
Burwell, J. Townsend, 188
Burwell, Nathaniel, 187-8
Byrd, Anne, 131
Byrd, Evelyn, sister of William Byrd, III, 113, 117-18
Byrd, Evelyn, sister of Mrs. A. DeJ. Hart, 131
Byrd, George H., 193
Byrd, Harry F., 203
Byrd, Maria, 53
Byrd, Col. William (fl. 1865), 193
Byrd, Col. William Evelyn, II, 113, 115-16
Byrd, William Evelyn, III, 113-16
Byrd House, Winchester, 193-4

Cabell, Caroline, 223

Cabell, Mrs. George W., 225
Cabell, Col. John, 213-14, 223
Cabell, Col. Samuel Jordan, 223-4
Cabell, Col. William, 213, 223
Cabell, Dr. William, 213
Cahill, Rev. Denis, 241, 244
Campbell County, 215-18
Candles, blown out by ghosts, 202
Capitol, Washington, D. C., 30
Caroline County, 55-8
Carpenter, ghost of a, 173
Carroll, Louisa Tilghman, 96
Carter, Elizabeth Hill, 113-15
Carter, John (fl. 1702), 48
Carter, John (fl. 1723), 112
Carter, Col. Landon, I, 53
Carter, Landon, II, 53
Carter Lucy Landon, 17
Carter, Robert ("King"), 48, 53
Carter, Robert Wormley, 53
Carter Hall, Clarke County, 187-8
Carter's Grove, near Williamsburg, 187
Cary, Constance, 8
Castle Hill, Albemarle County, 127-9
Catalepsis, 78
Catalpa, Culpeper County, 135
Catholics, 116, 239-44
Catlett, 162
Cattle and fowl, 240
Cavanaugh, Ethel, 179-180
Cawardin, Mrs. Charles O'Brien, 104
Cazenove, Charlotte, 5
Cazenove, Constance, 131
Cazenove, Harriet, 5
Cazenove, William, 131
Cedar Grove, near Farnham, 68-9
Cemetery(ies). *See* Graveyards
Center Hill, Petersburg, Dinwiddie County, 219-20
Chairs, rocking, 16, 37, 112, 125-6, 131, 160
Chandler, Ann, 34
Charles I, 34
Charles II, 84, 89
Charles City County, 107-18
Charlottesville, 126, 130-1
Chastellux, Marquis de, 219
Chatham, Stafford County, 27-9
Chellow Plantation, 219
Chesapeake Bay, 72, 83-4, 86
Chesterfield County, 119-21
Chew, Larkin, 20
Chew, Thomas, 20
Chewning, Dr. George, 150
Chewning, Mary Jeffries, 150

246

247

250

251

Rosewell Plantation, 187
Ross, Alexander, 201
Ross' Spring. See Waverley
Rowland, Elizabeth (Lizzie), 107-8
Rowland, Spencer, 107
Royalists, 83-4, 86
Rutledge, Mrs. Carleton, 157
Rye Cove Consolidated School,
    Scott County, 231-2

Sabine Hall, Richmond County, 53
Sailor(s), apparitions of, 87
Sailor's wife, ghost of, 1-2
Saint George's Church, Fred-
    ericksburg, 20-2, 36
Saint John's Church, Richmond,
    153
Salubria, Culpeper County, 140-1
Sanford, Lawrence, 178-9
Saunders, Elizabeth, 118
Saunders, John Loyall, 118
Scissors (invisible), cutting, 131,
    183, 240-1
Scott, Rev. Alexander, 23
Scotsmen, 13, 15, 30, 36, 49, 54,
    68-9, 115, 130, 153, 201, 221
Scott, Hannah, 225
Scott, Sir Walter, 215
Sea-bread baking, 107
Seawell, Henry, 24
Seawell, John B., 109
Seawell, John Tyler, 109
Seawell, Machen B., 109
Seawell, Molly Elliott, 109
Seddon, Leah, 73
Seldon, John, 118
Seldon, Martha Bland, 118
Selma, Staunton, 185-6
Seminary Hill. See Alexandria
Sewing machine, ghost-run, 218
Shaving, ghost of a man who
    didn't like to shave, 6-7
Shelton, John, 20
Shenandoah Valley, 189-90, 195
Sheridan, Gen. Philip Henry,
    192, 197
Ships, phantom, 62-3, 86-9
Shirley, Sir Thomas, 111
Shirley, Charles City County,
    111-12
Sinclair, James, 80
Skeletons, apparitions of, 25, 85,
    89, 102, 179, 234
Skipwith, Lady, 92
Skipwith, Lelia, 92
Skipwith, Sir Peyton, 92
Skulls, 85
Slaughter, Thomas, 135
Slaughter, Mrs. William, 57

Smith, Alfred E., 239
Smith, Rev. Charles, 221
Smith, Mary Peyton, 225
Smith, Richard, 225
Smith,Mrs. Thomas, 164
Smithfield. See Middleway
Smoot, Albert, 4
Smoot, W. A., 4
Snellings, Virginia Elliott Chiles,
    119
Snow, and the appearance of
    ghosts, 53, 77-8, 172-3, 206
Snow Creek, Spotsylvania County,
    178
Snow Hill, Fauquier County, 170-1
Sobbing. See Moaning
Soldier(s), spies, apparitions of.
    See Confederate Soldiers;
    Hession Soldiers; Redcoats
Soldier's Joy, Nelson County,
    223-4
Soul, freeing of the, 230
Southern Churchman, 74
Spotswood, Lady, 140-1
Spotswood, Sir Alexander, 13-14,
    41, 140
Spotswood, Dandridge, 140
Spotswood, Robert, 140
Spotsylvania County, 20-2, 38-9,
    40-2. See also Fredericks-
    burg
Stafford County, 23-37
Staunton, 185-6
Steele, Dr. John M., 183
Steele, Mary, 181-2
Steele, Mr. and Mrs. Thomas,
    181-2
Steele, Capt. William, 181
Steele, William (fl. 1889), 181-3
Stephens, Lewis and John, 199
Stepmother's tyranny, 164
Stevensburg, Culpeper County,
    140
Stoffegan, Mrs. Gilmer, 22
Stones, throwing, and falling,
    135-6, 181-4, 243
Storms, 44, 65, 79, 85-6, 148-9,
    167-8, 176, 223
Stribling, Taliaferro, 201
Stuart, T. C. and W. J., 233
Student, discouraged, ghost of, 67
Suicides, 1-2, 67, 92-3, 114-15, 145
Sunny Bank, Albemarle County,
    130-1
Surry County, 111, 227-8
Swift, Marie, 199-200
Swift, Jonathan, 3
Swishing of skirts, 71, 79, 93, 97,
    151-2

253